T0319806

Central Banks and Supervisory Architecture in Europe

Central Banks and Supervisory Architecture in Europe

Lessons from Crises in the 21st Century

Edited by

Robert Holzmann

Governor, Oesterreichische Nationalbank, Austria

Fernando Restoy

Chair, Financial Stability Institute, Bank for International Settlements, Switzerland

PUBLISHED IN ASSOCIATION WITH
OESTERREICHISCHE NATIONALBANK, AUSTRIA

Edward Elgar
PUBLISHING

Cheltenham, UK • Northampton, MA, USA

© Oesterreichische Nationalbank 2022

All rights reserved. No part of this publication may be reproduced, stored in a retrieval system or transmitted in any form or by any means, electronic, mechanical or photocopying, recording, or otherwise without the prior permission of the publisher.

Published by
Edward Elgar Publishing Limited
The Lypiatts
15 Lansdown Road
Cheltenham
Glos GL50 2JA
UK

Edward Elgar Publishing, Inc.
William Pratt House
9 Dewey Court
Northampton
Massachusetts 01060
USA

A catalogue record for this book
is available from the British Library

Library of Congress Control Number: 2022943097

This book is available electronically in the **Elgar**online
Economics subject collection
http://dx.doi.org/10.4337/9781802208894

ISBN 978 1 80220 888 7 (cased)
ISBN 978 1 80220 889 4 (eBook)
Printed and bound by CPI Group (UK) Ltd, Croydon, CR0 4YY

Contents

List of contributors   vii

1   Introduction to *Central Banks and Supervisory Architecture
    in Europe*   1
    Robert Holzmann and Fernando Restoy

PART I   TRENDS IN EUROPEAN BANKING
            SUPERVISION DESIGN

2   The puzzle of Europe's banking union: progress and missing pieces   14
    Thorsten Beck

3   Supervisory architecture in the EU: where should we go from here?   21
    Fernando Restoy

4   The architecture of supervision and prudential policy   34
    Angela Maddaloni and Alessandro Scopelliti

5   Trends in European banking supervision design: is there
    a path to an optimal architecture for financial supervision in
    the EU?   49
    Luís Silva Morais

PART II   THE ROLE OF CENTRAL BANKS
            (I): ASPECTS OF MONETARY AND
            MACROPRUDENTIAL POLICY INTERACTION

6   Can macroprudential tools ensure financial stability?   62
    Anne Epaulard

7   The interaction of monetary and financial tasks in different
    central bank structures   71
    Aerdt Houben, Jan Kakes and Annelie Petersen

8   Monetary and macroprudential policies: a troubled marriage   83
    Phurichai Rungcharoenkitkul

9   The architecture of macroprudential policy: delegation and
     coordination   96
     Charles Bean

10   Governance of financial sector policies in an era of climate change   108
     Daniel C. Hardy

PART III   THE ROLE OF CENTRAL BANKS (II):
            MICROPRUDENTIAL SUPERVISION AND
            FINANCIAL STABILITY

11   Entrusting central banks with microprudential supervision:
     implications for financial stability   122
     Anca Maria Podpiera

12   Is this time different? Synergies between ECB's tasks   135
     Karin Hobelsberger, Christoffer Kok and Francesco Paolo Mongelli

13   Money, supervision, and financial stability: a money-credit
     constitution entrusted to independent but constrained central banks   156
     Paul Tucker

14   Politicians, central banks and macroprudential supervision   170
     Donato Masciandaro

PART IV   THE FINTECH REVOLUTION: IMPLICATIONS
            FOR OPTIMAL SUPERVISORY ARCHITECTURE

15   Regulating and supervising BigTech in finance   181
     José Manuel González-Páramo

16   The emerging autonomy–stability choice for stablecoins   194
     Maarten R. C. van Oordt

PART V   LESSONS FROM THE COVID-19 CRISIS FOR
            THE OPTIMAL SUPERVISORY ARCHITECTURE

17   Some lessons from COVID-19 for the EU financial framework   206
     Ignazio Angeloni

18   Central banks as emergency actors: implications for
     governance arrangements   218
     David Archer

Index   231

Contributors

EDITORS

Robert Holzmann has been Governor of the Oesterreichische Nationalbank and member of the Governing Council of the ECB since September 2019. He is a full member of the Austrian Academy of Sciences and holds honorary positions at the Southwestern University of Finance and Economics in Chengdu, the University of Malaya in Kuala Lumpur and the University of New South Wales in Sydney. He served as Senior Economist at the OECD and the IMF. Furthermore, he was Sector Director of the Social Protection & Labor Department at the World Bank, leading the strategic work on pensions. Robert also served internationally as Senior Advisor on pensions, financial literacy and education as well as labour market and migration issues. He has published extensively on financial, fiscal and social policy issues.

Fernando Restoy became Chair of the Financial Stability Institute on 1 January 2017. He had been Deputy Governor of the Bank of Spain since 2012. Previously, he held other senior positions at the Bank of Spain, which he joined in 1991. From 1995 to 1997, he was Economic Advisor and Head of the Monetary Framework Section at the European Monetary Institute in Frankfurt. Fernando was Vice Chair of the Spanish Securities and Markets Commission (CNMV) from 2008 to 2012 and Vice Chair of the IOSCO Technical Committee (now Board). He was the Chairman of the Spanish Executive Resolution Authority (FROB) from 2012 to 2015 and was a Member of the Supervisory Board of the ECB's Single Supervisory Mechanism from 2014 to end 2016. He holds an MSc in Econometrics and Mathematical Economics from the London School of Economics and an MA and PhD in Economics from Harvard.

CONTRIBUTORS

Ignazio Angeloni is a Senior Fellow in the Mossavar-Rahmani Center for Business and Government of the Harvard Kennedy School and in the Leibniz Institute for Financial Research SAFE. From 2014–2019 he was member of the ECB supervisory board. From 2012–2013, as head of financial stability in the ECB, he coordinated the preparations for the single supervisory mechanism. In his earlier career he held positions in the Bank of Italy and Italy's Finance Ministry. Ignazio holds a degree from Bocconi University and a PhD from the University of Pennsylvania and has published books and articles in leading academic journals.

David Archer is Head of the Central Banking Studies unit at the Bank for International Settlements. He is also the Secretary to the Central Bank Governance Group, a group of Governors that meets regularly in Basel to consider issues relating to the organisation and governance of central banks. Prior to joining the BIS, Mr Archer was Assistant Governor at the Reserve Bank of New Zealand, where he was responsible for monetary policy analysis and advice, forecasting and research, as well as for the Bank's financial market activities. He was a member of the Bank's Governor's Committee, Monetary Policy Committee, Financial System Oversight Committee and Risk Management Committee. For a number of years in the late 1980s David was seconded to the International Monetary Fund.

Charles Bean is Professor of Economics at the London School of Economics and Chairman of the Centre for Economic Policy Research. Between 2016 and 2021, he was also an executive member at the Office for Budget Responsibility. From 2000 to 2014, he served at the Bank of England as Chief Economist and then Deputy Governor for Monetary Policy, sitting on both the Monetary Policy and Financial Policy Committees and representing the Bank internationally. Prior to that he was on the faculty at LSE and has also worked at HM Treasury. He was knighted in 2014 for services to monetary policy and central banking and was President of the Royal Economic Society from 2013 to 2015. He holds a PhD from the Massachusetts Institute of Technology.

Thorsten Beck is Director of the Florence School of Banking and Finance and Professor of Financial Stability at the European University Institute. He is a Research Fellow of the Centre for Economic Policy Research and the CESifo. He was Professor of Banking and Finance at Bayes Business School, Professor of Economics at the European Banking Center at Tilburg University and has been a consultant to several international institutions such as the European Central Bank, the Bank of England, the BIS, the IMF and the European Commission. His research and policy work have focused on the relationship between finance and economic development and on policies that are needed to build a sound and effective financial system. He holds a PhD from the University of Virginia and an MA from the University of Tübingen in Germany.

Anne Epaulard is Professor of Economics at Paris Dauphine University. Since 2016, she has also served as board member of the Autorité de contrôle prudentiel et de résolution (French Prudential Supervision and Resolution Authority) and as Director of its Scientific Committee. Previously, she was Deputy Assistant Secretary at the French Treasury (2005–2013) and Senior Economist at the IMF (2000–2004). Her research covers the impact of macroeconomic and structural policies and reforms on economic growth and stability.

José Manuel González-Páramo is Professor of Economics at IESE Business School University of Navarra and Chairman of European DataWarehouse GmbH. From 2013 to 2020 he was an Executive Board Director of BBVA (Chief Officer Economics, Regulation & Public Affairs) and Chairman of its International Advisory Board. He served as a member of the Executive Board of the European Central Bank (ECB) from 2004 to 2012 and was a member of the Governing Council of the ECB. Prior to that, José Manuel was a member of the Governing Council of Bank of Spain (1994–2004) and of its Executive Committee (1998–2004). He has advised public and private institutions including the IMF, the World Bank and the European Commission. José Manuel, a full professor in UCM (Madrid) since 1988, and an external professor at CEMFI (1987–2004), has published extensively on financial matters, monetary policy and the economy. He is a board member at Bruegel and a member of the advisory board of the Bretton Woods Committee. He holds a PhD, MPhil and MA in Economics from Columbia University and a PhD from Universidad Complutense.

Daniel C. Hardy is currently a Visiting Scholar at the Vienna University of Economics and Business, where he is researching political economy issues affecting the financial sector. For most of his career he was on the staff of the IMF, advising on policies and building capacity in a wide range of industrialised, emerging market and developing countries. Recently, he led work on European financial integration and the banking union, debt management, as well as sovereign debt restructurings. He has conducted research on such topics as cross-border policy coordination, credit market behaviour, and stress testing. He has also worked at the Austrian Financial Market Authority and the Deutsche Bundesbank. He studied at the University of Oxford and holds a PhD from Princeton University.

Karin Hobelsberger is a Research Associate at Columbia Business School. Prior to that she had been working as a Research Analyst in the Directorate General Macroprudential Policy and Financial Stability and the Directorate General Research at the European Central Bank. She holds a master's degree in Economics from Université de Liège and a master's degree in Finance from the University of Exeter.

Aerdt Houben is Director of Financial Markets at De Nederlandsche Bank (DNB), responsible for monetary and investment operations, risk management and market intelligence. He is Professor of Financial Policies at the University of Amsterdam. He chairs the Committee on Financial Markets at the OECD and is a member of the Committee on the Global Financial System and the Markets Committee at the Bank for International Settlements. He was DNB's Director for Financial Stability and headed the Supervisory Strategy and Monetary Policy Departments. He served on the IMF staff in the Policy Development and Review Department. He has been a member of the Basel Committee on Banking Supervision, the ECB's Financial Stability Committee and the International Organisation of Pension Supervisors. He has a PhD in Monetary Economics from the University of Groningen and has published broadly on financial issues.

Jan Kakes is Senior Economist in the Financial Markets Division at De Nederlandsche Bank. Prior to this, he was a (Senior) Economist in the Monetary and Economic Policy Department and the Financial Stability Division of DNB and a Researcher at the Faculty of Economics of the University of Groningen. He has also been seconded to the UK Financial Services Authority in London and the Financial Stability Board in Basel. He has been a member of various working groups in the context of the Eurosystem, the Financial Stability Board and the Bank for International Settlements. He has published on various subjects including monetary policy, financial stability and macroprudential policy. He holds a PhD in Economics from the University of Groningen.

Christoffer Kok is Head of the Stress Test Experts Division of the ECB's Directorate General Horizontal Line Supervision. His team is responsible for coordinating and carrying out the annual stress tests of the ECB/SSM. In addition to this he has had a leading role in the development of the ECB's top-down stress test models and its macroprudential policy analysis. During the sovereign debt crisis he was involved in stress test exercises in EU/IMF Programme countries. He has also been involved in a large number of quantitative impact studies of regulatory reforms, such as the macroeconomic assessments of Basel II and Basel III. He is also a short-term expert at the International Monetary Fund. Previously, he worked as a Deputy Head of Division and Adviser in the ECB's Directorate General Macroprudential Policy and Financial Stability, as Principal Economist in the ECB's Monetary Policy Directorate and as an Economist at Danmarks Nationalbank. He has published research on stress testing and monetary and macroprudential policy issues. He holds an MSc in Economics from Aarhus University and Université Paris 1 Panthéon-Sorbonne and an MSc in Finance from Copenhagen Business School.

Angela Maddaloni is Head of the Financial Intermediation Research Section in the Directorate General Research of the ECB, where she has worked since 2001. Her research and policy interests cover a wide range of topics related to macrofinancial linkages, the transmission of monetary policy, credit and business cycles and the impact of financial regulation. Recently, her work has focused on the interactions between monetary policy and financial stability as well as on the architecture of supervision. Her research has been published, inter alia, in *Journal of Money, Banking and Finance, Journal of Financial Economics, Review of Financial Studies, Review of Economic Dynamics* and *Journal of Business.* She holds a PhD in Finance from Columbia University in New York and a master's degree in statistics and economics from the University of Siena in Italy.

Donato Masciandaro has been Full Professor of Economics at Bocconi University in Milan since 2001, where he also holds a Chair in Economics of Financial Regulation. He is Director of the Baffi Carefin Centre for Applied Research on Banking, Finance and Regulation and served as the organisation's president from 2015 to 2017. Since 2011, he has been a member of the Management Board and Honorary Treasurer of the Société Universitarie Européenne de Recherches Financières (SUERF). Masciandaro also served as Consultant to the World Bank, the European Parliament, the Inter-American Development Bank and the United Nations. He was a Visiting Scholar at the IMF's Institute for Capacity Development and is Associate Editor of the *Journal of Financial Stability* and the *Italian Economic Journal.* His main research interests are in financial regulation and supervision, and central banking.

Francesco Paolo Mongelli is Senior Adviser in the Directorate General Monetary Policy at the ECB, and Honorary Professor at the Goethe University Frankfurt. He holds a master's degree and a PhD in Economics from the Johns Hopkins University in Baltimore. He has worked at the ECB since 1998, holding various positions, including as organiser of the analytical agenda of DG Economics, Editor of the ECB Occasional Paper Series, and in Directorate General Research. Prior to that he spent several years at the International Monetary Fund in Washington. His main area of research pertains to climate change and monetary policy, monetary policy transmission, financial integration, the effects of the euro on the functioning of EMU, and the links between economic integration and institutional integration. He also teaches Central Banking Elements and Economics of Monetary Unions at the Goethe University Frankfurt. His papers have been published in various scientific and policy-oriented journals, such as *Journal of Money Credit and Banking, Journal of Common Market Studies, Journal of Applied Economics, Integration and Trade Journal, Economie Internationale, Comparative Economic Studies* and *Journal of Economic Integration.*

Luís Silva Morais is Professor at Lisbon University Law School (FDUL). He is also Jean Monnet Chair for Economic Regulation in the EU, Chairman of the

Research Centre on Supervision and Regulation of the Financial Sector (www
.cirsf.eu), Vice Chair of the Appeal Panel of the Single Resolution Board (SRB)
and Chair of the Supervisory Council of the Portuguese Insurance and Pension
Funds Supervisory Authority (ASF). He was previously Vice President of the
Special Privatization Unit of the Portuguese Ministry of Finance (2001–2011),
a Member of the Executive Board of ASF (1998–2001) and Chief of
Cabinet of the Secretary of State of Treasury and Finance (1996–1998, XIII
Portuguese Constitutional Government). He is also Attorney-at-law, founder
and Managing Partner of LSM Advogados, a law firm based in Lisbon (www
.lsmadvogados.com). He holds a PhD and master's degree in law from Lisbon
University Law School.

Annelie Petersen is ECB Governing Council Coordinator and Monetary
Policy Advisor at the Monetary Policy Department of De Nederlandsche Bank.
Prior to that she worked as a Financial Economist at the Financial Markets
Directorate of DNB. She is specialised in the interaction between monetary
policy and financial markets. Annelie holds an MSc in Economics from the
University of Amsterdam.

Anca Maria Podpiera is a Senior Consultant for the World Bank where
she worked on numerous projects, including Financial Sector Assessment
Programmes, in Europe & Central Asia and South Asia. Her research focuses
on institutional structures for prudential supervision, financial sector development and strategies, systemic risk, and the impact of financial shocks. Since
2019, she has also served as Associate Director for Macroeconomics for D3P
Global Pension Consulting. From 2002–2010 she was an economist with
the Czech National Bank, where she conducted research on monetary policy
transmission mechanism, competition and the efficiency of the banking sector.
She holds a PhD in Economics from the Center for Economic Research and
Graduate Education, Prague, Czech Republic.

Phurichai Rungcharoenkitkul is a Principal Economist in the Monetary
and Economic Department at the Bank for International Settlements (BIS).
In his previous career at the Bank of Thailand, he led a team responsible for
providing policy recommendations to the Monetary Policy Committee. His
other central banking experiences include forecasting, macro-modelling and
reserve management. He spent several years at the IMF in the Asia & Pacific
Department, working on macroeconomic research and country missions. He
holds a DPhil and MPhil in Economics from the University of Oxford.

Alessandro Scopelliti is an Assistant Professor of Finance at KU Leuven, in
the Faculty of Economics and Business. He is also an Economist (part-time) at
the European Central Bank and a Research Fellow at the University of Zurich.
At the ECB, he contributes to the design of macroprudential policy and the

analysis of financial stability issues. His research focuses on financial intermediation, regulation and stability, macroprudential and monetary policies, sustainable finance, and capital markets. Combining research and policy, he has collaborated with central banks (Bank of England, Banca d'Italia), macroprudential bodies (ESRB) and international institutions (IMF). He holds a PhD in Economics from the University of Warwick, an MSc in Economics from Pompeu Fabra University and an MRes in Economic Analysis and Policy from Paris School of Economics.

Paul Tucker is a Research Fellow at Harvard Kennedy School, and author of *Unelected Power: The Quest for Legitimacy in Central Banking and the Regulatory State* (Princeton University Press, 2018). His forthcoming book, *Global Discord*, on international institutions during fractured geopolitics, will be published by Princeton University Press in late 2022. He was formerly at the Bank of England, a director of the Bank for International Settlements, chairing its Committee on Payment and Settlement Systems, and a member of the G20 Financial Stability Board, chairing its group on resolving too-big-to-fail groups. He is President of the UK's National Institute for Economic and Social Research, a Senior Fellow at the Minda de Gunzburg Center for European Studies at Harvard, a member of the advisory board of the Yale Program on Financial Stability, a governor of the Ditchley Foundation, and a director at Swiss Re.

Maarten R. C. van Oordt is an Associate Professor of Finance at Vrije Universiteit Amsterdam. He is an expert in the areas of digital currencies and financial risk management. Previously, he worked as a Research Advisor in the Banking and Payments Department of the Bank of Canada on the topic of digital currency. He gained experience in various roles in the Financial Stability Department and the Currency Department of the Bank of Canada, and in the Economics and Research Division of De Nederlandsche Bank. He received his PhD from Erasmus University Rotterdam. His research has been published in leading academic journals.

1. Introduction to *Central Banks and Supervisory Architecture in Europe*

Robert Holzmann and Fernando Restoy

WHY THIS BOOK NOW?

The debate on how to best organise supervisory tasks is relatively recent. Until the last quarter of the 20th century, with bank financing dominant in most jurisdictions, banking and financial supervision were almost synonymous. The mandates of most central banks around the globe reflected a combination of monetary policy functions and banking oversight responsibilities. Yet the development of capital and insurance markets soon generated the need to establish sectoral supervisors for other financial intermediaries.

As the 20th century drew to a close, a debate emerged over central banks' role in financial stability. In their pursuit of an explicit, delegated mandate normally focused on price stability, central banks were gaining independence from governments. At the same time, financial institutions became active in different sectors. In a number of jurisdictions, the notion of an integrated financial supervisor separate from the price stability-oriented central bank gained traction, notably after the creation of the UK's Financial Services Authority in 1997.

Soon after, the idea was put forward to organise supervision around functions rather than types of entities. At the turn of the century, several jurisdictions followed Australia's example and introduced a 'twin peaks' model. Under such a model, one agency – in most cases the central bank – assumes prudential responsibility for all financial institutions, while a separate agency takes over the supervision of the conduct of business of all regulated entities.

In the European Union (EU), national jurisdictions deciding on the institutional architecture opted for different formulas. When European agencies were established to deal with newly centralised tasks and to facilitate consistent national implementation of common rules, the EU authorities followed a sectoral approach, differentiating between banks, insurance companies and securities markets. Though rare among member states, a sectoral organisation of supervision proved more effective in accommodating diverse domestic arrangements. Assigning microprudential responsibilities to the European Central Bank (ECB) in 2013 was, to some extent, another pragmatic decision, that made use of existing treaty provisions to address the perceived urgency to centralise banking supervsion. The great financial crisis of 2008–9 exposed the lack of a euro area-wide supervision structure, and the subsequent euro debt crisis laid bare the doom loop between sovereign and bank fragility. Both events ushered in the development of EU-wide supervision structures and pointed towards a close link with the ECB.

The current framework comprises a complex set of arrangements with varying degrees of decentralised supervisory responsibilities (high for banks, low for insurance and capital market entities) and heterogeneous institutional set-ups at the domestic and European levels. It has certainly not facilitated progress in integrating European financial markets. At the same time, the lack of integration helps to justify idiosyncratic organisational structures at the national level that match the relevant national specificities. It is therefore a sort of suboptimal equilibrium that might need to be revisited.

The COVID-19 pandemic has heightened the need for a review. Both European and national financial authorities have adopted a wide range of actions that have helped to cope with the potentially large impact of the health crisis on economic and financial stability. Such actions, however, largely entailed the application of new instruments by different national and European policymakers for which there were often no explicit normative provisions and which sometimes implied stretching the mandates of the established agencies.

The pandemic shock illustrates the need to put in place robust institutional frameworks that could help deal with different types of unforeseen events in an orderly manner. At the current juncture, it is therefore opportune to reflect on how to improve the European supervisory architecture.

GENERAL ISSUES

This book revisits the arguments for and against different institutional arrangements for financial sector oversight.

Several chapters focus on the role of central banks in financial supervision. The debate has traditionally revolved around balancing the synergies and conflicts between price (or economic) stability on the one hand, and financial stability on the other. In principle, the more important the synergies (conflicts) are, the stronger (weaker) is the case for institutional integration of both functions within the same agency.

The evidence at hand, such as that included in this volume, suggests that the complementarities are more important than the conflicts, particularly in times of crisis. In light of their lender of last resort function for solvent banks, central banks are well suited to be responsible for the vigilance of credit institutions' safety and soundness and the stability of the financial system.

At the same time, the terms of the debate have changed on account of the development of macroprudential policy frameworks. Indeed, this new function opens up the possibility of using different instruments – which could be managed by different agencies – to achieve either price or financial stability, thereby giving additional support to assigning central banks a narrow price stability mandate. Yet, as discussed in this book, there is as yet no compelling evidence that macroprudential instruments on their own deliver the financial stability objective. More importantly, standard monetary policy instruments (like interest rates) and macroprudential tools (such as regulatory capital buffers) affect both macroeconomic and financial developments. It is therefore necessary to coordinate both policy functions to simultaneously achieve both price and financial stability. That need for coordination somewhat limits the scope for the conduct of monetary and macroprudential policies by separate agencies.

Furthermore, supervisory oversight may need to be broadened to cope with new developments in the financial industry. Specific regulatory and supervisory attention may need to be paid to risks posed by large financial services technology providers, so-called Big Tech companies. Moreover, some adjustments of the supervisory function may also be implied by the role the financial system is meant to play in facilitating the transition towards a more sustainable economy. While such adjustments may not require supervisors to stretch their current mandates, the implications of climate-related financial risks for the safety and soundness of financial institutions should be accounted for in an adequate manner.

Overall, the above-mentioned debate and recent developments suggest that central banks are set to play a greater role in monitoring the financial system. What is very important in this context and as highlighted in several chapters of this book is that authorities need to be well equipped to cope with unforeseen developments along the lines of the COVID-19 pandemic. To this end, they should be empowered to act discretionally in emergency situations.

This raises issues about accountability and democratic legitimacy. The book discusses how an institutional framework – properly established by legislation – should articulate the delegation of tasks to central banks. Such a framework should include governance rules aimed at controlling potential conflicts across objectives and should facilitate regular reporting on each of the objectives. Moreover, legislation should also establish the types of actions that central banks can take in both normal and emergency situations. Last, but not least, it should also establish adequate controls by elected officials – both ex ante and ex post – whenever central banks need to make use of extraordinary powers.

EUROPEAN ISSUES

Beyond the issues analysed above, any debate in the EU about what the desirable supervisory architecture may look like inevitably touches on the degree to which supervisory powers may or should be centralised.

Since monetary policymaking has already been centralised, much of the debate is about what other powers should be assigned to the European Central Bank. Since the creation of the banking union, the ECB has been given supervisory responsibility for all significant institutions in the monetary union. The book presents analyses that show that the centralisation of microprudential policy has so far proven beneficial to financial stability.

The banking union has yet to meet its objectives, however. First, the third pillar of the project, a European deposit guarantee scheme, has not yet been developed and much uncertainty remains about when that will happen. Second, European banking markets have remained largely fragmented as the provision of cross-border banking services or the pan-Europeanisation of banks' business models remain stalled. As argued in the volume, the permanence of ring-fencing strategies by host authorities may partly explain this unfavourable development. And, third, recent experience with banking crises suggests that the doom loop between banks and sovereigns has not been deactivated despite the creation of the Single Resolution Mechanism.

Another topical issue in the European context is how to organise the macro-prudential function. Currently, it is largely decentralised, although the ECB can top up some of the measures taken at the national level. In principle, this might seem to be a good compromise as it helps to recognise the specificities of the domestic economic and financial cycles and correct a possible inaction bias by national authorities.

However, the ECB's macroprudential powers are confined to using a subset of (capital-based) instruments which may not be so effective in smoothing out fluctuations in the credit cycle. Given that monetary and macroprudential policy complement each other in promoting both price and financial stability in the euro area, a critical review of the division of labour between the ECB and member countries seems warranted.

Finally, the full development of the capital markets union may also require revising the powers currently assigned to the European agencies in relation to the supervision of the current (largely common) rules that govern capital market activity.

FIVE THEMATIC PARTS, 18 CHAPTERS AND AN OUTLOOK

Providing a diverse set of conceptual and empirical arguments on the issues touched upon above, the 18 chapters of this book are grouped into five thematic parts.

Part I discusses *trends in European banking supervision design* from different angles.

Thorsten Beck (Chapter 2) zeroes in on the time after the global financial crisis, which saw significant regulatory reforms and endeavours to build a European financial safety net. While progress has been made, in particular with regard to the banking union, the reforms have fallen short of the original objectives of eliminating bail-out and the 'deadly embrace' between banks and sovereigns, and of creating a single market in banking. The governance of banking regulation is still far from optimal. Beck recalls well-known episodes of failing banks having been resolved at the national level – mostly with taxpayer money. According to Beck, prerequisites for a truly European banking system are completing the banking union with a European deposit insurance scheme and a backstop for the resolution fund as well as establishing stronger resolution powers on the European level. At the same time, it will also be imperative to reduce political influence over regulatory decisions, both at the national and at the European level.

This mixed assessment of reform progress is broadly shared by Fernando Restoy (Chapter 3), but Restoy's arguments differ from Beck's. According to Restoy, political economy and governance issues are probably as important as technical aspects of supervision and regulation. He emphasises the complexity of the supervisory architecture in the European Union: heterogeneity at the national level, ranging from integrated supervisors to 'twin peaks' models, coexists with the allocation of some functions to European bodies, while other responsibilities are vested in national authorities. This diversity in institutional supervisory arrangements across Europe impedes both adequate financial oversight and the integration of the financial industry. Additionally, this architecture seems to be ill-suited to effectively deal with deep technological transformations of the financial services industry, climate-related financial risks, and unprecedented challenges, such as the coronavirus pandemic. These more recent phenomena have further strengthened the case for close coordination between monetary, microprudential and macroprudential policies. Furthermore, the rise of non-bank financial activities and intermediaries in the market for financial services and the need to favour, as much as is warranted, a level playing field tend to support models based on a functional rather than a sectoral distribution of supervisory responsibilities. In the European case, the above arguments support the expansion of the ECB's responsibilities and tools in macroprudential policies. Moreover, the need to advance the capital markets union favours the transfer of more direct responsibilities to European authorities.

In their contribution, Angela Maddaloni and Alessandro Scopelliti (Chapter 4) discuss various aspects of the supervisory architecture in Europe. They elaborate on the pros and cons of having a central bank in charge of both central banking and supervisory functions and conclude that the integration of both functions provides benefits arising from better information flow and an internalisation of spillovers of their policies. The model for the euro area, which is not fully integrated, reaps those benefits while avoiding conflicts of interest between the monetary policy and supervisory functions by taking due account of a strict separation principle between the two tasks. The costs and benefits of centralised, as opposed to national, supervision are also examined in the euro area context. As noted by Maddaloni and Scopelliti, the centralisation of banking supervision – together with the new macroprudential policy framework – has been decisive in safeguarding the resilience of the banking system and avoiding procyclical adjustments by deleveraging during the COVID-19 crisis. The authors argue, however, that the decentralised structure of macroprudential policies may have contributed to the limited availability of counter-cyclical capital buffers when the coronavirus crisis hit. Whether this justifies their call for a more centralised governance with regard to macroprudential policies remains debatable.

Finally, Luís Silva Morais (Chapter 5) gives a detailed account of the recent key evolutionary trends in the financial supervisory architecture. Amid the recent pandemic and international trends, he then critically examines the main benefits and costs of important options available to further optimise the institutional architecture of financial supervision in Europe. The author envisages a more structured organisation of the EU architecture and, above all, a new overall balance between national and European supervisory authorities.

Part II puts the spotlight on *aspects of the interaction of monetary and macroprudential policy*.

Anne Epaulard (Chapter 6) kicks off the debate by critically reviewing the evolution of the pre-2008 and post-2008 consensus on the topic. The post-2008 consensus has been highly influenced by empirical work on credit cycles (that for many remain much more damaging than stock market bubbles, property price hikes and commodity price exuberance) and macroprudential measures that were developed and gradually implemented also in industrial countries. As noted by Epaulard, the prevailing consensus that monetary policymakers are in charge of price stability – while macroprudential policymakers are in charge of financial stability – rests on the prerequisite of macroprudential measures being more effective in containing more granular credit surges and related financial stability risks. After reviewing the main empirical literature on the effectiveness of macroprudential measures, which is constrained by the fact that only short time series are available, the author concludes that first empirical evidence certainly points to effectiveness, but many issues remain unresolved.

Aerdt Houben, Jan Kakes and Annelie Petersen (Chapter 7) explore the cross-country heterogeneity of the institutional set-up of monetary and financial stability tasks in Europe amid centralisation towards European agencies (e.g. the ECB), while at the national level prudential tasks were transferred to national central banks in some cases. The authors discuss how these policies interact and assess pros and cons of central bank involvement. They argue that while a noticeable central bank role improves operational synergies, oversight and policy coordination, it may also involve conflicts of interest, concentration of power and reputation risk. Interestingly, they note that in jurisdictions where central banks are responsible for macroprudential policies inaction bias seems to be less prevalent. At least, this was the experience during the pandemic. Preliminary evidence shows that central banks with a prominent role in macroprudential policies were easing capital buffers somewhat more than others. The authors argue that the literature has not yet reached a consensus on whether monetary policy should explicitly incorporate financial stability considerations ('lean against the wind'). They mention the overhaul of the ECB's strategy as an example of policy change. While macroprudential policies are still considered to be a first line of defence against financial imbalances, in the ECB's recent strategy review financial stability considerations were recognised more explicitly in view of their impact on price stability.

In the wake of the rapid ascent of macroprudential policy, Phurichai Rungcharoenkitkul (Chapter 8) asks whether the 'separation approach' of one policy tool for one policy objective, on net, has delivered in terms of financial stability or whether 'leaning against the wind' through interest rate policy is a necessary complement or even viable alternative. A review of the main literature reveals that studies doubtless point to the effectiveness of some of the macroprudential measures. However, a number of features – such as regulatory arbitrage, risk migration to non-bank entities and financial activities, risk-taking and search-for-yield behaviour, rising asset (in particular housing) prices (despite the output slump during the pandemic) – may nevertheless indicate that macroprudential policies cannot single-handedly achieve financial stability. The author concludes that too big a burden is placed on macroprudential policy, especially if monetary policy focuses too narrowly on near-term macroeconomic outcomes. But he also argues, and this is relevant for 'optimal' governance, that it is critical to internalise the tight connections between the two policy objectives and the two instruments – monetary and macroprudential policies. He sees a shift in this direction in the recent strategy reviews of both the Federal Reserve and the European Central Bank.

Charles Bean (Chapter 9) first puts the spotlight on governance issues that are rarely elaborated on, such as the nature of legitimacy of delegating macroprudential policies to independent agencies. While technical and political economy reasons clearly speak in favour of delegation, a point which is also made by other contributors to this volume, the absence of measurable objectives impedes accountability. Furthermore, distributional effects of some borrower-based measures raise questions of political legitimacy. Second, the author asks whether macroprudential policies need to be coordinated with monetary policy and, if so, if they need to reside within the same agency. Following the experience of the Bank of England, he concludes that the latter may be helpful and practical as it allows acting on a common basis of information and being well informed about each other's thinking. Finally, he notes that the COVID-induced financial market turbulence in spring 2020 as well as the ascent of new financing technologies underline that stress may arise beyond the regulatory perimeter. For him that makes it even more important for macroprudential authorities to have access to relevant information on upcoming threats as well as sufficiently wide representation to understand them properly.

The final contribution to Part II is devoted to the governance of financial sector policies in light of climate change. Central banks and supervisory authorities have implemented measures to ensure that the financial system is more robust in the face of the adverse consequences of climate change. However, as highlighted by Daniel Hardy (Chapter 10), questions arise about what actions are consistent with the mandates of the competent agencies. Maintaining good governance practices may be challenging but is essential for measures to be accepted. Hardy explores whether such action may come into conflict with the attainment of other objectives and how good governance practices can be maintained. These questions, he argues, become more pressing when proposals are made for more radical action that goes beyond the traditional areas of monetary stability, financial stability, and consumer protection. Measures to mitigate or cope with emerging climate risk are conjectured to be more in line with good governance than measures that aim at reducing such risks through preferential use of monetary and regulatory instruments; this may be a bridge too far and the start of mission creep.

Part III deals with *the role of central banks in microprudential supervision and financial stability*.

Since the global financial crisis, many countries have fundamentally changed their microprudential supervisory structures. Anca Maria Podpiera (Chapter 11) records a significant increase in the number of countries that have assigned the prudential mandate, for banking as well as for other financial sectors, to the central bank or merged a unified prudential supervisor with the central bank. Reviewing the benefits and drawbacks of an integrated model, Podpiera sees significant coordination benefits in having microprudential supervision under the roof of central banks, specifically for systemic risk management, crisis preparedness and crisis resolution. She adds that recent empirical research, albeit limited, shows that central bank involvement in microprudential supervision improves bank soundness and has a mitigating effect on systemic risk. But the author also conjectures that more effort is still needed towards clear objectives, resources and robust governance frameworks for microprudential supervision regardless of whether this function is vested within or outside the central bank.

The second chapter in this part by Francesco Paolo Mongelli, Christoffer Kok and Karin Hobelsberger (Chapter 12) traces the main regulatory and supervisory reforms in the EU and the euro area vis-à-vis the unfolding of three crises: the financial turmoil in mid-2007 and the 2008 global financial crisis; the sovereign debt crisis of the euro area in 2010–12; and the ongoing COVID-19 crisis that started in early 2020. Some of the most important financial reforms include the Single Regulatory Framework (Single Rule Book), the implementation of Basel III in Europe, the establishment of the European System of Financial Supervision (ESFS), and ultimately the banking union with the Single Supervisory Mechanism (SSM) and the Single Resolution Board (SRB) and eventually a European Deposit Insurance Scheme (EDIS). Among other things, the authors conclude that the expansion of the ECB's tasks and responsibilities, in particular the establishment of microprudential supervision at the ECB by setting up the SSM, was decisive in mitigating the sovereign-bank nexus and improving the overall resilience and resolvability of the EU banking sector. Moreover, they maintain that these reforms helped to counter the COVID-19 crisis with a swift, concerted crisis response. While the reforms were undoubtedly helpful, it has to be acknowledged that the remarkable resilience of the financial sector in the course of the pandemic was also instigated by significant fiscal and monetary policy interventions.

In his contribution on the part's topic, Paul Tucker (Chapter 13) starts by citing Paul Volcker, who wrote in 1990, 'I insist that neither monetary policy nor the financial system will be well served if a central bank loses interest in, or influence over, the financial system.'[1] Tucker then provides a detailed account of why Volcker was right. Preserving price stability and financial stability are intimately intertwined, he argues, with the joint goal being 'monetary system stability'. To effectively accomplish this goal, a central bank needs to have a bearing on financial regulation and supervision and to be in a position to track, for instance, the health of individual financial institutions. But in a constitutional democracy this in turn requires that the central bank's role in supervision and regulation is formalised. Tucker envisages a 'money-credit constitution' that, grounded in shared principles, stipulates 'what central banks must do (their mandate), may do and may not do'. Only then, he concludes, can accountability be ensured without undermining central banks' independence.

Rather than exploring the relative economic merits of the integration view versus the separation view, Donato Masciandaro (Chapter 14) takes a political economy perspective. He examines the political determinants of (changes in) the supervisory setting and finds that, among other things, central banks acting as microprudential supervisors are more likely to be given macroprudential powers. In contrast, greater central bank independence, which may increase the risk of a powerful monetary authority, is associated with less involvement in macroprudential supervision. Supervisory reforms, in general, are mainly driven by systemic banking crises and reforms undertaken by peers ('bandwagon' effect). In light of the rise in populism, the author cautions, more attention should be paid to changes in political preferences, in particular with regard to central bank independence that may increasingly become contested.

Part IV deals with the *implications of the fintech revolution for the optimal supervisory architecture*.

While the presence of Big Tech platforms in finance may bring many benefits, such as cost reductions, higher productivity or financial inclusion, their activities may inhibit competition, impair consumer protection and incur financial stability risks. In his contribution, José Manuel González-Páramo (Chapter 15) argues that two main features are driving this potential outcome: Big Tech's business model itself – such companies also offer non-financial services and may become 'too big to fail' – as well as regulatory and supervisory asymmetries created by the current supervisory practices. At the same time, supervisors overlook the financial stability risks of the growth potential and interconnectedness of Big Tech platforms. González-Páramo then critically assesses various initiatives that could mitigate some of the supervisory asymmetries and rebalance the playing field. But in order to effectively address the unfavourable effects of Big Techs on competition, and the operational resilience risks of platforms, he notes that it could be justifiable to recalibrate regulation towards a more entity-based framework. This would imply treating Big Techs as entities that perform financial and non-financial roles of crucial importance for financial and economic stability.

Finally, Maarten van Oordt (Chapter 16) discusses regulatory control over stablecoin issuers. Stablecoin arrangements are typically discussed in the context of their compliance with regulations aimed at financial consumer protection, investor protection, operational resilience and the prevention of money-laundering, terrorist financing and other illicit activities. But less attention, as noted by van Oordt, has been raised to the fact that stablecoin transactions are processed by decentralised networks that may operate outside the sphere of control of the relevant authorities. Hence, he focuses on the importance for the issuer of a fiat-backed stablecoin to maintain reliable access to the domestic payment system of the jurisdiction that issues the fiat currency in order to maintain a stable peg. The chapter provides several empirical illustrations that show how substantial deviations of the one-to-one peg could occur for the most prominent fiat-backed stablecoin when its access to the domestic payment system was interrupted. Van Oordt then discusses the implications for the extent to which regulators will be able exercise control over stablecoin issuers.

Part V elaborates on the *challenges for monetary policy and supervision design against the lessons of COVID-19 and future known and unknown uncertainties.*

Without doubt, the young 21st century has already seen a partial disruption of our economies and societies on account of a sequence of crisis episodes that are quite diverse in nature. Ignazio Angeloni (Chapter 17) mentions terrorism, the global financial crisis and the pandemic – while a fourth is in the making: the climate crisis. The author thus makes a case for building 'systems' that are resilient and sustainable in the face of unforeseen events. This, in turn, necessitates thinking of scenarios and safeguards which may protect us against imponderable incidents. Angeloni zeroes in on the European financial architecture and the monetary policy framework and asks himself where both need rethinking. On the one hand, a main challenge lies in the need to significantly rely on discretionary decisions delegated to independent agencies – e.g. the ECB as monetary policymaker and banking supervisor. Rigid rules constraining discretion may hamper swift decision-making in times of crises. On the other hand, policy discretion by independent, unelected authorities requires strict accountability processes regarding the way in which such authorities pursue their objectives.

David Archer (Chapter 18) poses a question related to Angeloni's considerations: How to best prepare an instrument set now to counter another crisis yet unforeseeable at the current juncture? In the course of the most recent crises, central banks considerably widened their operational toolkits and interpreted their mandate in a flexible way. As a result, legitimacy concerns were raised as central bank discretionary power was to a high degree exercised by unelected officials. According to Archer, many central bank constitutions miss explicit emergency mandates. Drawing on debates among constitutional theorists about how best to provide emergency powers, the author of the final chapter explores the potential value and policy options of explicit emergency mandates for central banks.

OUTLOOK

It is no small feat to analyse issues relating to the financial supervisory architecture. After all, we are dealing with a complex combination of theoretical arguments, empirical evidence and political economy considerations.

This volume does not aim at providing definitive answers to all relevant aspects. It does, however, bring together a series of contributions by prominent experts in the field. They tackle some of the key issues through the lens of the most recent academic research and practical experience. The lessons learned are especially relevant as new developments affect the terms of the debate on different institutional arrangements, be it technological disruption, greater awareness of the importance of climate change for the financial sector, or the COVID-19 pandemic. In Europe, the supervisory architecture needs to evolve further, not only to cope with new developments, but also to effectively advance economic and financial integration. Cases in point are completing the banking union and making fast progress in the area of the capital markets union. The European supervisory architecture stands to benefit from conceptual and empirical advances in many areas, but four areas are of particular importance. First, revisiting and taking a novel approach to the governance of monetary policy, microprudential and macroprudential policies: after all, good governance is the basis for any successful policy. Second, evaluating the effectiveness of supervision under different settings: rigorous monitoring and assessment of the impact of reforms will enhance our understanding of what works (and what does not) for what reason. Third, monetary and supervisory institutions in Europe possess a treasure of data whose potential has yet to be fully used. Here, it is key to provide broader access – to non-sensitive data – to both institutional and academic researchers. Fourth, empowering supervisors to be at least one step ahead of rapidly changing financial markets and institutions: in an optimal institutional setting only this will allow them to react swiftly to changes.

NOTE

1.   Paul Volcker, 'The Triumph of Central Banking?' The 1990 Per Jacobsson Lecture, Per Jacobsson Foundation, 1990.

PART I

Trends in European banking supervision design

2. The puzzle of Europe's banking union: progress and missing pieces

Thorsten Beck

1.   INTRODUCTION

The Global Financial Crisis has clearly shown the tension between the global footprint of banks and close cross-border integration of national banking systems, on the one hand, and the national stability focus of regulators, on the other hand. Large cross-border banks, such as Fortis and Dexia, were at the core of the crisis. While there was cross-border cooperation between supervisors, in the form of Memorandums of Understanding governing exchange of information and Colleges of Supervisors convened by parent bank supervisors, these arrangements turned out to be insufficient. Memorandums of Understanding are not legally binding; when cross-border banks get into trouble, the value of these agreements rises and falls with the banks' value – as cross-border banks are about to fail, non-binding agreements lose their usefulness as each supervisory authority is focused on stability in its jurisdiction. Similarly, Colleges of Supervisors are not decision takers – in a crisis, each supervisor is on her own. This is not to say that cooperation agreements such as memorandums and colleges are not useful and necessary, but they are simply not sufficient when cooperation is needed most – during times of fragility. This experience has resulted in an extension of supervisory cooperation to resolution and crisis management, at the bilateral level and global level.

The crisis revealed another major shortcoming: the lack of bank resolution frameworks across Europe. There are several reasons why the corporate insolvency regime is inadequate to deal with failing banks. First, the failure of a financial institution results in negative externalities beyond the private costs of failure; it imposes external costs on other financial institutions and the economy at large. Second, the opacity of banks' balance sheets, the market sensitivity of assets, and the ability to rapidly change the structure of balance sheet and thus capital position call for an early and swift intervention, not available under a court-based system. The experience of the Global Financial Crisis has consequently resulted in the establishment of bank resolution frameworks at the national and European level, with the Bank Recovery and Resolution Directive (BRRD) forcing a certain harmonisation in the principles and tools of bank resolution across EU members.

The Eurodebt crisis in 2010/2011 brought a third problem to the forefront: the doom-loop between sovereign and bank fragility. Failing banks require government support, which might make government debt unsustainable, as seen in Ireland in 2009. But sovereign fragility can also hurt the banking sector: the restructuring of Greek government debt in 2011 required in turn a bail-out of Greek banks and contributed to the Cypriot crisis in 2013, with both Greek and Cypriot banks heavily exposed to Greek government bonds. The Spanish government tapped European funding to resolve problems in its banking system, mainly in the *cajas* segments and related to the boom-bust construction cycle. The fear during the Eurodebt crisis that Italy might be next also prevented the Italian government from acting more decisively in addressing the problems in the banking sector. However, this delay ultimately turned into a growth problem, as Italian enterprises had increasing problems tapping a weakened banking sector for funding. Breaking the doom-loop between sovereign and bank fragility was the motivation for starting work on a common financial safety net, the banking union.

Finally, the limited institutional and fiscal capacity to resolve failing banks has incentivised many national supervisors into actively pushing their banks into ring-fencing, which ultimately undermined the Single European Market in Banking. This is complemented with a tragedy of commons character of the euro area, stemming from the tension between national supervision but European access to liquidity support, where the costs of keeping zombie banks alive can be shared across the common currency. As the doom-loop between sovereign and bank fragility, this tragedy of commons problem was a motivation for the establishment of common supervision and resolution.

The question arises whether the regulatory reforms of the past decade, including the banking union, have fulfilled their objectives, including addressing the four problems mentioned so far. My argument in the following is that we have made progress, but still have a long way to go, and that some decisions made along the way have made further progress more difficult.

2.   FROM BAIL-OUT TO BAIL-IN

While economists were quick to call for a European regulatory framework if not financial safety net after the Global Financial Crisis, it was not until the Eurodebt crisis that European governments focused on creating the foundations for what is now referred to as banking union. While initially designed with three legs, only supervision and resolution have been partly delegated to the euro area level, with plans for a common deposit insurance scheme so far not implemented.

2.1   Moving from National to Supranational Supervision

On 29 June 2012, the heads of government of all euro area countries issued a statement announcing that the Commission would present proposals for the creation of a Single Supervisory Mechanism (SSM), underpinned by the necessity to break the vicious circle between banks and sovereigns. The regulation on the SSM mandates the European Central Bank (ECB) to exercise prudential supervision of all banks located in the euro area, whether directly by the ECB's own supervisory arm for the significant banks, or indirectly for less significant banks, supervised by the national prudential supervisors but under the general guidance of the ECB.

An important step in preparing the SSM to become fully operational was the Comprehensive Assessment that took place between November 2013 and October 2014, a year-long effort to assess capital positions across the largest banks in the Eurozone and apply stress tests to these capital positions to establish their resilience. Before that, in October 2013, the criteria guiding the classification of euro area banks into significant institutions (SIs, supervised directly by the SSM) and less significant institutions (LSIs, supervised by national authorities) was published.

In late October 2014, the ECB published the results of the Comprehensive Assessment. This test was seen as entry point for the ECB assuming its responsibility as Single Supervisory Mechanism on 4 November 2014.

The Comprehensive Assessment showed quite some variation in asset reclassification. For example, more than 20 per cent of the reviewed debtors were reclassified as non-performing in Greece, Malta and Estonia. Slovenia even saw a 32 per cent reclassification, with one bank hitting 43 per cent. The large variation in loan reclassification across countries and the rather high number in some countries suggest that this is not simply due to different national loan classification regimes but rather a high degree of regulatory forbearance.

Joint supervisory teams are tasked with the day-to-day supervision of significant institutions, composed of both ECB and national supervisory staff. The SSM exercises supervision both at the group level as well as at the individual entity level within the banking union, for example, ensuring that the subsidiary has sound levels of capital and liquidity and that its internal governance is effective. However, supervisors still work with different legal frameworks across countries.

Overall, and even though European supervision is still work in progress, one can consider the SSM as a success, paving the way towards a common supervisory culture and approach within Europe. It can also be considered a great success given the political and legal resistance against any form of centralising the financial safety at the European level in the wake of the 2008 crisis.

2.2   The Single Resolution Mechanism – A Political Compromise and Halfway House

Resolution frameworks across Europe were strengthened after the Global Financial Crisis, at the national level, but also – with the bail-in clause introduced under the Bank Recovery and Resolution Directive (BRRD) – at the European level. Complementing the SSM, the Single Resolution Mechanism (SRM), coming into effect in 2016, aims to coordinate resolution of failing banks on the level of the banking union. However, centralisation is much less than in the case of bank supervision. The Single Resolution Board (SRB) has not only the national resolution authorities (NRAs) as its constituent members but also the European Commission and the ECB as observers, and the European Council in cooperation with the European Commission with veto powers for certain decisions. There is a strong role for the NRAs in the execution of resolution decisions as well as in the planning phase. NRAs, as part of internal resolution teams led by the SRB, are deeply involved in drafting resolution plans, resolvability assessments, communicating with banks, engaging with them, addressing their doubts, but in accordance with the general policies and criteria approved by the SRB. The euro area NRAs concerned, together with the SRB, make up the internal resolution team. They jointly perform all the activities required to conduct resolution planning, and hence host country resolution authorities, even from small hosts, are also fully involved in the planning process. Parallel to SRB, a Single Resolution Fund is being built up over a period of eight years (2016–2023) and will reach at least 1 per cent of the amount of covered deposits of credit institutions. From 2022 onwards the backstop to the SRF will be introduced, in the form of revolving credit line from the ESM that doubles the size of the SRF.

The SRM – with all the caveats stated below – is an important first step. One major gap is that currently resolution options are only available for banks where such resolution is in the public interest (focusing mostly on financial stability concerns). All other banks have to be sent into national insolvency proceedings, which vary quite a lot across member countries, some of them court-based and others of administrative nature. This, however, is not only inefficient but also leaves gaps, such as when the regulator declares a bank failing or likely to fail but the court finds the bank still solvent, and thus it can not enter insolvency proceedings. One example was the Latvian ABLV Bank where the ECB's declaration that it was failing was followed by the assessment of the Single Resolution Board that a resolution procedure was not in the public interest. While the Latvian parent shareholders decided to liquidate the bank voluntarily, the Luxembourg subsidiary was initially not declared insolvent. Further, such loopholes give space for political interference into the process, pressure for taxpayer support on the national level, thus leading us back to the bank-sovereign linkage that the banking union was supposed to eliminate.

2.3   The Banking Union's Original Sin

To what extent has the banking union succeeded? To answer this question, we have to go back to the original objectives. A first objective was to better handle the failure of cross-border banks. A second objective was to reduce if not eliminate this 'deadly embrace' of governments and banks. A third was to move from bail-out to bail-in and a fourth (and overarching) objective was to create a European Single Market in Banking with no risk of national ring-fencing. One can argue that the banking union, as it currently stands, has been allowed to make careful steps towards these goals, but has ultimately fallen short.

Concerning better crisis management of failing cross-border management, global regulatory reforms (increasing the capital buffer through Total Loss Absorbing Capacity, TLAC; establishment of crisis management groups; bank recovery and resolution plans) as well as SSM and SRM have certainly contributed to a better preparation for such cases and possibly reduced the likelihood of such failures (Beck et al., 2021). However, the ultimate proof is still out and will only come in the case of another major financial crisis. So far, the banking union has not had to deal with the failure of a major cross-border bank and has thus not really been put to test in this regard.

Has the banking union contributed to a better functioning of the Single Market and prevented ring-fencing? While microprudential regulation is at the European level, macroprudential regulation is not. And a clash could be seen in 2020 when the ECB and the European Systemic Risk Board (ESRB) asked banks across Europe not to pay out profits at the group level, while macroprudential authorities in some member countries asked all banks in their jurisdictions, including subsidiaries of European banking groups, not to pay any profits to their parent banks, which is a disruption to free capital flows within the Single Market. On the other hand, these authorities correctly pointed out that the subsidiaries benefited indirectly from national fiscal support and that risk sharing across Europe is far from complete (ESRB, 2020). This episode clearly points to the incomplete nature of the banking union and thus risk sharing within Europe. More generally, and as also argued by Dewatripont et al. (2021), prepositioning of internal Minimum Requirements for own funds and Eligible Liabilities (MRELs), even though banking groups within the banking union are considered as a Single Point of Entry for resolution purposes, effectively constitutes barriers to the free allocation of capital within the group and thus the banking union.

Take next the 'deadly embrace' of governments and banks. Banks still hold an extensive, large share of their sovereign bond portfolio in the bonds of their home country, and after a long period of decline this has been increasing again during the COVID-19 crisis (Lozano Guerrero et al., 2020). Attempts to create synthetic safe assets, such as ESBies (Brunnermeier et al., 2017), have not taken off and regulatory restrictions such as concentration limits have not been imposed. While following the 'whatever it takes' announcement in 2012 and extremely lose monetary policy, the spectre of sovereign distress has faded in the euro area, and the structural constraints have not been addressed.

This brings me to the third criterion: failing banks are still resolved at the national level and mostly with taxpayer support, be it in Germany (Nord LB) or in Italy (Monte dei Paschi di Siena). True, there is a Single Resolution Mechanism; however, there have been few cases where it has become active. This is also a problem of regional banks and their close connection with local politicians, clearly seen in Italy, but also in Germany with the *Landesbanken* and in Spain, with the *cajas*. Yes, supervision has been Europeanised; however, banks' connections with local and national politicians have kept the resolution effectively at the national level and bail-outs still the default solution.

Finally, and related to the previous two points, there has been little progress towards a truly Single Market in Banking across Europe. Banking markets are still predominantly national, especially in the larger markets of Germany, France, Italy and Spain. Cross-border mergers (such as in the run-up to the Global Financial Crisis) have become less numerous and consolidation attempts are often focused on the national level (e.g., politically encouraged merger talks between Deutsche and Commerzbank in Germany).

Ultimately, this reflects what I would call the original sin of the banking union: the above-mentioned Comprehensive Assessment showed several significant European lenders to have significant capital shortfalls. Rather than address legacy losses and force an effective restructuring of European banking in 2014, the new regulatory framework was applied to a banking system still working through the aftermath of the Global Financial and Eurodebt crises and – in the case of Italy – a triple-dip recession. Such restructuring through, for example, a European bad bank would have put the European banking system on a sounder footing and would have enabled an important first step towards a truly European banking system (Beck and Trebesch, 2013). An important opportunity lost.

3.   LOOKING FORWARD – THE NEXT STEPS

There is increasing consensus on what needs to be done: (1) completing the banking union with a European deposit insurance and backstop for the resolution fund; (2) stronger resolution powers at the European level that allow quicker and more decisive interventions.

Ultimately, all these are necessary but not sufficient conditions for a truly European banking system. Regulations and regulators can provide the framework for a Single Market in Banking but cannot create it. Only a reduction in political influence over regulatory decisions, both at a national and European level, can help here. Importantly, the same forces that are reluctant to give up political influence over the banking system are resisting attempts to take the next step towards completing the banking union.

REFERENCES

Beck, Thorsten and Christoph Trebesch (2013). A Bank Restructuring Agency for the Eurozone – Cleaning up the Legacy Losses. VoxEU, 18 November.
Beck, Thorsten, Consuelo Silva-Buston and Wolf Wagner (2021). The Economics of Supranational Bank Supervision. *Journal of Financial and Quantitative Analysis*, forthcoming.
Brunnermeier, Markus, Sam Langfield, Marco Pagano, Ricardo Reis, Stijn Van Nieuwerburgh and Dimitri Vayanos (2017). ESBies: Safety in the Tranches. *Economic Policy* 32 (90), 175–219.
Dewatripont, Mathias, Marie Montigny and Gregory Nguyen (2021). When Trust is Not Enough: Bank Resolution, SPE, Ring-fencing and Group Support. European Corporate Governance Institute – Finance Working Paper 759/2021.
European Systemic Risk Board (2020). System-wide Restraints on Dividend Payments, Share Buybacks and Other Pay-outs. Frankfurt a.M., Germany.
Lozano Guerrero, Silvia, Julian Metzler and Alessandro D. Scopelliti (2020). Developments in the Sovereign-bank Nexus in the Euro Area: The Role of Direct Sovereign Exposures. Published as part of the Financial Stability Review, November 2020, European Central Bank.

3. Supervisory architecture in the EU: where should we go from here?

Fernando Restoy[1]

1. INTRODUCTION

The financial industry is currently characterized by a large number of entities offering a wide range of services and by a diverse set of rules that aim at protecting social objectives such as financial stability, consumer protection and market integrity. Given the diversity of the financial industry and the numerous public policy objectives of regulation, the design of an adequate institutional framework for the supervision of financial firms' requirements and obligations is both an essential and a complex task.

Traditionally the debate on the design of a supervisory architecture has focused on whether central banks should be involved in prudential oversight and whether supervision should be organized according to a sectoral, a functional or an integrated approach. More recently, the debate has also included the adequate allocation of macroprudential and resolution responsibilities.

From a technical point of view, the selection of a supervisory model from various alternatives should take into account both the synergies and the conflicts that assigning different objectives to a specific agency can create (Kremers et al. 2003). Moreover, it should assess whether there is a neat association between the available instruments and specific policy objectives (Restoy 2020). Experience shows, however, that political economy considerations are at least as important as the technical arguments. In particular, as in modern societies supervisors must be able to operate independently from elected officials; there is a logical interest in constraining the powers and functions that each independent agency receives upon delegation from governments (Tucker 2018).

The debate is still far from conclusive. Indeed, the concrete arrangements differ markedly across jurisdictions. Even within the European Union, the diversity of institutional supervisory arrangements is quite large, ranging from integrated supervisors to 'twin peaks' models. Central banks do also play quite different roles in the various jurisdictions. Moreover, the new oversight functions (resolution and macroprudential) have been assigned to existing or newly created agencies following heterogeneous approaches. That heterogeneity at the domestic level coexists with the allocation of responsibilities to European bodies in some areas (monetary policy, microprudential, resolution) but not (or only partially) in others (macroprudential, securities, insurance).

While an optimal institutional model may not exist, the current fragmentation of supervisory responsibilities across national and European agencies following highly diverse structures can hardly contribute to adequate financial oversight and further integration of the industry. Moreover, recent developments, such as the disruption created by the new technological players in the market for financial services and the increased attention to climate-related financial risks, call for a consistent supervisory approach that may be difficult to achieve under the current fragmented organization. The quest for policy consistency is further motivated by the unprecedented challenge provoked by the COVID-19 pandemic for the adequate conduct of macroeconomic and financial policies.

This chapter reviews different aspects of the supervisory architecture in the EU and analyses the case for possible reforms in a post-pandemic framework characterized by a deep technological transformation of the industry and increased awareness of climate-related-risks (CRR).

The structure of the rest of the chapter is as follows. Section 2 briefly describes some relevant aspects of the current European supervisory architecture. Section 3 reviews the terms of the debate on three concrete issues, namely, the role of central banks in financial stability, the comparison between sectoral and functional organization of supervision, and the distribution of responsibilities between European and national authorities. Section 4 explains how technological developments, climate change considerations and the lessons extracted from the pandemic affect the debate. Finally, Section 5 provides some concluding remarks.

2.   THE CURRENT ARCHITECTURE

In the current institutional framework in the European Economic and Monetary Union (EMU), financial regulation is largely harmonized through EU directives and regulations, although some national specificities still exist that prevent the achievement of a complete 'single rule-book' (Enria 2019, Restoy 2019).

By contrast, oversight responsibilities are shared between European and national authorities. National authorities remain fully in charge of the supervision of most regulated capital market entities (such as investment firms and asset managers), insurance companies and firms offering payment services (such as Payment Institutions (PIs) and Electronic Money Institutions (EMIs)).

European authorities have taken over responsibilities in the area of banks' microprudential supervision (undertaken by the European Central Bank (ECB)), resolution (Single Resolution Board (SRB)) and some capital market activities like credit ratings (European Securities and Markets Authority (ESMA)). In all areas in which European agencies have direct supervisory responsibilities, national authorities also play a role, particularly in relation to the oversight of smaller (less significant) institutions.

In the field of macroprudential policies, responsibilities in the euro area (EA) are shared between the ECB and national authorities, although the former can only top up macroprudential measures taken at the domestic level. That framework is designed to facilitate a swift policy reaction to nation-specific macro-financial imbalances and correct somehow the inaction bias by national authorities. However, the ECB can deploy only some specific policy instruments (the so-called capital-based tools) but not others (like constraints on loan-to-value or debt-to-income ratios) which are available for national authorities.

The functions that remain at the domestic level are organized following a variety of approaches (see Table 3.1). In particular, Germany applies an integrated supervisory model around a single financial supervisor (Bafin). At the other extreme, Spain follows a sectoral model with different regulators for banks, insurance companies and securities markets. Belgium and the Netherlands have put in place a functional twin peaks model with separate agencies in charge of prudential and conduct of business supervision of all regulated entities. Finally, France and Italy operate a hybrid (two-agency) model in which one agency monitors both the safety and soundness and the conduct of business of banks and insurance companies, while a second agency supervises securities markets.

As for the new oversight functions, for the most part jurisdictions have tended to assign resolution functions to the prudential banking supervisory authority and the macroprudential responsibilities to cross-agency financial stability committees with government participation.

Despite the heterogeneity of the prevailing institutional framework in European jurisdictions, a common feature is the assignment of key oversight responsibilities to the central bank. Indeed, among the six largest European jurisdictions, in five of them the central bank conducts microprudential supervision, acts as a resolution authority and oversees PIs and EMIs. Moreover, while in most countries the formal macroprudential authority is not the central bank, in all cases in which it has microprudential responsibilities it also acts as the competent authority for the deployment of the macroprudential tools foreseen in European legislation (ESRB 2021).

Table 3.1   *Supervisory regimes in selected Euro area countries*[a]

Country	Model	Micropru (banking)	Macropru	Resolution	Payments (PI, EMI)
Belgium	TP	CB	CB	CB	CB
France[b]	TA	CB	FSC	CB	CB
Germany	Integrated	SA	FSC	SA	SA
Italy	TA	CB	CB	CB	CB
Netherlands	TP	CB	FSC	CB	CB
Spain[c]	Sectoral	CB	FSC	CB/RA	CB

Note: [a] TP: twin-peaks; CB: central bank; SA: dedicated supervisory agency; RA: dedicated resolution agency; FSC: cross-agency financial stability council; PI: Payment Institutions; EMI: Electronic Money Institutions; TA: two-agency model consisting of an agency overseeing both prudential and conduct of business for banks and insurance companies and a different agency looking after securities markets. [b] In France, microprudential supervision and resolution is performed by ACPR, an agency working under the auspices of the Banque de France and chaired by its Governor. [c] In Spain, the central bank is the planning resolution authority, while a dedicated agency (FROB) is the executive resolution authority.
Source: Calvo et al. (2018); author's compilation.

3.   THE TRADITIONAL TERMS OF THE DEBATE

While the debate on the institutional organization of financial supervision has covered a large variety of aspects, there are two which have attracted special attention: (1) the involvement of central banks in financial stability; and (2) the choice between a sectoral and a functional organization. In the European context, a third, and possibly more relevant, issue is the distribution of supervisory responsibilities between European and national authorities.

3.1   Central Banks and Financial Stability

The original mandates of most central banks included – when they were created – a financial oversight function, which has traditionally been considered as a natural complement of central banks' key role as a lender of a last resort. The debate on whether there might be drawbacks to involving them in financial stability has arisen rather recently. This essentially coincides with the adoption by central banks – mostly in the last two decades of the 20th century – of price stability mandates accompanied by statutory independence from governments and parliaments (Padoa-Schioppa 2002). The main argument against giving central banks any sort of responsibility in the area of financial stability is that this objective would not always be aligned with the primary price stability objective, thereby leading to socially suboptimal monetary policy.

Indeed, although in the long run economic stability and financial stability are closely linked to each other, over the regular horizon of monetary policy actions, some conflicts can and often do occur. This is particularly the case whenever a consumer price stability-oriented interest rate policy may contribute to exacerbate or abruptly correct macro-financial imbalances.

It could be argued that the post-Great Financial Crisis (GFC) establishment of macroprudential authorities with dedicated policy tools and a clear financial stability mandate strengthens the case for central banks to focus on a narrow price stability mandate. However, the allocation of two different objectives to two separate authorities should not only depend on whether each of the two objectives can be achieved by applying two distinct sets of instruments. It also requires that the instruments designed to achieve one objective have no significant effect on the other objective. It is clear that the standard monetary policy instruments directly affect credit developments, asset prices and banks' margins. Thus, they have an impact on the prospects for financial stability. Likewise, macroprudential instruments, such as capital requirements or restrictions on credit availability, directly affect financial conditions, which in turn affect consumption and investment decisions and hence the prospects for economic stability.[2]

These arguments imply that monetary and macroprudential policies should not be conducted by separate institutions unless there are sufficiently effective coordination mechanisms in place (Carstens 2019, Restoy 2020). In game-theory terms, the non-cooperative equilibrium (each authority pursuing its own objective independently of the other) is likely to become, under those conditions, socially suboptimal (Cao and Cholletec 2017).

Similar arguments could be applied to the discussion on the allocation of microprudential and macroprudential responsibilities. In fact, micro- and macroprudential policies share the same objective: to preserve financial stability. They do, however, pursue this common objective from two different perspectives: either entity by entity (microprudential) or system-wide (macroprudential). In principle, those two perspectives can work together effectively but can occasionally clash with each other. This is particularly the case in cyclical downturns.

The potential frictions between macroprudential and microprudential could argue for assigning these two functions to different agencies.

Yet, as discussed above, that approach could only work well if the instruments needed to achieve the respective objectives of each agency could be neatly differentiated. But this kind of demarcation is difficult to make, as both functions operate through similar instruments such as capital requirements or controls on banks' exposures. Since macroprudential and microprudential policies share the same ultimate objective and much of their respective toolkits, the option to house them in separate agencies is unlikely to be socially preferable to the alternative.

The involvement of central banks in bank resolution could be discussed as a possible complement to their participation in prudential supervision. The terms of the debate will then depend on the balance of conflicts and synergies between those two functions.

Supervision focuses on crisis prevention for banks as going concerns, while resolution aims at ensuring adequate management of banks of gone concern status. Synergies between those functions are significant as they require a similar set of information on individual institutions and similar technical capabilities for staff involved in both areas.

There are also some potentially relevant conflicts across those two functions. In particular, it has been often argued that supervisors may have an interest in delaying resolution and, for that purpose, applying excessive forbearance, while resolution authorities may prefer earlier action in order to reduce costs for creditors or external fund providers. These conflicts could, in theory, be addressed by separating the two functions in different agencies. However, even in countries where this is the case, the trigger for resolution (e.g. the declaration that a bank is failing or likely to fail) typically remains with the supervisory authority (Baudino et al. 2021) given their superior analytical ability to assess the situation and prospects of supervised institutions. Separation, therefore, does not necessarily disactivate the main potential source of conflicts between objectives, while it may reduce the ability to take advantage of the existing synergies.

3.2   Sectoral vs. Functional

The debate on a sectoral versus a functional organization of supervision closely follows the synergies-conflicts logic (Kremers et al. 2003). A sectoral model – characterized by different supervisors for different financial sectors (banking, insurance, securities markets) – can be justified based on possible complementarities between prudential and conduct of business oversight and the operational convenience of having a single supervisory entry point to each financial institution. The defence of this needs, however, to attach little importance to potential conflicts between pursuing entities' financial soundness and consumer protection.

The functional approach is best represented by the twin peaks model, consisting in organizing supervision around two agencies with authority over all financial institutions: one is in charge of the prudential supervision, while the other focuses on conduct of business. This model weighs prominently the conflicts that could eventually arise between protecting the solvency of financial institutions and ensuring their clients and investors are properly treated. At the same time, it acknowledges the relevant synergies that exist in the monitoring of the prudential situation or the conduct of business of different types of institutions.

In general, the academic literature tends to lend support to the functional model (e.g. Group of Thirty 2008, Fischer 2008). Moreover, this model seems to have proven more robust than alternative approaches during the GFC (Kremers and Schoenmaker 2010).

Despite this, in the banking union only two of the six largest countries follow a pure twin peaks model (Belgium and the Netherlands). The limited adoption of supervisory models based on a functional approach in the EU may be partly linked to the sectoral focus of most European conduct of business regulation.[3] The current EU institutional framework – inspired by the de Larosière Report (2009) – contains specific consumer protection rules for financial products depending on the type of entity that offers them. In addition, it establishes specialized authorities for banking (EBA), insurance (EIOPA) and securities (ESMA), with relatively soft coordination mechanisms among them.

Yet, both the de Larosière Report (2009) and the subsequent EU regulation themselves envisage a future revision entailing the transformation of the current architecture to create two agencies with functional responsibilities, in line with the twin peaks model.

3.3   European vs. National

The process of transferring competences from national agencies to European institutions has broadly followed the quest for a progressive integration of the EU economy. However, the timing of the process has also been shaped by the perception of the need to ensure the sustainability of the integration achieved by fostering the transfer of yet additional powers and functions.

The sense that an insufficient transfer of responsibilities from national jurisdictions to European bodies could challenge the stability of the whole European construction process became evident at the time of the European sovereign debt crisis initiated in 2010 in the midst of the GFC.

The perverse feedback loop between the domestic sovereign and banking risks threatened the sustainability of the monetary union as markets started pricing redenomination risks. The response was a series of interlinked policy actions – aimed at mitigating the national character of banking risks – that shaped what we know as banking union. The creation of the Single Supervisory Mechanism (SSM) and the Single Resolution Mechanism (SRM), and the associated transfer of competences by EU member states to European agencies, can therefore be considered as primarily motivated by the need to ensure the stability of the monetary union.[4]

Those developments show that, despite divergent national interests, there has so far always been a clear determination to adopt the required institutional reforms for the preservation of the European construction project. Yet it would be helpful to adopt in quiet times reforms that could strengthen the European integration process by reducing its vulnerability against destabilizing events that could affect specific member states.

A major objective in this regard would be the strengthening of pan-European private risk-sharing mechanisms. The common banks' supervisory and resolution mechanisms and the capital markets union project already contribute to the integration of financial markets by facilitating more homogenous conditions for the conduct of business in different member states. However, in order to achieve the desired integration additional efforts are required, particularly to complete the banking union (with a European deposit insurance scheme) and to achieve more homogenous supervision of the common rules for capital markets activity. Indeed, there is a case for assigning ESMA more responsibilities (in cooperation with national authorities) in the supervision of large capital market players and large market operations (such as IPOs or takeovers). Assigning ESMA the supervision of the conduct of business of significant commercial and investment banks could also be considered. That would make the EU institutional arrangement closer to a functional – as opposed to the current mostly sectoral – allocation of supervisory responsibilities (Schoenmaker and Veron 2017). Notice that those actions would not require any modification of the Treaty. Recent rulings by the European Court of Justice[5] effectively enlarge the scope of delegation of responsibilities, under the current Treaty, to European authorities (Botopoulos 2020).

Finally, in the euro area the case for integrating both macroprudential and microprudential policies within the ECB is even more compelling. The current rather decentralised framework severely constrains the ECB's ability to deploy macroprudential instruments that could complement monetary policy (and sometimes microprudential) actions aimed at fostering the stability of the euro area economic and financial system. This is likely to generate tensions between the centralised functions (monetary policy and microprudential) and the ones that remain largely decentralised (macroprudential).

4.   THE NEW ELEMENTS

4.1   The Pandemic

The policy response to the economic impact of the COVID-19 pandemic highlighted relevant complementarities across policy domains. As the economy faced a large adverse shock, both monetary and macroprudential policies had to adopt a highly supportive stance in order to preserve economic and financial stability.

Interestingly, microprudential policies also played, probably for the first time, an explicit stabilization role. After the COVID-19 outbreak, supervisory authorities worldwide relaxed capital requirements, invited firms to adopt a pragmatic approach to recognize impairments and expected credit losses, postponed regulatory reforms and reduced supervisory intensity. All that with the purpose of mitigating the risk of excessively procyclical behaviour by financial institutions that could lead to a sharp credit contraction (Borio and Restoy 2020).[6]

The pandemic has therefore shown relevant synergies between monetary and prudential policies and between the macroprudential and microprudential policy functions. The latter has been key, as a narrow focus by prudential supervisors on individual banks' resilience – for instance by forcing banks to reduce risk exposures or accumulate capital – would have left macroprudential authorities with no firepower to prevent a credit crunch. As discussed above, those synergies certainly support the case for promoting a supervisory architecture that facilitates close coordination across policy domains.

It is true, though, that we have seen consistent policy actions undertaken by authorities in jurisdictions with different supervisory models and often lacking formal coordination procedures among responsible agencies. However, that spontaneous coordination across separate agencies seems to be caused by the unprecedented size and nature of the shock. It may certainly be more challenging to decide how rapidly prudential requirements should be normalised if the recovery does not take place at a sufficient speed.

Ensuring the required consistency in all phases of the economic and financial cycle may require, once again, the ECB's macroprudential functions and policy toolbox to be enlarged.

4.2   Technology

There is currently an active debate on how best to address the challenges posed by the new technological developments for the adequate functioning of the financial system. A specific aspect of that debate is the regulatory approach that should be adopted to control the risks associated with the increasing presence of tech companies (fintech and especially big techs) in the market for financial services.

Until recently, most commentators tended to support an activity-based approach under the principle *same activity, same regulation* as the best formula to prevent regulatory arbitrage and contribute to a level playing field. Yet there are strong arguments that a superior approach would be to combine activity-based rules with entity-based ones.[7] While activity-based rules would be warranted in policy domains (like consumer protection or anti-money laundering and combating the financing of terrorism (AML/CFT)) where all providers of financial services roughly generate the same type of risks, an entity-based approach should be preferred in those areas (like competition or financial stability) where different entities generate different risks when performing the same activity (Restoy 2019). On those grounds, entity-based rules would therefore be justified not only for banking institutions but also for big techs as a way to address the risk they pose for adequate market functioning (Restoy 2021, Carstens et al. 2021).

So far there has been less discussion on what the adequate supervisory structure to accompany the regulatory reform should be. In principle, for policy areas in which an activity-based approach should be preferred, there seems to be a case to ensure also that all entities performing the same function should be supervised by the same agency. In the EU, regulations regarding consumer protection or AML/CFT largely follow an activity-based approach. Yet, in many cases, separate agencies monitor the way different entities comply with the relevant requirements and often apply different degrees of stringency. As this may jeopardize the objectives of the regulation and generate unwarranted competitive distortion, it provides additional arguments for adopting a functional rather than a sectoral approach for supervision of activity-based rules.

In some policy domains where an entity-based approach is preferable, a functional supervisory regime could also be a sensible option. In the area of competition, some countries are already developing specific rules aiming at preventing damage to market contestability by big techs (Crisanto et al. 2021). As we already have a functional supervisor in this policy domain (competition authorities at the national and EU levels), that should be the one overseeing big techs' compliance with those rules. This is the approach followed by the European Commission's (EC) proposal for a Digital Markets Act (DMA), which also assigns direct competences to the EC for applying the rules to large platforms offering services in different countries.

In other areas, where there could be special, big tech-specific risks, a pure functional approach may not be entirely satisfactory. In particular, big techs can create major disruptions if they fail to satisfy the required operational continuity of the different services they provide to the public or to financial institutions (like cloud computing services). The EC's recent proposal for a Digital Operational Resilience Act (DORA) largely follows an activity-based approach and does not foresee a specific supervisory regime for big tech groups, although it envisages the oversight of some significant third-party providers of services for financial institutions. Big techs' operational risks may well be associated with the failure of the systems used in different business lines – which include the provision of both financial and non-financial services – and they could be rather different than the ones posed by other entities (like banks or insurance companies). That not only supports the adoption of entity-based rules but may also provide arguments for a specific supervisory regime aimed at addressing the operational resilience and other relevant risks posed by big techs.

4.3   Climate

There is now emerging consensus that climate-related risks (CRRs) pose significant challenges to individual banks and the financial system. In particular, financial institutions are exposed to climate change not only through physical risks (e.g. extreme weather events) but also through transition risks, as changes in government policies, in technology and in consumer and investor behaviours could affect the value of some banks' exposures.

For the time being, most prudential authorities have adopted a cautious approach aimed at analysing the impact of the main climate risk drivers in their own jurisdictions and fostering a better understanding of the implications of CRRs by financial institutions. Yet more direct normative action may be warranted as knowledge develops further about the nature and magnitude of climate-related financial risks and the ability of different policy instruments to address them. That would imply an adaptation to the current microprudential framework.

CRRs also have a macroprudential dimension. Beyond the pure microprudential objective, regulators could, at least theoretically, adjust requirements in order to help orient banks' lending towards specific sectors or firms with the purpose of mitigating physical and transitional risks for the financial system.

Implementing a macroprudential approach to CRRs entails significant practical challenges and poses trade-offs between the microprudential and the macroprudential framework, which are likely to be much more significant than the traditional ones described above. For example, imposing higher risk weights with a (micro-) prudential motivation for climate-related exposures may exacerbate the financing difficulties for firms in specific sectors, thereby generating larger (macro-) transition risks.

In any event, as long as the instruments used for micro- and macroprudential actions are likely to both be based on capital requirements for different firms or sectors, following the logic in Section 3, the need for a prudential policy response to climate-related risks further supports the integration (or strict coordination) of the microprudential and macroprudential functions. As discussed before, in the euro zone that would provide additional arguments for enlarging the ECB's macroprudential responsibilities.

The experience of the years after the outbreak of the GFC has shown that the intersection of the policy instruments used with different policy objectives makes the strict coordination between monetary, microprudential and macroprudential responsibilities more relevant than the conflicts that could occasionally arise among them. The potential impact of the pandemic and the increasingly perceived relevance of climate change for economic and financial stability have further strengthened the case for close coordination across those policy domains.

Technological developments and the disruption they are creating in the financial system also affect the strengths and weaknesses of different supervisory models. In particular, the larger set of entities which are now active in the market for financial services and the need to favour, as much as is warranted, a level playing field among them tend to support models based on a functional rather than a sectoral distribution of supervisory responsibilities.

5.   CONCLUDING REMARKS

In the European case, the above arguments support the enlargement of the ECB's responsibilities and tools in the area of macroprudential policies. Moreover, the need to substantiate the capital markets union speaks in favour of seeking to transfer more direct responsibilities to European authorities, particularly in the area of the supervision of consumer protection, capital market activities and AML/CFT and on the oversight of rules affecting the activity of big techs.

NOTES

1.   I am grateful to Patricia Baudino, Rodrigo Coelho, Julio Segura and Helene Schuberth for helpful comments on an earlier draft and to Marie-Christine Drexler and Christina Paavola for excellent secretarial support. The views expressed are solely my own and do not necessarily reflect those of the BIS or the Basel-based standard-setting bodies.
2.   This argument can be challenged if cross-objective effects of each policy instrument are considered to be substantially less pronounced than their own-objective effects (Svensson 2018).
3.   Regulations 1093/2010 for EBA, 1094/2010 for EIOPA and 1095 for ESMA.
4.   See Restoy (2019) for a more detailed description of the logic followed to develop the banking union.
5.   The so called short-selling decision: Judgement C-270/2012, United Kingdom v. Parliament and Council of the EU.
6.   See e.g. press releases by the ECB Banking Supervision of 12 March and the joint statement by the US Supervisory Agencies of 27 March 2020.
7.   See Restoy (2021), Carstens et al. (2021) and Crisanto et al. (2021).

REFERENCES

Baudino, P, C Sánchez and R Walters (2021): 'Institutional arrangements for bank resolution', FSI Insights on Policy Implementation, No. 32, May.

Borio, C and F Restoy (2020): 'Reflections on regulatory responses to the Covid-19 pandemic', FSI Briefs, No. 1, April.

Botopoulos, K (2020): 'The European Supervisory Authority: role models or in need of re-modelling', *ERA Forum* 21: 177–198.

Calvo, D, J C Crisanto, S Hohl and O P Gutiérrez (2018): 'Financial supervisory architecture: what has changed after the crisis?', FSI Insights on Policy Implementation, No. 8, April.

Cao, J and L Cholletec (2017): 'Monetary policy and financial stability in the long run: a simple gametheoretic approach', *Journal of Financial Stability* 28, February: 125–142.

Carstens, A (2019): 'The new role of central banks'. Speech at the Financial Stability Institute's 20th anniversary conference, 'A cross-sectoral reflection on the past, and looking ahead to the future', Basel, 12 March.

Carstens, A, S Claessens, F Restoy and H S Shin (2021): 'Regulating big techs in finance', *BIS Bulletin* 45, August.

Crisanto, J C, J Ehrentraud, A Lawson and F Restoy (2021): 'Big tech regulation: what is going on?' FSI Insights on Policy Implementation, No. 36, September.

Enria, A (2019): 'On supervisory arquitecture'. Panel remarks at the Financial Stability Institute's 20th Anniversary Conference, March.

European Systemic Risk Board (2021): 'List of national macroprudential authorities and national designated authorities in EEA Member States'.

Fischer, S (2008): 'Remarks about financial supervision authorities'. Remarks at 'The Marker' Capital Markets Conference, Tel Aviv, 21 May.

Group of Thirty (2008): The structure of financial supervision: approaches and challenges in a global marketplace.

Kremers, J and D Schoenmaker (2010), 'Twin Peaks: experiences in the Netherlands', Special Paper, 196, LSE Financial Markets Group, London.

Kremers, J, D Schoenmaker and P Wierts (2003): 'Cross-sector supervision: which model?', in R Herring and R Litan (eds), *Brookings-Wharton Papers on Financial Services: 2003*, Brookings Institution, Washington DC.

The de Larosière Report (2009): Report by the High-Level Group on Financial Supervision in the EU, 25 February.

Padoa-Schioppa, T (2002): 'Central banks and financial stability: exploring the land in between', Second ECB Central Banking Conference, October.

Restoy, F (2019): 'The European Banking Union: achievements and challenges', Annual Yearbook, 2018. Fundación ICO.

Restoy, F (2020): 'Central banks and financial stability: A reflection after the Covid-19 outbreak'. FSI Occasional Paper, No. 16, August.

Restoy, F (2021): 'Fintech regulation: how to achieve a level playing field', FSI Occasional Papers, No. 17, February.

Schoenmaker D and N Veron (2017): 'A twin peaks version for Europe', Policy contribution No. 30, Bruegel.

Svensson, L (2018): 'Monetary policy and macroprudential policy: different and separate?', *Canadian Journal of Economics/Revue canadienne d'économique* 51 (3): 802–827.

Tucker P (2018): *Unelected Power: The Quest for Legitimacy in Central Banking and the Regulatory State*, Princeton University Press.

4. The architecture of supervision and prudential policy[1]

Angela Maddaloni and Alessandro Scopelliti

INTRODUCTION

The *architecture of supervision and prudential policy* is defined by the allocation of prudential policy powers to different institutions. This allocation has implications for policy conduct and for the economic and financial environment in which the policies are implemented. This chapter addresses three main issues related to the architecture of supervision and prudential policy. First, it analyses the implications arising from an integrated model of the functions of central banking and prudential supervision. Afterwards, the consequences of centralised supervision, as opposed to national supervision are also examined. The implications are also broadly discussed in the euro area context and in relation to the design of the Single Supervisory Mechanism (SSM). Next, the article discusses the design for macroprudential policy in the EU and in the euro area. The last section is devoted to the prudential response in Europe during the COVID-19 crisis. Key successes and shortcomings of the current architecture for supervision and prudential policy in Europe are then analysed.

1. CENTRAL BANKING AND SUPERVISION: INTEGRATED OR SEPARATED FUNCTIONS

This section outlines the pros and cons of having the same institution – a central bank – in charge of both central banking and supervisory functions. Then it explicitly addresses how monetary and prudential policies interact and show the results of some cross-country analysis suggesting that there might be important synergies to leverage on.

1.1   A Cost Benefit Analysis

When analysing the costs and benefits of having an integrated or separated model for the architecture of supervision, the possible consequences that the setup has on the reputation and the independence of the central bank are central to the debate.

In terms of benefits, in an integrated structure supervisors can benefit from the independence and reputation of the central bank, thus limiting the risks of political pressure and regulatory capture. The proximity of supervisors to national authorities, local stakeholders and special interest groups can influence their decisions and result in them being too lenient. In the euro area the advantages of an integrated model may be significant because of the monetary union setup and the high degree of independency granted to the European Central Bank.

At the same time, an integrated model entails risks to reputation for both functions, which are then more strictly linked. For example, the bad reputation of supervisors stemming from a bank failure can transfer to the central banking function, affecting its credibility and effectiveness in implementing monetary policy. However, it is not clear that a separated structure would shield the central bank from this risk, especially when a crisis erupts and the central bank is the lender of last resort (LOLR).[2]

An integrated structure may foster better coordination of policies aimed at price and financial stability. Indeed, consolidated responsibilities can help avoid coordination failure and account for the interdependencies of the two policies. Central bank and supervisory authority residing in different institutions may not fully internalise the spillovers existing between their own policies and objectives (*push-me/pull-you* conduct). The resulting non-cooperative allocation entails a welfare loss.

But coordination may also be difficult since price stability and financial stability may be conflicting objectives. In these cases, policy makers may deviate from the optimal path of monetary policy in an attempt to preserve the stability of the financial institutions (*financial dominance*). Central banks in charge of both monetary policy and prudential supervision may have therefore an inflation bias (Di Noia and Di Giorgio, 1999; Copelovitch and Singer, 2008). Similarly, supervisors may be more lenient (*excessive forbearance*) in order to reduce possible losses to central banks arising from exposure towards the banking sector for example.

Another important dimension to consider when evaluating different setups for the architecture of supervision is the impact that this may have on the easiness of transferring information. Easier transfer of information is beneficial for supervisors and monetary policy makers. Central banks can benefit from supervisory information when assessing the impact of monetary policy decisions. Better knowledge of the banking sector improves information on financial conditions prevailing in the economy. Supervisors benefit from central banking knowledge of the economic and financial environment. LOLR interventions are also more effective and conducive to financial stability if the central bank has better information on the state of the financial sector.

There is also evidence that monetary policy can benefit from access to *aggregate supervisory information*, including soft information in the form of supervisory assessment. Evidence based on US data shows that an aggregate index calculated using individual supervisory information (including supervisory assessment) *improves the forecasting of inflation and unemployment* (Peek, Rosengren and Tootell, 1999). Similar information also *significantly improves the fit of a policy rule explaining short term rates* (Peek, Rosengren and Tootell, 2016). A similar indicator constructed for the euro area provides suggestive evidence in the same direction. A Financial Stress Indicator (FSI) constructed by aggregating supervisory information on euro area banks helps to improve the statistical and out-of-sample forecast properties of a Taylor rule, compared with an estimated benchmark rule.[3]

1.2   Interaction of Policies

As already described in the previous section, researchers have suggested that an integrated model of a central bank in charge of both monetary policy and supervision may be more conducive to price and financial instability. An empirical analysis using data from 98 countries worldwide during the period 1999–2012 sheds some light on this topic.[4] The analysis investigates the link between the institutional structure of supervision and the economic growth and inflation performances across countries. It also looks at the likelihood that a credit boom turns into a full financial crisis. Based on different fixed and random effects models, including control variables such as a corruption control index, log (GDP/capital) and time fixed effects, results point to no evidence that an integrated structure is related to a worse growth performance. Similarly, there is no evidence that in countries where the integrated model is prevailing there are higher deviations from the inflation target, therefore providing no support to the notion that an integrated structure is associated to an inflation bias.

Turning to the impact on financial stability, the analysis suggests that in countries where bank supervision is outside the central bank there is a higher probability of a credit boom turning into a banking crisis. In countries and years where bank supervision is in the central bank, there is a higher likelihood that loan-to-value ratios are used as macroprudential tools during credit booms and that credit booms are less likely to turn into a crisis. Thus, there seems to be no evidence that an integrated structure is associated to more financial instability or inaction bias.

This suggestive cross-country evidence therefore does not support arguments against unifying responsibilities for monetary and financial stability into one institution. At the same time, the analysis is mostly inconclusive on the optimal structure, but it suggests that monetary policy and supervision integrated in the same structure may result in benefits arising from better information flow and policy coordination, which could result in potential financial stability gains.

1.3   The Setup in the Euro Area

The choice whether to separate bank supervision and central banking functions involves a complicated trade-off between different objectives. The design chosen in the euro area represents a compromise between a model of full separation or full integration. The model for the euro area is not fully integrated. Supervisory responsibilities are carried out by the SSM which is part of the ECB. However, to prevent conflicts of interest between the monetary policy and supervisory functions, legislators introduced a *separation principle*, which translates in certain legal and administrative barriers (separation of objectives, decision-making and tasks) and strict separation of Governing Council's meetings.

In the previous section, it has been argued that in an integrated structure the information may be channelled in a more efficient and transparent way. It is important to stress that in the euro area setting, much of this information can still be collected while respecting the separation principle.

Concerning the supervisory function, there is a unique model of supervision for significant and less significant financial institutions. However, the SSM performs direct centralised supervision only of significant institutions, while the supervision of less significant institutions is a responsibility of the national supervisors based on a common rule book. The following section will address the likely implications of this setup.

2.   CENTRALISED AND DECENTRALISED SUPERVISION

The occurrence of the Great Financial Crisis induced important changes in the architecture of supervision, and more generally in the design of prudential policy around the world. In the euro area in particular, this translated into the implementation of the Banking Union, with the centralisation of the supervisory powers to the ECB, which directly supervises the significant banks of the euro area. In the next sections, a discussion on the difference between local and central supervisors is outlined and the reactions that can be expected from the financial sector – banks in particular – when changes to the structure occur.

2.1   Local and Central Supervisors

Local and central supervisors are subject to different incentives and possibly conflicts of interest. First, they have different costs in acquiring the important information from the banks that they are supervising. Academic literature has shown that geographical proximity matters for the effectiveness of supervision (Delis and Staikouras, 2011; Quintyn and Taylor, 2003; Gopalan, Kalda and Manela, 2021). One of the main factors explaining this result could be the easiness of information acquisition, coupled with higher specialisation and cultural closeness of local supervisors, which improves knowledge of local credit markets and their specificities.

Empirical evidence on the effectiveness of supervision also supports the importance of resources for supervisors (see Rezende, 2011), for example a large budget allowing a higher number of onsite visits but also more staff to supervise large, more complex banks. While local supervisors may have an advantage in onsite inspections, they are often more budget constrained and may have less resources than central supervisors.

In general, there are important economies of scale to be reaped in banking supervision, including a better sense of macroeconomic conditions and how these affect the banking sector as a whole, which support the move towards centralised supervision. Central supervisors have more resources, have a better macro view on the state of the financial sector and can use more peer comparisons. Centralisation of supervision may also limit incentives' distortions related to resource constraints, which may be particularly pronounced for supervisory institutions entirely financed with fees.

Apart from resource constraints and differences in cost of information acquisitions, local and central supervisors are also facing different incentives, stemming from different responsibilities and objectives. Generally, centralised supervisors face lower costs – also politically – in deciding to intervene in a bank or take a liquidation decision (Repullo, 2018). At the same time, removing decision power from the local supervisors may lead to worse information collection and possibly more bank risk-taking (Carletti et al., 2021). Still, stricter central supervisors may call for higher regulatory standards and thus increase the effectiveness of supervision overall.

Bringing supervision at the supranational level aligns incentives of supervisors vis-à-vis domestic and foreign shareholders and creditors, thus removing supervisory bias against foreign creditors. Overall, this is likely to result in tougher supervision.

2.2 Moving Towards Centralised Supervision

Changing the way in which supervision is organised and performed in a region will also change the way in which the supervised institutions behave.

Academic literature suggests that banks expect central supervisors to be generally tougher compared to local supervisors. For example, in the US, where there is a system of supervision in which banks change their supervisors between federal and state, it has been shown that federal supervisors tend to be stricter (Agarwal, Lucca, Seru and Trebbi, 2014).

The move towards the implementation of the SSM in the euro area provides some evidence pointing in the same direction. Banks expected the SSM's supervision to be tougher than national competent authorities. In the run-up to the SSM the most significant banks reduced their lending (Fiordelisi, Ricci and Lopes, 2017). SSM banks also reduced their asset size and reliance on wholesale debt (Eber and Minoiu, 2016).

Banks under SSM surveillance reported higher risk weights, higher probability of default and lower collateral to loan ratios for exposures to the same firm as compared to banks under national supervision (Haselmann et al., 2019).

During the period preceding the implementation of the SSM, 30% of the banks around the threshold strategically reduced size to avoid SSM supervision (see Figure 4.1). Compared to peers, banks with strategic behaviour had worse asset quality and liquidity position.

Centralised supervision is likely to have an impact also on financial integration. The central supervisor is less nationally oriented. Centralised supervision removes the bias against foreign creditors and therefore may allow banks to borrow more easily, and at lower rates, internationally. Banks that are supervised by a central supervisor may enjoy a positive signalling effect which overall lower their cost of funding. Indeed, banks supervised by the SSM pay lower deposit rates to their customers – both households and non-financial corporations (Barbiero, Colliard and Popov, 2017) compared to other euro area banks. They also have partly changed the composition of their liabilities, reducing reliance on deposits and increasing securities issuance, which is consistent with positive market signalling effect arising from the SSM 'certification' (Barbiero, Colliard and Popov, 2017).

Central supervision can have additional effects on financial integration through the structure of multinational banks (MNBs), which have subsidiaries and branches in different countries. A supranational supervisor optimally exerts more monitoring than a local supervisor to foreign units (subsidiaries) of a bank (monitoring externality). Therefore, centralisation of supervision may create incentives for banks to expand abroad through cross-border branches. In turn, the shift from subsidiaries to branches would increase the burden on the deposit insurance fund of countries that host more banks' headquarters.

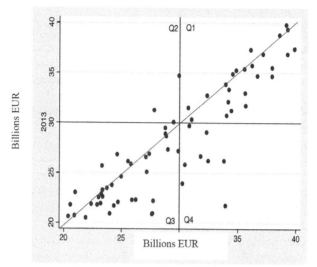

Note: Dots in this figure depict euro area banks with the total assets ranging from EUR 20 to 40 billion. For each bank, the Y axis shows its total assets in 2013 while the X axis represents its total assets in 2012.
Source: Ben-David et al. (2018).

Figure 4.1   Change in bank size during the implementation of the SSM

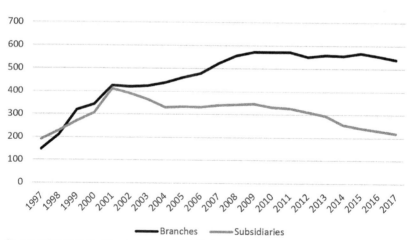

Source: ECB, Banking Structural Financial Indicators.

Figure 4.2   Cross-border branches and subsidiaries in the euro area

Recent developments in the euro area suggest that changes in the structure of big banking groups are somewhat limited (see Figure 4.2).

3.   THE SETTING OF MACROPRUDENTIAL POLICY

The developments of the Global Financial Crisis in 2008 and following years induced a substantial rethinking of the design of prudential policy across the globe, in particular concerning the establishment of a framework for the macroprudential policy in addition to the existing microprudential supervision. While supervisory authorities monitor the risks and oversee the soundness of individual financial institutions, macroprudential authorities pursue the goal to mitigate systemic risk for the overall financial sector. In order to prevent procyclical developments and amplification mechanisms which may trigger financial crises, macroprudential policy is supposed to act countercyclically, by moderating credit expansion in boom times and by supporting credit provision in recession times. It can be implemented via different instruments: capital-based, liquidity-based and borrower-based measures. These measures target the build-up of risks in the system from the viewpoints of lenders and borrowers respectively.

The explicit introduction of macroprudential policy also required the creation or the designation of the authorities in charge of this responsibility. Macroprudential authorities have to assess risks, determine the macroprudential stance and decide the activation and/or the release of macroprudential policy measures. As for the microprudential policy, the assignment of macroprudential tasks also spurred the debate about the separation or integration with central banking tasks and, in the context of the EU, about the centralisation or decentralisation of these prerogatives.

Differently from the decision taken for microprudential supervision, the model adopted for macroprudential policy in the EU is largely based on the decentralisation of powers to national authorities, although the ECB has a top-up power for euro area countries and banks supervised by the SSM (see Figure 4.3 and Constancio et al., 2019). This institutional design is relevant, in particular, for the determination of the capital-based measures, which are aimed at ensuring that credit institutions have sufficient loss-absorbing capacity.

The economic rationale behind the choice of this decentralised design was that financial cycles may follow different patterns across countries and therefore national authorities would be better suited to address these potentially asymmetric shocks in a way consistent with the features of the national banking sectors. At the same time, the assignment of the top-up power allows the ECB to tighten the measures adopted by national authorities in case they

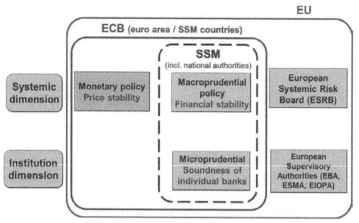

Source: Constancio et al., 2019.

Figure 4.3   Monetary and prudential policies at the ECB

are deemed as not adequate to prevent the build-up of systemic risks in individual countries.[5]

The capital-based measures include different types of capital buffers, which can address cyclical or structural risks – such as the Countercyclical Capital Buffer (CCyB) and the Systemic Risk Buffer (SyRB), respectively.[6] Capital buffers are also intended to address the 'too-big-to-fail' problem posed by large and complex institutions – like the capital buffers for global (GSII) or other systemically important (OSII) institutions. Capital buffers are designed in order to allow credit institutions to use them in stress periods, subject to certain restrictions on distribution (Behn et al., 2020).

4.   PRUDENTIAL POLICY DURING THE COVID-19 CRISIS

The COVID-19 crisis, with its significant consequences on the real economy and then on the financial sector, has provided the opportunity to test the functioning of the prudential framework designed after the Global Financial Crisis, across the globe and particularly in Europe.[7]

To support the provision of credit to firms and then to promote the recovery after the outbreak of the pandemic, policy authorities – also in the euro area – implemented a large set of monetary, fiscal and prudential policy measures. The ECB introduced a new asset purchase programme designed for the pandemic and eased significantly the conditions for central bank liquidity provision.[8] Governments introduced various schemes of loan guarantees to shield banks from the potential losses on the loans extended to the corporate sector.

In the prudential domain, both banking supervisors and macroprudential authorities adopted various measures to provide capital relief to euro area banks, supporting them in absorbing losses and providing credit.[9] Indeed, prudential authorities assessed that banks could face pressures to maintain their capital ratios and constrain credit access exactly when households and firms would need financial support. In this environment, if banks had undertaken procyclical adjustments by deleveraging or de-risking in their loan portfolio, this could have exacerbated the negative consequences of the pandemic on the real economy.

Thanks to the reforms of financial regulation since the Global Financial Crisis, and to the effectiveness of the centralised banking supervision, euro area banks entered the COVID-19 crisis in a much stronger capital position. In addition, the flexibility of the prudential framework allowed authorities to address the distress due to the pandemic, complementing monetary and fiscal policies.

The ECB, in its role of supervisory authority, took three types of measures. First, it frontloaded the legislative change in the composition of the Pillar 2 Requirement (P2R), supposed to enter into force by 1 January 2021, by allowing banks to fulfil the requirement also with Additional Tier 1 and Tier 2 instruments.[10] Second, it allowed banks to operate below the level of the Pillar 2 Guidance (P2G) and of the Capital Conservation Buffer. Third, the ECB asked significant institutions not to pay out dividends for the financial years 2019 and 2020 and to refrain from conducting share buybacks until at least 1 October 2020.[11]

At the same time, several national macroprudential authorities decided to release (or to revoke the previously announced increase of) the countercyclical capital buffer. In addition, they decided to lower some structural buffers, like the Systemic Risk Buffer, and to reduce (or to delay the phase-in of) some buffers for Other Systemically Important Institutions.

The microprudential adjustments allowed to free up EUR 120 billion of Common Equity Tier 1 (CET1) Capital, while the macroprudential measures made available EUR 20 billion of the same capital type. This difference was due to the relatively limited amount of releasable capital available to national macroprudential authorities, given the insufficient build-up of the cyclical buffers in the pre-COVID period.

In the existing macroprudential framework, the CCyB is the cyclical capital buffer which is meant to be built up in phases of credit expansion, and to be released in times of credit contraction. The other macroprudential buffers were designed as structural buffers and not meant to be released to face economic downturns. However, given that only some countries had activated positive

CCyB rates before the pandemic, national macroprudential authorities had to lower also structural buffers to provide capital relief. Moreover, given that the responsibility for macroprudential policy is assigned to national authorities, all these measures were adopted by designated authorities according to a somehow staggered timeline. In this context characterised by limited *macroprudential space*, the actions of banking supervisors in providing capital relief were therefore important to pursue also macroprudential goals.

5.   LESSONS FROM THE COVID-19 CRISIS FOR THE DESIGN OF THE PRUDENTIAL FRAMEWORK

The experience of the COVID-19 crisis induces some reflections for the overall design of the prudential framework in Europe and in the euro area, in particular concerning the responsibilities for microprudential supervision and macroprudential policy.

First, the centralisation of banking supervision has proved effective in fostering immediate capital relief for banks as well as in supporting synergies with monetary policy conduct. Thanks to the centralised structure of banking supervision in the euro area, the ECB was able to undertake prompt release measures for the significant banks and to promote the adoption of corresponding measures by national authorities for the less significant institutions.

The supervisory measures of capital relief implemented during the COVID-19 pandemic were however of different types and as such affected differently banks' capital management and lending behaviour. For instance, measures implying a permanent reduction in capital requirements produced larger positive effects on bank lending volumes and rates than other measures providing temporary capital relief based on supervisory forward guidance (Couaillier et al., 2022, 2021). Indeed, the effectiveness of these measures may be conditional on the credibility of the timeline for the future replenishment: banks may adjust their capital targets and their balance sheet behaviour, also in terms of lending, to the extent that the policy measures change their expectations about the capital demand by supervisory authorities.

Second, the decentralised governance of macroprudential policy required the actions of national designated authorities in releasing the countercyclical capital buffers, when available, or in decreasing existing structural capital buffers. The effectiveness of these policies was partly constrained by the limited macroprudential space that could be released.

The decentralised governance of macroprudential policy in the EU seems to have contributed to the inaction of national authorities (Edge and Liang, 2020; Babic, 2018). In a decentralised setting, the decision-making of national authorities is influenced by different types of incentives related to national banking systems. National authorities may be reluctant to activate counter-cyclical capital buffers, to the extent that this increase in capital requirements may raise a competitive disadvantage for domestic banks versus foreign banks. Moreover, in countries with significant presence of cross-border banking groups, macroprudential authorities may undertake some ring-fencing measures, by increasing the structural capital buffers for the subsidiaries of these banking groups (Bengtsson, 2020).[12] The combination of these incentives may have contributed to the limited availability of cyclical capital buffers that could be released when the COVID-19 crisis started. Moreover, on similar ground, there could have been a shift in the composition of capital buffers towards structural buffers.

CONCLUDING REMARKS

The introduction of the SSM has been the largest change in recent years in the supervisory architecture across developed countries. The current setup reflects, at least to some extent, the economics of supervisory architecture and the many trade-offs that have to be taken into account. It reflects a compromise between models of integration versus separation of bank supervision and monetary policy functions. It also reflects a middle ground in the choice between local versus central supervision and centralisation versus delegation of information collection versus decision-making and rule-setting.

Overall, the centralisation of banking supervision in the euro area has provided an effective institutional setting. This setting improved the resilience of the banking sector in the previous years and fostered the implementation of prompt capital actions during the COVID-19 crisis.

The significant capital releases implemented via the decisions of macro- and microprudential authorities and the extensive liquidity support provided via monetary policy allowed banks to satisfy the increasing credit demand – particularly from corporations – at the onset of the pandemic, especially for banks with ex ante smaller buffers above their regulatory requirements. Going forward, the experience of the COVID-19 crisis suggests that the effectiveness of the prudential policy in the EU could benefit from increasing the releasable macroprudential capital in crisis times, particularly to address systemic shocks affecting large parts of the Banking Union. In such cases, the euro area-wide nature of systemic shocks could support the arguments in favour of a partially centralised governance for the build-up and the release of some capital buffers in macroprudential policy.

NOTES

1.   This chapter is based partly on a presentation given at the workshop 'How Do Monetary, Micro- and Macroprudential Policies Interact?', organised by the Osterreich National Central Bank on 1 December 2019. It draws also on the ECB Discussion Paper No. 2287 'The architecture of supervision' published in May 2019 (Ampudia et al., 2019). The views expressed in this paper are solely those of the authors and do not necessarily reflect the views of the European Central Bank or the Eurosystem.

2.   A recent example on this is offered by the UK experience in the context of the failure of the Northern Rock bank. In the UK, after 1997, supervisory powers were assigned to the Financial Service Authority (FSA). However, the Bank of England (BoE) still retained the lender of last resort function. On this basis, the BoE was considered largely responsible for the bankruptcy of Northern Rock, lacking a swift intervention of the central bank in providing emergency liquidity when needed.

3.   See Box 1 of the ECB Discussion Paper No. 2287, 'The architecture of supervision'.

4.   For detailed results on this analysis see the Annex of the ECB Discussion Paper No. 2287, 'The architecture of supervision'.

5.   Importantly, this prerogative in macroprudential policy is assigned to the ECB on an asymmetric basis, only to top up national measures, and not to release them. Moreover, the ECB can only act by topping up capital-based measures and cannot deploy or modify other measures of different type, such as caps on loan to values or debt to income ratios.

6.   On operationalising the countercyclical capital buffer in the EU, see Detken et al. (2014). See Constancio et al. (2019) on the framework and the strategy for macroprudential policy at the ECB.

7.   While the Global Financial Crisis originated from the financial sector and then spread across the real economy, the COVID-19 crisis developed first in the real economy and then affected the financial system. This structural difference between the two crises also highlights the difference in the required policy responses and raises the question of whether the policy frameworks designed after the Global Financial Crisis are fully effective in addressing the new challenges from the current crisis.

8.   On 18 March 2020 the ECB announced the Pandemic Emergency Purchase Programme, initially designed for an envelope of EUR 750 billion, and then extended with an additional EUR 600 billion on 4 June 2020 and EUR 500 billion on 10 December 2020, for an overall amount of EUR 1,850 billion. Moreover, the ECB recalibrated the parameters for the Targeted Long-Term Refinancing Operations (TLTRO-III): it reduced the rate by 25 bps on 12 March 2020, and by a further 25 bps on 30 April 2020, bringing the funding cost down to -0.5% and as low as -1% for banks meeting the lending threshold of 0%. To ensure that banks could take full advantage of the liquidity measures, the ECB introduced several measures of collateral easing, expanding the set of the Additional Credit Claims and reducing valuation haircuts. For more details, see the ECB press releases: 'Monetary policy decisions', 12 March 2020; 'ECB announces easing of conditions for targeted longer-term refinancing operations (TLTRO III)', 12 March 2020; 'ECB announces €750 billion Pandemic Emergency Purchase

Programme (PEPP)', 18 March 2020; 'ECB announces package of temporary collateral easing measures', 7 April 2020.

9.   For more details, see the description of the prudential measures in Chapter 5 of the ECB's Financial Stability Review from May 2020.

10.   Based on this change, banks can now partially meet the requirement with Additional Tier 1 and Tier 2 instruments up to 43.75% of the required P2R (as opposed to 100% Common Equity Tier 1 capital previously).

11.   For more details, see the press release of ECB Banking Supervision (2020): 'ECB Banking Supervision provides temporary capital and operational relief in reaction to coronavirus', 12 March 2021.

12.   This approach of some macroprudential authorities, aimed at preserving the stability of their banking sectors from adverse developments affecting cross-border banking groups in other markets, may however further distort the incentives of banking groups in the direction of branchification (see also section 2). Cross-border groups may prefer to establish branches instead of subsidiaries in other countries, to ensure that these banking activities are subject to the prudential authorities of the country of the holding company (Singh, 2020).

REFERENCES

Agarwal, S., Lucca, D., Seru, A. and Trebbi, F. (2014): 'Inconsistent regulators: Evidence from banking', *Quarterly Journal of Economics*, 129(2).

Ampudia, M., Beck, T., Beyer, A., Colliard, J.-E., A Leonello, A., Maddaloni, A. and Marques-Ibanez, D. (2019): 'The architecture of supervision', ECB Discussion Paper No. 2287, May 2019.

Babic, D. (2018): 'Use of the countercyclical capital buffer – a cross-country comparative analysis', in *A Review of Macroprudential Policy in the EU in 2017*, ESRB, August 2018, pp. 68–82.

Barbiero, F., Colliard, J.E. and Popov, A. (2017): 'Prudential supervision and bank funding: Evidence from the implementation of the SSM', Mimeo.

Behn, M., Rancoita, E. and Rodriguez D'Acri, C. (2020): 'Macroprudential capital buffers – objectives and usability', *ECB Macroprudential Bulletin*, October.

Ben-David, I., Cerulli, G., Fiordelisi, F. and Marques-Ibanez, D. (2018): 'Seeking my supervisor: Evidence from the centralization of banking supervision in Europe'. Mimeo.

Bengtsson, E. (2020): 'Macroprudential policy in the EU: A political economy perspective', *Global Finance Journal*, 46, 1–19.

Carletti, E., Dell'Ariccia, G. and Marquez, R. (2021): 'Supervisory incentives in a banking union', *Management Science*, 67(1), 455–470.

Constancio, V. et al. (2019): 'Macroprudential policy at the ECB: Institutional framework, strategy, analytical tools and policies', ECB Occasional Paper Series, No. 226.

Copelovitch, M.S. and Singer, D.A. (2008): 'Financial regulation, monetary policy, and inflation in the industrialized world', *The Journal of Politics*, 70(3), 663–680.

Couaillier, C., Reghezza, A., Rodriguez d'Acri, C. and Scopelliti, A. (2022): 'How to release capital requirements during a pandemic? Evidence from euro area banks', ECB Working Paper Series, Forthcoming.

Couaillier, C., Lo Duca, M., Reghezza, A., Rodriguez d'Acri, C. and Scopelliti, A. (2021): 'Bank capital buffers and bank lending in the euro area during the pandemic', Special Feature A, *Financial Stability Review*, European Central Bank.

Delis, M.D. and Staikouras, P.K. (2011): 'Supervisory effectiveness and bank risk', *Review of Finance*, 15(3), 511–543.

Detken C. et al. (2014): 'Operationalising the countercyclical capital buffer: Indicator selection, threshold identification and calibration options', ESRB Occasional Paper, No. 5.

Di Noia, C. and Di Giorgio, G. (1999): 'Should banking supervision and monetary policy tasks be given to different agencies?', *International Finance*, 2, 361–378.

Eber, M. and Minoiu, C. (2016): 'How do banks adjust to stricter supervision?', Working Paper.

Edge, R. and Liang, J.N. (2020): 'Financial stability committees and the countercyclical capital buffer', Deutsche Bundesbank, Working Paper No. 4/2020.

Fiordelisi, F., Ricci, O. and Lopes, F.S.S. (2017): 'The unintended consequences of the launch of the single supervisory mechanism in Europe', *Journal of Financial and Quantitative Analysis*, 52(6), 2809–2836.

Gopalan, Y., Kalda A. and Manela, A. (2021): 'Hub-and-spoke regulation and bank leverage', *Review of Finance*, 25(5), 1499–1545.

Haselmann, R., Singla, S. and Vig, V. (2019): 'Supra(national) supervision,' Working Paper.

Peek, J., Rosengren, E.S. and Tootell, G.M.B. (1999): 'Is bank supervision central to central banking?', *Quarterly Journal of Economics*, 114(2), 629–653.

Peek, J., Rosengren, E.S. and Tootell, G. (2016): 'Does Fed policy reveal a ternary mandate?', Working Papers 16–11, Federal Reserve Bank of Boston.

Quintyn, M. and Taylor, M.W. (2003): 'Regulatory and supervisory independence and financial stability', *CESifo Economic Studies*, 49(2), 259–294.

Repullo, R. (2018): 'Hierarchical bank supervision,' *SERIEs – Journal of the Spanish Economic Association*, 9(2018), 1–26.

Rezende, M. (2011): 'How do joint supervisors examine financial institutions? The case of state banks', in *Handbook of Central Banking, Financial Regulation and Supervision – After the Financial Crisis*, ed. by S. Eijffinger and D. Masciandaro, Edward Elgar.

Singh, D. (2020): *European cross-border banking and banking supervision*, Oxford University Press.

5. Trends in European banking supervision design: is there a path to an optimal architecture for financial supervision in the EU?

Luís Silva Morais[1]

1. OVERALL PERSPECTIVE[2]

1.1 Preliminary Observations and Sequence of Analysis

Financial crises understandably lead us to question the existing *institutional architectures* of *financial supervision* and to a considerable soul-searching in terms of the *alternative models* that may be adopted in this field. By those standards, we are experiencing a crucial moment in this everlasting debate. In fact, not much longer than a decade after the great financial crisis (GFC), which in the EU evolved towards a sovereign debt crisis, intertwined with a banking crisis, a new crisis arising from the COVID-19 pandemic has unexpectedly erupted. Although, the current COVID-19 crisis is fundamentally different from the GFC,[3] it nonetheless enhances once again the crucial importance of an *optimal design* of *supervisory architecture* to safeguard *financial stability*. Furthermore, beside such overall goal of financial stability, the institutional architecture of financial supervision should also ensure the capacity to timely adopt *exceptional supervisory measures* that may contribute to prevent contagion to the financial sector.

Within this context, this succinct chapter purports to (1) identify the key evolutionary trends of supervisory architecture, arising from the aforementioned crises, building on such analysis to (2) discuss, from a comparative perspective, the chief advantages and drawbacks of the main options available; and, finally, (3) to give a broad picture about the current crossroad of the European architecture of financial supervision.

1.2   Key Evolutionary Trends of Financial Supervisory Architecture

Before dwelling on the intricacies of the major evolutionary trends of supervisory architecture, it is perhaps sober to start with a comprehensive, albeit
generic, assessment of the impact and relevance of such architecture. Actually,
experience drawn from the most recent crises seems to indicate that the
architecture of financial supervision is not a 'silver bullet' for the prevention
of serious supervisory failures. In a nutshell, no model of supervision ensures
the absolute stability of the financial system or prevents the eruption of crises.
Conversely, the design of the supervisory architecture is a relevant element
for the functioning and effective scrutiny of the financial system. In effect, it
contributes to the establishment of a more effective framework that both limits
potential supervisory failures and ensures a proper handling of financial crises
whenever these cannot be prevented.

     Another point which may be anticipated is the emergence of a new trend in
this domain. It is characterised by the development of what we may designate
as *hybrid models*, which are mostly flexible and tailored to the features of
each financial system so that they can be continuously adjusted to the highly
dynamic changes of transnational interconnected financial systems. These
hybrid variations of the architecture of supervision are somehow driven by
prevailing needs of devising *coordination mechanisms* for the *timely exchange
of information* – in connection with an overall and prevailing safeguard of
financial stability. This in turn leads to a key role of what we may loosely designate as a *coordination function*, which is of paramount importance in every
model of financial supervision.

     An overall comparative analysis of the institutional evolution of the past
two decades shows that the reform movement of supervision architectures was
triggered in the wake of the creation of single supervisor models. This involved
the combination of different supervisory functions in a single authority chiefly
in two alternative sub-models: (1) separation of the single financial supervisory
authority from the central bank (with its monetary policy responsibilities); or
(2) appointment of the central bank as the single financial supervisory authority.

     This movement started with the creation of a single supervisor in Singapore
in 1984, rapidly followed by the Scandinavian countries, with ensuing reforms
in Norway (1986), Denmark (1988) and Sweden (1991). However, it was
only with the in-depth reform in the United Kingdom in 1997, leading to the
establishment of the Financial Services Authority (FSA), that the movement
gained wider recognition given the UK status as a major international financial
centre.[4] This reform trend, marked by the integration of supervisory functions,
evolved over the following decade in accordance with an alternative paradigm
of supervision specialised by objectives. This alternative approach was first
conceptualised by Michael Taylor in his ground-breaking study Twin Peaks:

A Regulatory Structure for the New Century, of 1995.[5] Taylor's study put forward a model based on two financial supervisory authorities specialised in the fields of prudential control, (financial soundness) and market conduct supervision. This model forged a second wave of reforms, starting in Australia in 1997, in the aftermath of the Report published by the Wallis Commission of Inquiry, and closely followed by the Netherlands in 2002.

In the wake of the GFC, the 'Twin Peaks' model encroached relatively swiftly, as it became widely viewed as an answer to a series of disadvantages of the single supervisor model, whilst preserving the core set of advantages that in theory derive from the integration of supervisory functions. This led a number of experts to support the adoption of 'Twin Peaks' models post-financial crisis, although with some institutional variants: e.g. concentration of the prudential pillar in the central bank or the unbundling of the central bank from financial supervisory functions. However, the implementation of these models is far from confirming the claim that the 'Twin Peaks' model is capable of overcoming a series of disadvantages attached to the concentration of financial supervisory functions. For these reasons, it may be argued that putting forward the idea of 'Twin Peaks' as a predominant model is manifestly premature, on the basis of a critical analysis of supervision architectures in the more developed financial systems.

As things stand, and in the wake of two major crises (the GFC and the COVID-19 crisis), comparative analysis should systematically address three basic model alternatives for financial supervision architecture, namely: (1) the traditional sectoral model (organised on a tripartite basis, involving the traditional breakdown of the financial system into the subsectors of banking, insurance and pension funds and securities markets), (2) the single supervisor model, and (3) the 'Twin Peaks' model. Complementarily, such analysis should also take into account the *hybrid* components and sub-variants that give rise to different combinations between these basic models and other systematic frameworks.

2. CHIEF ADVANTAGES AND DRAWBACKS OF THE MAIN INSTITUTIONAL MODELS OF FINANCIAL SUPERVISION – WHAT LESSONS FOR THE EU?

2.1 General Perspective and Critical Balance Concerning the Single Supervisor Model vis-à-vis other Models and Hybrid Elements of Supervisory Architecture

Bearing in mind these trends, it is of paramount importance to ponder the chief advantages and drawbacks of the prevailing alternative models, in light of evolution that took place in some EU Member States and also in some jurisdictions that played a leading role in these reforms.[6] Underlying the shift towards the establishing of single supervisory authorities are concerns over how to prevent or eliminate potential problems associated with the existence of multiple supervisory authorities. These potential problems include: (1) competitive disadvantages or distortions, (2) overall inconsistency in the various supervisory approaches, and (3) two opposing tensions – one due to overlapping intervention problems and the other resulting from a higher risk of enforcement gaps in the context of an increasingly widespread universal banking business model as well as other types of cross-currents among financial activity segments. Regardless of the initial expectations of efficiency surrounding the single supervisor model, especially after the establishment of the FSA in 1997, its actual operation shed a light over its potential disadvantages and inherent risks. First of all, the assumption of efficiency associated with this model was not always confirmed. In fact, the establishment of large bodies tends to increase bureaucracy, making their action less flexible. Furthermore, the experience accumulated using this model and a critical analysis of it revealed major risks stemming from the fact that the expected scale economies are often negatively offset by an institutional incentive to over-accumulate functions, often only marginally related to the core financial supervision functions and objectives (so called 'Christmas tree effect').[7]

In fact, as illustrated by the UK case – which in 2013 reversed the 1997 reform establishing then the FSA – the institutional integration of chiefly prudential and market conduct objectives does not *per se* guarantee a more balanced weighting of these objectives and of its prioritisation. Conversely, the concentration of supervisory functions in a single supervisor may give rise to risks of imbalance between the prudential and market conduct supervisory components, often to the detriment of prudential supervision (as pointed out in the so called 2009 Turner Review).

Another much discussed risk relates to the elimination of a number of virtuous factors which result from *regulatory competition*. In fact, provided that efficient levels of *coordination* between multiple supervision interventions are effectively ensured, the combined action of different authorities may give rise to a virtuous tension between them, actually enabling a more accurate perception of specific problems.

In other words, the single supervisor model may lack a true system of checks and balances that can mitigate the issues arising from the failure to detect problems, which are more likely to occur in direct proportion to the growing complexities of financial activities (thus involving the risk of a 'single point of failure' in terms of financial supervision). The single supervisor model may also entail the risk of excessive formal simplification and of generating a bias towards organisational matters to the detriment of the actual financial supervision tasks. In fact, some level of specialisation will still be required, even within the context of a single organisation that combines prudential and market conduct supervision and monitors a wide array of financial institutions. Such specialisation constraints may well lead to the reintroduction within a single authority of functional supervisory intervention 'silos'.

Issues of communication and *coordination* between different types of supervisory intervention and, also, other areas of public policy (chiefly *monetary policy* and related *lender of last resort function*) remain key, even in the case of single supervisors. In fact, and somewhat paradoxically, coordination risks may end up being more acute in single supervisor settings, if only because they are less noticeable and therefore less tackled. This key issue of *coordination* also became more pressing in the context of the interplay between macroprudential supervision and the various types of market conduct and microprudential supervision, in the wake of the GFC. In most major single supervisor systems, the overall macroprudential supervision, due to its intrinsic characteristics, usually goes beyond the remit of that single supervisor and is also ensured by the central bank and government representatives.

The experience of Germany and the UK in terms of single supervisor model is paradigmatic in this regard and sends mixed messages about the importance of the coordination of supervisory activities.

The German experience, especially after the 2012 reform of the supervision system,[8] somehow contrasts with the negative experience of the single supervisor model in the UK. In particular, it highlights the key importance of coordination problems and shows that these are not automatically solved under a single supervisor model. What the case of Germany shows is that it is possible to effectively combine, to some extent, this institutional model with a *hybrid* component, through the establishment of new coordination bodies – in this case, the German Financial Stability Committee (Ausschuss für Finanzstabilität) – comprised of the single supervisor (BaFin) and representatives of the Deutsche Bundesbank and the Federal Ministry of Finance. By contrast, in the UK, the Turner Review, the 2009 report released by the House of Lords Banking Supervision and Regulation, and the November 2015 report released by the Bank of England on The Failure of HBOS plc revealed that the FSA favoured market conduct supervision, in operational terms, to the detriment of *prudential* supervision, with major negative consequences in terms of *prudential supervision* failings. These *ex post* analyses of UK supervisory failures also enhance the need for greater clarity over the division of responsibility and better coordination between the central bank in charge of the *lender of last resort function* and the financial supervisor. On the whole, it may be argued that the FSA failed to ensure a proper balancing of: (a) prudential supervision, (b) market conduct supervision, and, more recently, at a particular level (c) macroprudential supervision and *overall financial stability* in connection with *monetary policy* and the provision of liquidity (which implies proper and prompt communication channels between the financial supervisor and the institution in charge of lender of last resort function).[9] Actually, this may indicate that such balance depends to a large extent on a set of more *hybrid institutional elements* coexisting in any architecture of supervision, associated with reinforced coordination mechanisms.

The importance of these *hybrid* and *coordination* elements is clear when comparing the UK and the German cases. In fact, one of the key differences between these two single supervisor experiments was the somehow hybrid nature of the German supervisory design. The difference between the two cases largely resulted from Bundesbank's non-negligible role and continuous exercise of a number of financial supervisory functions (particularly in banking); and from the recognition of the crucial importance of *coordination* functions across supervisory components, also associated with the new concepts of the safeguard of financial stability. Such *hybrid* elements of the German single supervisor model were even reinforced with the 2012 reform, which both consolidated the central role played by the Bundesbank in macroprudential supervision and financial stability matters and established a new body (the aforementioned Ausschuss für Finanzstabilität) formed by representatives of the Deutsche Bundesbank, the BaFin and the Federal Ministry of Finance.

The 2012 reform also provided this body with a wide set of responsibilities, including the safeguarding of overall financial stability (namely with powers to intervene in causes for potential future financial crises), and ensuring coordination and cooperation among authorities with financial supervisory powers. Besides supporting new macroprudential supervisory tasks, the Committee chiefly works as a mechanism for reinforced cooperation and information exchange among supervisors that never found an adequate institutional support in the UK approach to the single supervisor model, including as regards proper articulation between financial supervision and monetary policy.

2.2 Successive Waves of Twin Peaks – A Critical Balance as a Benchmark for the Evolution of EU Supervisory Architecture

The so-called 'Twin Peaks' model, which somehow corresponds to a second wave of reforms of supervisory architectures, was designed to preserve the key set of benefits usually associated with the relative integration of supervisory functions, while avoiding, at the same time, a number of disadvantages brought about by the single supervisor model. Therefore, the 'Twin Peaks' model essentially addressed the same concerns underlying the single supervisor model, while creating a new institutional paradigm of integration of supervisory functions that would decisively contribute to bridging the gaps of the first model in terms of risks and imbalances. The starting point of Michael Taylor's ground-breaking Twin Peaks concept is an analysis of the increasing mismatch between regulatory structure and market reality, leading to regulatory failures and dysfunctions.[10]

In a nutshell, the Twin Peaks model is said to present two main advantages in comparison to other models: (1) clarity of the key objectives to be pursued by each supervisory authority, free from flawed prioritisations; and (2) sounder accountability of each supervisory authority in terms of performance in the pursuit of the priority goals assigned to it. In other words, the theoretical goal of 'Twin Peaks' is to enhance the quality levels of conduct of business supervision by answering to the novel challenges posed by the need to protect consumers of complex financial products, without jeopardising the intensity of prudential supervision, which typically adopts a more long-term perspective.

There is, however, a risk of over-simplification when describing the 'Twin Peaks' model as a virtuous alternative that combines the advantages of an integrated single supervisor model, without its disadvantages in terms of conflicts and tensions. In fact, the tensions associated with the *integration* of financial supervisory functions are not eliminated, to a large extent, by the 'Twin Peaks' model, but simply moved to a different institutional level. Furthermore, the GFC made clear that the broader 'systemic protection' objective required an enhanced macroprudential supervision, as well as a deeper proper knowledge and scrutiny of the financial sector, involving as such an institutional dynamic that the 'Twin Peaks' model alone could not address. At the same time, the new pressures to which supervisory systems are subject also require an enhanced coordination between the various supervisory interventions at the core of these systems, which the standard 'Twin Peaks' model cannot automatically ensure. This overall context leads to what Michael Taylor has recently termed as a 'third episode of Twin Peaks' in the wake of the GFC and, we may add, also intersecting the current COVID-19 crisis. It is characterised by the prominence of macroprudential supervisory approaches and the safeguarding of financial stability,[11] leading frequently to an increasing identification of the prudential 'peak' with autonomous units within central banks or, at least, with increased coordination with central banks with a pivotal role for safeguarding financial stability.[12]

3.   THE INTERNATIONAL EXPERIENCE AND
      COROLLARIES FOR THE EU – IS THERE
      AN OPTIMAL PATH FOR THE EUROPEAN
      ARCHITECTURE OF FINANCIAL SUPERVISION?

3.1   The Gradual Emergence of the European Financial Supervisory Architecture – A Convoluted Process

After a phase of accelerated integration of financial services, based on minimum harmonisation and the so called *Single Passport Framework* –

relying on cooperation of national supervisory authorities[13] – in the wake of the 1989 *Second Banking Directive* methodology and the Lamfalussy approach, the GFC has led to the quick emergence, after the Larosière Report, of three European Supervisory Authorities (ESAs), established under the traditional sectoral lines (banking, capital markets and insurance and pension funds). Furthermore, these three European authorities established in 2010 (EBA, ESMA and EIOPA) were conceived as predominantly *regulatory* authorities (producing *guidelines and technical rules* which supplement applicable Directives and Regulations), while to a large extent the *enforcement* actions of financial *supervision* were kept decentralised at the level of national supervisory authorities (NSAs), albeit under reinforced European coordination. Furthermore, in quick succession, the problems of financial fragmentation experienced in particular in the banking sector in the context of the doom loop and vicious circle of the banking and sovereign debt crises led in the banking subsector to the launching after 2012 of the European Banking Union project (EBU) and, as one of its pillars, to the establishment of a new supranational European authority in charge of banking supervision, *maxime* prudential banking supervision – the Single Supervisory Mechanism (SSM) within ECB (whose normative support was found in Article 127 (6) of TFEU).

3.2   Possible Short-term and Longer-term Developments of the Current Incomplete European Supervisory Architecture in Light of Evolutionary Trends in this Field

As arises from the merely schematic considerations *infra*, the EU architecture of financial supervision evolved rapidly after the GFC in a rather convoluted manner and is still a work in progress. Currently, a recent Public Consultation launched by the Commission as part of the new Capital Markets Union (CMU) Action Plan on EU Supervisory Convergence and the Single Rule Book covered a very wide range of matters which had been pondered before, with very limited results, in the process that led to a first ESAs revision in 2019, including namely: (a) concrete measures to achieve further progress on supervisory convergence, (b) the adequacy of ESAs governance, and (c) possible additional direct supervisory powers for the ESAs, particularly in the case of ESMA (which had already received supervisory powers, e.g. as regards rating agencies).

Against this background, and given the multiple factors conditioning the evolution of a European architecture of financial supervision, it is pertinent to consider both a short-term and a medium- and longer-term perspective.

As regards the former, the 2021 Public Consultation brings back the delicate debate between further *centralisation* or the sufficiency of current tools to achieve supervisory *convergence* in Europe in the context of a rather complex structure which involves the three ESAs (in coordination with NSAs), the ESRB and the SSM. Within this shorter-term approach a possible second review of ESAs may involve three crucial aspects. These comprehend (1) developments towards more or enhanced supervisory coordination across National Competent Authorities (NCAs). Among other aspects, the ESAs could enhance this convergence by reinforcing specific guidelines, leaving less room for interpretative divergences among NCAs. Also, as part of this enhanced supervisory coordination, a more recurrent and perhaps more structured use of the so-called Peer Review tool could be considered;[14] (2) a second major development, although duly calibrated in realistic political terms, could involve granting further powers to the ESAs (especially to ESMA in the context of the CMU Project), e.g. somehow increasing responsibilities of ESMA as regards data collection and sharing – a function which is made even more relevant in times of crisis or tensions and, also, much relevant in a context in which the EU is considering the establishment of a new *European Single Access Point (ESAP) for companies' financial and sustainable-investment-related information*; (3) a third possible development could involve some limited changes to the governance of ESAs, again, singling out ESMA here, on account of the CMU Project, and considering that, in terms of banking, the EU architecture has already evolved towards further centralisation going beyond the ESAs, with the SSM.

In fact, within this overall context, the Commission has already announced a report to be produced in the first half of 2022 largely oriented towards enhancing the single rulebook for capital markets, but also contemplating measures for stronger supervisory convergence by the ESAs.

This undeniable short-term prioritisation of *supervisory convergence* and apparent lack of willingness for further *supervisory centralisation* and *institution-building* should not make us oblivious of a necessary longer-term perspective. In fact, we should not regard the two perspectives as contradictory, but should endeavour to begin conceptualising longer-term avenues for deepening financial integration without unduly tensions. For that, we may take stock of the international experience and evolutionary trends on financial supervisory architecture (as discussed *infra*, 2.1–2.2). Accordingly, in spite of the fact that (1) politically it might be too early to meet the proper conditions and (2) the legal basis in the Treaty may still need further testing and refinement,[15] we should start envisaging the direction of travel in this domain: a direction towards a *more structured organisation of the EU architecture* within a new overall balance between national and European authorities. This might involve a discussion on a potential merge between the SSM, EBA and EIOPA (using as legal basis, failing a new Treaty provision, Article 114 instead of Article 127(6) which has specific limitations on insurance supervision), as a mainly (a) prudential European supervisory arm to be combined with (b) a restructured and reinforced ESMA, and possibly (c) a coordinating body dedicated to financial stability in the whole financial sector and relying heavily on the ECB. On the whole, this would imply a gradual movement towards a European architecture approaching a *new and largely reinvented episode of Twin Peaks*, although with particular and hybrid features due to (1) the need of establishing a *network system with NSAs* and to (2) the need of establishing an *effective overall coordination function* (capable of addressing limitations and even setbacks of the 'Twin Peaks' model worldwide) combined with a truly effective *macroprudential arm* of the system, somehow relying on more *institutional building within the ECB or related with the ECB* (and different from the current ESRB). The pondering of such long-term potential redesign of the European financial supervisory architecture is, however, much beyond the limited purview of this chapter.[16] It represents the beginning of a new whole chapter of analysis in this field (to which we purport to return through a more in-depth analysis), but that should be in the EU agenda for the incoming years.

NOTES

1. The cut-off date for relevant information and developments included therein is 30 September 2021 (only exceptional later developments until 30 November will be considered).
2. The views in this chapter are entirely personal and academic and do not arise in any manner whatsoever from the author's institutional affiliations at SRB (Single Resolution Board) and ASF (Portuguese Insurance and Pension Funds Supervisory Authority).
3. On the financial sector tensions arising from the COVID-19 crisis in contrast with the GFC see, for all, Morais (2021).
4. On these developments see, in general, Masciandaro (2005).
5. See Taylor (1995). Michael Taylor reassessed this concept a decade later in *Twin Peaks Revisited ... A Second Chance for Regulatory Reform* (Taylor 2009).
6. For an overall perspective see Morais (2017), available at: www.bportugal.pt/en/publications/banco-de-portugal/all/133. See also Calvo et al. (2018).
7. See on such types of risks, Abrams and Taylor (2000).
8. See on these developments, Financial Stability Board (FSB) (2014).
9. See in particular on the failures occurring in the UK single supervisor system related with proper *coordination* between the *financial supervisory function* and *monetary policy* functions, which we have no room to develop *ex professo* here, Hauser (2014).
10. Taylor presented in his already quoted *'Twin Peaks': A Regulatory Structure for the New Century* (1995) four main arguments in this domain to which *brevitatis causae* we refer here.
11. See Michael Taylor (2021), 'The Three Episodes of Twin Peaks', in Godwin and Schmulow (eds) (2021), p. 17.
12. On this pivotal role of central banks for safeguarding financial stability, see Restoy (2020).

13. For a comprehensive view of all these developments, see, in general, Teixeira (2020).
14. On this specific Peer Review Tool concerning the ESAs and its use to address potential supervisory failures of national supervisory authorities, see Botopolous (2020), p. 177.
15. We refer here mainly to the potential legal obstacles still arising from the *Meroni* doctrine, which we have no room to cover here. However, there seems to be an evolution of ECJ case law paving the way to overcoming such obstacles. See, e.g., ECJ ruling in Case C-270/12, *UK* v. *Council and Parliament*.
16. On these longer-term developments see Ringe, Morais, Ramos (2019) in Colaert, Busch and Incalza (eds) (2019), chapter 17, p. 405.

REFERENCES

Abrams, R. and Taylor, M. (2000). *Issues in the Unification of Financial Sector Supervision*, International Monetary Fund, No. 213.

Botopoulos, K. (2020). 'The European Supervisory Authorities: Role-models or in Need of Re-modelling?', *ERA Forum* 21, 177–198. https://doi.org/10.1007/s12027 -020-00609-7

Calvo, D., Crisanto, J.C., Hohl, S. and Gutiérrez, O.P. (2018). *Financial Supervisory Architecture: What has Changed after the Crisis?* FSI Insights on Policy Implementation, No. 8.

Colaert, V., Busch, D. and Incalza, T. (eds) (2019). *European Financial Regulation – Levelling the Cross-Sectoral Playing Field*. Hart, Bloomsbury.

Godwin, A. and Schmulow, A. (eds) (2021). *The Cambridge Handbook of Twin Peaks Financial Regulation*. Cambridge University Press.

Gortsos, C. and Ringe, W. (eds) (2021). *Financial Stability amidst the Pandemic Crisis*. EBI, Ebook.

Hauser, A. (2014). *Lender of Last Resort Operations during the Financial Crisis: Seven Practical Lessons from the United Kingdom*, BIS Papers No. 79.

Masciandaro, D. (ed.) (2005). *Handbook of Central Banking and Financial Authorities in Europe, New Architectures in the Supervision of Financial Markets*. Elgar.

Morais, L. (2017). *Models of Financial Supervision in Portugal and the European Union – Executive Summary – Part VI of White Paper on Regulation and Supervision of the Financial Sector*. Published by Banco de Portugal/Bank of Portugal. www .bportugal.pt/en/publications/banco-de-portugal/all/133

Morais, L. (2021). 'A Post-Covid Reformed EU: New Fiscal Policies Preserving Financial Stability and the Future of the Banking Sector', in C. Gortsos and W. Ringe (eds), *Financial Stability amidst the Pandemic Crisis*. EBI, Ebook.

Restoy, F, (2020). *Central Banks and Financial Stability: A Reflection after the Covid-19 Outbreak*, Financial Stability Institute, Occasional Paper No. 16.

Ringe, W., Morais, L. and Ramos, D. (2019). 'A Holistic Approach to the Institutional Architecture of Financial Supervision and Regulation in the EU', in V. Colaert, D. Busch, and T. Incalza (eds), *European Financial Regulation – Levelling the Cross-Sectoral Playing Field*. Hart, Bloomsbury.

Taylor, M. (1995). *'Twin Peaks': A Regulatory Structure for the New Century*. CSFI.

Taylor, M. (2009). *Twin Peaks Revisited ... A Second Chance for Regulatory Reform*. CSFI.

Taylor, M. (2021). 'The Three Episodes of Twin Peaks', in A. Godwin and A. Schmulow (eds), *The Cambridge Handbook of Twin Peaks Financial Regulation.* Cambridge University Press, p. 17.

Teixeira, P.G. (2020). *The Legal History of the European Banking Union – How European Law Led to the Supranational Integration of the Single Financial Market.* Hart, Bloomsbury.

Institutional Reports

Financial Conduct Authority (FCA), Prudential Regulation Authority (PRA) (2015). *The Failure of HBOS Plc (HBOS).*

Financial Services Authority (2009). *Turner Review – A Regulatory Response to the Global Banking Crisis.*

Financial Stability Board (FSB) (2014). *Peer Review of Germany – Review Report.*

Select Committee on Economic Affairs. *Banking Supervision and Regulation* (HL Session 2008–09, 101-I).

The Group of Thirty (2008). *The Structure of Financial Supervision – Approaches and Challenges in a Global Marketplace*, Washington, DC.

Wallis, S., Beerworth, B., Carmichael, J., Harper, I. and Nicholls, L. (1997). *Financial Stability Inquiry.* Series edited by the Treasury of the Commonwealth Government of Australia, The Treasury, 31 March 1997.

European Commission Documents

Commission (2021). 'Targeted Consultation on the Supervisory Convergence and the Single Rulebook' (Consultation). https://ec.europa.eu/info/consultations/finance-2021-esas-review_en

Case Law

Case C-270/12 *UK v Council and Parliament* [2014] ECR.

PART II

The role of central banks (I): aspects of
monetary and macroprudential policy
interaction

6. Can macroprudential tools ensure financial stability?

Anne Epaulard

---

1. THE CURRENT CONSENSUS: MONETARY POLICY IS IN CHARGE OF PRICE STABILITY, WHILE MACROPRUDENTIAL POLICY IS IN CHARGE OF FINANCIAL STABILITY

In late 2019, more and more European countries, within or outside the euro zone, had implemented macroprudential measures to try to tame the credit cycle in their economy. According to data published by the European Systemic Risk Board (ESRB), by late November 2019 11 countries had introduced Counter Cyclical Buffers (CCyBs) that increased capital requirements for banks; 20 countries had implemented a maximum Loan to Value Ratio (Max LTV) that limits the size of a mortgage loan; and 15 countries had implemented other borrower based macroprudential measures that limit the capacity of households to borrow (Debt Service to Income – DSTI; Debt to Income – DTI; Loan to Income – LTI). At the same time, monetary policy remains accommodative: monetary policy rates are low, and central banks, notably the ECB, continue their asset purchase programmes.

In response to the pandemic, regulatory constraints were temporarily relaxed with the idea that this would facilitate bank support to economic activity. The loosening of macroprudential policy took different forms but most tools were used: from regulatory constraints on bank capital and liquidity to borrower-based tools. Of course, the size of the loosening depended on the pre-pandemic level of macroprudential tools (see Bergant and Forbes, 2021). This is for example the case for a CCyB that was cut by 2.5 basis points in Sweden and by only 0.25 basis points in Germany (see Nier and Olafsson, 2020).

The consensus on which these policies have been implemented rests on the idea that there is a clear separation between the goal of monetary and macroprudential policies. Monetary policy is in charge of price stability while macroprudential policy is in charge of financial stability. This consensus results from lessons of the 2008–2009 Global Financial Crisis (GFC) and departs from the pre-crisis consensus.

1.1   The Pre-2008 Consensus

Before the GFC, most economists and central bankers agreed that the interest rate was too blunt a tool to deal with stock market bubbles. This was for example also reflected in the academic work by Bernanke and Gertler (2001) as well as in several speeches by Bernanke when he was Governor at the Federal Reserve Bank (Bernanke, 2002). This consensus also had some roots in the 'natural experiment' of the US in 1929, when the stock market crash followed successive increases in the federal funds rate in 1928.[1] Finally, and probably more importantly, before the GFC there was a general trust regarding the ability of financial markets to self-regulate.

This pre-2008 consensus does not imply that the central bank was not concerned with financial stability, but rather that the goal of financial stability had to be achieved with other tools than the policy rate (the then standard monetary policy tool), namely regulation, supervision and last resort lending (Bernanke, 2002). In 1996, when Alan Greenspan, then Chair of the US Federal Reserve, spoke of irrational exuberance to describe what was happening in the US financial markets, he was trying to warn investors about dot.com asset valuations that he believed were much too high. However, in accordance with the doctrine of the Federal Reserve and the consensus of the time, the course of monetary policy was unaffected, with the central bank remaining committed to its dual mandate: price stability and low unemployment. After the dot.com bubble burst in 2001, the Federal Reserve lowered its interest rate: the damage to the real economy was limited and the post-crash economic slowdown relatively short.

1.2   Empirical Research after the 2008 Financial Crisis has Changed the View Regarding the Causes of Financial Crises: Credit Cycles are Potentially More Damaging than Stock Market Bubbles

The financial crisis has spurred a long list of theoretical and empirical analyses that tried to challenge each part of the pre-crisis consensus. A first set of empirical work aims at identifying the specific characteristics of financial cycles that result in financial crises compared to other financial cycles. Schularik and Taylor (2012) and Dell'Arricia et al. (2017) conclude that the threat to financial stability comes more from large credit expansions rather than from booming stock markets or property bubbles.

One focus of post-2008 empirical research has been on better describing past financial crises and developments in financial markets, indebtedness and the economy before, during and after the financial crises. An article by Schularick and Taylor (2012) focused on the outbreaks of financial crises that took place from 1870 to 2008 in 14 economies. It provides a wealth of information about financial crises that simply cannot be summarized here. With respect to the role of monetary policy before and/or after financial booms, their main conclusions are: (a) after the Second World War, central banks were more inclined to intervene following financial crises. As a result, the post-crisis periods were less often characterized by deflation and a tightening of credit conditions in the economy, but (b) the post-war crises were nevertheless more costly in terms of activity and unemployment. They also note (c) that the pace of credit growth is a good predictor of the imminence of a financial crisis, and that the probability of a financial crisis is greater when debt levels are high. Finally, Schularik and Taylor conclude (d) that a rise in the price of financial assets in the pre-crisis years does not help to predict financial crises. Financial crises are therefore rather episodes of credit booms going bad than episodes of runaway financial markets alone, a hypothesis that had been prevalent before but which was difficult to validate empirically for developed countries due to the relative rarity of financial crises. Expanding on this work using long historical data, Jorda, Schularick and Taylor (2013) showed that the severity of a crisis is linked to the expansion of credit in the pre-crisis period, which had already been shown by Cerra and Saxena (2008) and Reinhart and Rogoff (2009) on shorter samples.

These empirical studies, which are very useful for understanding the genesis and consequences of crises, also provide orders of magnitude for quantifying the macroeconomic gains associated with financial stability. Above all, they help to rethink the hierarchy of effects: it is the surge in credit to individuals (in particular household debt) that, in the past, has been the main trigger of financial crises. Spectacular as they are, record levels reached by the stock market indices and the bursting of the bubbles that sometimes follow them are far from being so devastating. The threat to financial stability comes more from large credit expansions than from bursting stock market or property bubbles.

1.3   Whose Job is it to Tame the Credit Cycle?

If debt and credit cycles are dangerous for financial stability, the question is then: is it the job of monetary policy or that of macroprudential policy to tame credit cycles? To answer this question, we can hardly rely on real-life experiments. Rather researchers have built models to simulate policy experiments. They then compare the net gain associated with 'preventive' monetary policy actions – the increase in the policy interest rate above what is needed to maintain price stability reduces both the amplitude of the credit cycle and the probability of a burst at the cost of reducing economic activity today – to the net gain associated with 'reactive' monetary policy consisting in lowering the policy interest rate only after the credit cycle has turned and hurt the economy. These types of experiments help answer the question of whether monetary policy should be on the front line to ensure financial stability. It appears that across a large range of macroeconomic models[2] – from a 3-equation-new-keynesian model to more sophisticated DSGE[3] models – it is difficult to identify occurrences where a preventive monetary policy action is welfare improving.

In addition to these model simulations, an interesting episode of preventive monetary policy took place in Sweden in 2010–2011. Worried by the potential consequences of household debt and property price developments in Sweden, the Sveriges Riskbank increased its policy rate from 0.25% to 2% in a succession of 25 basis point hikes. At the time of these interest rate hikes, Swedish inflation was on target and did not require any monetary policy actions. The consequences of these hikes have been documented by Lars Svensson (2016): inflation plummeted, unemployment stayed at high levels compared to other developed economies, and neither property prices nor household debt decreased. In 2012, because of the damage to the real economy, the Sveriges Riskbank reversed its monetary policy and became one of the first central banks to implement negative interest rates.

All these studies and policy experiments led to the conviction that the interest rate was not the right policy tool to deal with rampant credit cycles. But if standard monetary policy tool is not available to ensure financial stability, whose job is it to ensure financial stability? All the hopes are with macroprudential policies. And this is the new consensus: monetary policy is in charge of price stability while macroprudential policy is in charge of financial stability.[4]

2.   HOW COMFORTABLE ARE WE WITH THIS CONSENSUS?

One of the appeals of macroprudential instruments is that they look sufficiently granular to target a given market, institution or behaviour and deal with any glaring imbalances in specific markets. And this is precisely this granular characteristic that the monetary policy rate lacks. Still, we do not know that much about the actual ability of these tools to have a significant impact on specific market dynamics or behaviours.

2.1   Our Knowledge Regarding the Efficiency of Macroprudential Policies to Tame the Credit Cycle is Still Imperfect

Central banks can rely on a large body of empirical results regarding the size of the impact of changes in policy rates on the economy. By contrast, we don't know much about the effectiveness of most macroprudential tools. There are many reasons for this ignorance. First of all, there are many different instruments: some of them target banks (for example the CCyB), others target borrowers (Debt Service to Income – DSTI; Debt to Income – DTI; Loan to Income – LTI). In addition, data are scarce because these instruments were rarely used in the past. When we do have data, they mostly cover emerging economies, not developed economies. Finally, the empirical methodology to measure the implementation of these tools and their effectiveness needs to be improved. For example, most empirical papers are just counting the number of macroprudential measures in place (no matter their intensity) and/or the overall stance of the policy (tightening vs. loosening). Another concern about the results of these empirical papers is that they show correlations as opposed to causalities.

2.1.1   Macroprudential instruments appear capable of reducing the debt cycle

Already before the outbreak of the GFC, Borio and Shim (2007) studied the implementation of prudential measures to limit credit growth and rising real estate prices across 15 countries. Based on an event study, they found that these measures reduce credit growth and property prices rapidly after being introduced. On a broader panel of 49 developed and emerging economies observed from 1990 to 2011, Lim et al. (2011) identified 53 episodes where at least one macroprudential tool was used. Only nine countries in the sample did not use any macroprudential tool over the period. They concluded that a number of macroprudential instruments are effective at reducing the procyclicality of credit, regardless of the country's exchange rate regime or the size of its financial sector. This is the case of limits on debt relative either to the value of the property it finances, the Loan to Value Ratio (LTV), or to income, the Loan to Income Ratio (LTI), banks' reserve requirement ratio, countercyclical capital requirements and dynamic provisioning (provisions grow more than proportionally to assets). Using an even more extensive database in terms of both the number of countries (57) and years (from 1980 to 2011), Kuttner and Shim (2016) showed that the Debt Service to Income ratio (DSTI) is the most universally effective instrument for reducing the rise in mortgages. On the other hand, this tool does not seem to have any effect on the dynamics of real estate prices, which rather tend to respond to the taxation of real estate property. These results are consistent with what has been estimated for Hong

Kong (He, 2014) and in emerging economies (Jacome and Mitra, 2015) where the use of LTV limits succeeded in containing household debt but had a limited impact on the rise in real estate prices, which are held down instead by higher transaction taxes.

Again, it is worth noting the coarse nature of these impact assessments, which do not shed much light on the appropriate mix of macroprudential instruments. In most impact studies, policies are represented by discrete variables (e.g. 0 if no action is taken, +1 if the macroprudential tool is introduced or its intensity increased, and -1 if the use of the macroprudential tool is relaxed, as is the case in the analysis of Kuttner and Shim, 2016), with the intensity of the macroprudential measure itself not being taken into account.

2.1.2 There are even fewer empirical results regarding the impact of macroprudential measures on the risks taken by banks

Claessens et al. (2013) analysed the use of macroprudential policies aimed at reducing vulnerabilities in banks. From a sample of 2,300 banks observed over the period 2000–2010, they concluded that debt limits (LTV and DSTI) are effective in reducing the banks' debt ratio and the growth of their debt in boom periods. Once again, the variable representing the use of the macroprudential tool is binary (0 or 1) and does not take into account the intensity with which the macroprudential policy is applied.

2.1.3 The cost of macroprudential policies

While it is one thing to show that macroprudential tools do have an impact on the behaviour they target, another is to evaluate whether or not these measures have spillovers that are costly to the rest of the economy. Richter et al. (2019) try to quantify the effects of changes in maximum LTV ratios on output and inflation. They show that there are, indeed, some spillovers from these macroprudential measures. According to their empirical results, a 10-point decrease in the maximum LTV ratio (a tightening of the macroprudential policy) generates a 1.1% loss in output, more or less the same impact as a 25-basis-point increase in the monetary policy rate.

2.2 We are Learning Fast

2.2.1 More data, better methodologies

As more and more European countries are implementing macroprudential measures, more data is becoming available for empirical research to assess their effectiveness. Meanwhile, policy makers are in the difficult situation where they have to implement measures without clear knowledge regarding their impact. At the same time, empirical methodologies are refined. For example, Richter et al. (2019) are able to use the intensity of the macroprudential policy in place and not only its pace. Also, they try to come up with a strategy to confirm the causal relationship from maximum LTV ratios to output losses and property prices.

2.2.2   The long list of questions waiting for answers

To be comfortable with the current consensus – that macroprudential policies can achieve financial stability and monetary policy keeps its narrow objective of price stability – we need to have answers to quite a long list of questions.

First of all, we need to know better what type of credit booms call for a macroprudential response. As shown by Asriyan et al. (2019), not all credit booms are alike and those that are relying on extensive use of collateral are more likely to shake financial stability than those that are fuelled by productivity shocks. Only the credit booms of the first type are calling for a macroprudential response.

Secondly, we need to know whether macroprudential measures once in place gradually lose their effectiveness. After the introduction of a macroprudential measure economic agents might (will) be tempted to find ways to circumvent them either by regulatory trade-offs or by creative financial engineering (Aiyar et al., 2014; Jeanne and Korinek, 2014), especially when policies are not coordinated at the international level. This is the argument often made by advocates of the use of monetary policy rather than macroprudential tools for ensuring financial stability. For example, Borio and Drehmann (2009), Cecchetti and Kohler (2012) and Stein (2014) argue that since the interest rate is a universal price, it hits regulated sectors and non-regulated sectors alike (including shadow banking).

Thirdly, the question of coordination of macroprudential policies within the euro area needs to be examined. On the one hand, the granularity of macroprudential tools makes them particularly suitable to deal with local conditions – to the point where they are sometimes implemented with different intensity within a given country. That is a reason not to coordinate within the euro area. However, in the case of a common situation within the euro area, some research shows that there would be benefits from coordinated actions (Rubio and Carrasco-Gallego, 2016), while other research concludes there is no need for it (Poutineau and Vermandel, 2017).

Finally, one limitation of the use of macroprudential tools lies in the difficulty in using them. Direct intervention in specific markets can have a high political cost, especially when it affects specific interest groups. The limits on household debt (limits on LTV ratios, DTIs or DSTIs) that do appear effective when they are used are also largely unpopular, especially as they are likely to affect the poorest households more. Indeed, looking at 58 countries over 2000–2014 Müller (2019) concludes that macroprudential regulation exhibits a predictable electoral cycle. Notably policies restricting mortgages and consumer credit appear to be looser before elections. It is reassuring though that no electoral cycle can be detected in the data in countries where macroprudential decisions are made by financial stability committees comprised of multiple stakeholders.

NOTES

1. Whether these fed fund increases actually caused the stock-market collapse is a related but slightly different question.
2. See for example Woodford (2012), Ajello et al. (2016), Gourio et al. (2016) and Epaulard (2018) for a review.
3. DSGE models (which stands for Dynamic Stochastic General Equilibrium model) are the now standard tools to analyse responses of economies to policy shocks.
4. Collard et al. (2017) propose a macroeconomic model that illustrates this divide between monetary policy and macroprudential policy.

REFERENCES

Aiyar, S., C. W. Calomiris and T. Wieladek, 2014, 'Does Macroprudential Leak: Evidence from a UK Policy Experiment', *Journal of Money, Credit and Banking,* 46(1).

Ajello, A., T. Laubach, J. D. Lopez-Salido and T. Nakata, 2016, 'Financial Stability and Optimal Interest-Rate Policy', *Finance and Economics Discussion Series,* 2016-067, Board of Governors of the Federal Reserve System (U.S.).

Asriyan, V., L. Laeven and A. Martin, 2019, 'Collateral Booms and Information Depletion', ECB Working Paper, No. 2266.

Bergant, K. and K. Forbes, 2021, 'Macroprudential Policies During the COVID-19: The Role of Policy Space', NBER Working Paper, No. 29346.

Bernanke, B. S., 2002, 'Asset-Price "Bubbles" and Monetary Policy', Remarks before the New York Chapter of the National Association for Business Economics, Federal Reserve, 15 October 2002.

Bernanke, B. S. and M. Gertler, 2001, 'Should Central Banks Respond to Movements in Asset Prices?', *American Economic Review,* 91(2): 253–257.

Borio, C. and M. Drehmann, 2009, 'Assessing the Risk of Banking Crises – Revisited', *BIS Quarterly Review,* March: 29–44.

Borio, C. and I. Shim, 2007, 'What Can (Macro-)Prudential Policy Do to Support Monetary Policy', BIS Working Paper, No. 242.

Cecchetti, S. and M. Kohler, 2012, 'When Capital Adequacy and Interest Rate Policy are Substitutes (And When They are Not)', BIS Working Paper, No. 379.

Cerra, V. and S. C. Saxena, 2008, 'Growth Dynamics: The Myth of Economic Recovery', *American Economic Review,* 98(1): 439–457.

Claessens, S., S. R. Ghosh and R. Mihet, 2013, 'Macroprudential Policies to Mitigate Financial System Vulnerabilities', *Journal of International Money and Finance,* 39(4): 1661–1707.

Collard, F., H. Dellas, B. Diba and O. Loisel, 2017, 'Optimal Monetary and Prudential Policies', *American Economic Journal: Macroeconomics,* 9(1): 40–87.

Dell'Ariccia, G., L. Laeven and G. Suarez, 2017, 'Bank Leverage and Monetary Policy's Risk-taking Channel: Evidence from the United States', *Journal of Finance*, 72(2): 613–654.

Epaulard, A., 2018, 'What Should Monetary Policy do in the Face of Soaring Asset Prices and Rampant Credit Growth?', Revue de l'OFCE, No. 157.

Gourio, F., A. K. Kashyap and J. Sim, 2016, 'The Tradeoffs in Leaning against the Wind', Federal Reserve Bank of Chicago, NBER Working Paper, No. w23658.

He, D., 2014, 'Les effets de la politique macro-prudentielle sur les risques du marché de l'immobilier résidentiel: le cas de Hong Kong', Banque de France, *Revue de la stabilité financière*, 18: 115–130.

Jacome, L. I. and S. Mitra, 2015, 'LTV and DTI Limits – Going Granular', IMF Working Paper, No. 15/154.

Jeanne, O. and A. Korinek, 2014, 'Macroprudential Policy beyond Banking Regulation. Macroprudential Policies: Implementation and Interactions', Banque de France, *Financial Stability Review*, 18: 163–171.

Jorda, O., M. Schularick and A. M. Taylor, 2013, 'When Credit Bites Back', *Journal of Money Credit and Banking*, 45(2): 3–28.

Kuttner, K. N. and I. Shim, 2016, 'Can Non-interest Rate Policies Stabilize Housing Markets? Evidence from a Panel of 57 Economies', *Journal of Financial Stability*, 26: 31–44.

Lim, C. H., A. Costa, F. Columba, P. Kongsamut, A. Otani, M. Saiyid, T. Wezel and X. Wu, 2011, 'Macroprudential Policy. What Instruments and How to Use them? Lessons from Country Experiences', IMF Working Papers, 11/238, International Monetary Fund.

Müller, K., 2019, 'Electoral Cycles in Macroprudential Regulation', ESRB Working Paper Series No. 2019/106.

Nier, E. and T. T. Olafsson, 2020, 'Main Operational Aspects for Macroprudential Policy Relaxation', IMF Special Series on COVID-19, September.

Poutineau, J. C. and G. Vermandel, 2017, 'Global Banking and the Conduct of Macroprudential Policy in a Monetary Union', *Journal of Macroeconomics*, 54: 306–331.

Reinhart, C. M. and K. S. Rogoff, 2009, *This Time Is Different: Eight Centuries of Financial Folly*, Princeton University Press.

Richter, B., M. Schularick and I. Shim, 2019, 'The Costs of Macroprudential Policy', *Journal of International Economics*, 118: 263–282.

Rubio, M. and J. A. Carrasco-Gallego, 2016, 'Coordinating Macroprudential Policies within the Euro Area: The Case of Spain', *Economic Modelling*, 59: 570–582.

Schularick, M. and A. M. Taylor, 2012, 'Credit Booms Gone Bust: Monetary Policy, Leverage Cycles, and Financial Crises, 1870–2008', *American Economic Review*, 102(2): 1029–1061.

Stein, J. C., 2014, 'Incorporating Financial Stability Considerations into a Monetary Policy Framework', Speech delivered at the International Forum on Monetary Policy, Washington DC, March.

Svensson, L. E., 2016, 'Cost-Benefit Analysis of Leaning against the Wind: Are Costs Larger Also with Less Effective Macroprudential Policy?', IMF Working Paper, No. 16/3.

Woodford, M., 2012, 'Inflation Targeting and Financial Stability', NBER Working Paper, No. 17967.

7.   The interaction of monetary and financial tasks in different central bank structures[1]

Aerdt Houben, Jan Kakes and Annelie Petersen

1.   INTRODUCTION

In response to the Global Financial Crisis, central banks substantially expanded their monetary and financial policy toolkits. Monetary tasks – here defined as monetary policy and the lender of last resort (LOLR) function – have been supplemented by unconventional tools, such as asset purchases, long-term lending operations for banks, negative interest rates and forward guidance. Moreover, non-monetary policy areas have been expanded in many central banks. Microprudential banking supervision has been strengthened by a tightening of capital and liquidity requirements. Macroprudential policy and banking resolution have been developed as (relatively) new areas with specific policy mandates and designated authorities. These extensions have enhanced the financial sector's resilience and increased the scope for stabilization policy and crisis resolution. At the same time, the interaction between policy instruments has become more challenging. These developments and challenges have been further accentuated by the COVID-19 pandemic in 2020, which resulted in a myriad of policy adjustments in monetary operations and prudential tools.

This chapter describes how the institutional set-up of monetary and financial policies differs across Europe and discusses central bank involvement. In some jurisdictions (like Austria) the central bank continues to focus on its core monetary tasks, whereas in other jurisdictions (like the Netherlands) the central bank also plays a prominent role in non-monetary policy fields. The European Central Bank's (ECB) tasks have been broadened in recent years by responsibilities for microprudential and macroprudential policy, whereas financial stability considerations will be more on the forefront in monetary policy decision-making following the ECB's recent strategy review. The purpose of this article is to (1) map out how traditional and new policy tools are organized across Europe, (2) discuss how these policy instruments interact, (3) review the pros and cons of central bank involvement, (4) discuss how the organization of policies – particularly the role of the central bank – may be related to country-specific features, and (5) discuss initial experiences with the policy response to the COVID-19 pandemic.

2.   HOW ARE NON-MONETARY TASKS ORGANIZED ACROSS EUROPE?

The current institutional set-up of regulatory policies was established in the aftermath of the 2008–2009 Global Financial Crisis (GFC). Following a rec-ommendation by the European Systemic Risk Board (ESRB, 2011), European Union (EU) jurisdictions established designated authorities that are responsi-ble for setting macroprudential policy tools. Similarly, the Banking Resolution and Recovery Directive, adopted in 2014, requires EU member states to estab-lish national resolution authorities. Some countries also changed the set-up of microprudential supervision, for instance by moving to a twin peaks model in which the central bank is also responsible for banking supervision (Belgium, United Kingdom) or to an integrated supervisor for banks and non-banks outside the central bank (Finland).[2]

The involvement of central banks with non-monetary tasks differs across jurisdictions but is most prominent for macroprudential policy. In the vast majority of countries, the central bank is directly responsible for macropruden-tial policy or chairs a committee that sets macroprudential instruments (Table 7.1). In many cases, central banks are also responsible for microprudential supervision and resolution, but several jurisdictions have designated these tasks to a separate regulator or resolution authority. In some jurisdictions, the resolution task has been assigned to existing bodies that were already responsible for elements of resolution, such as a deposit guarantee fund. There are also jurisdictions with two or more resolution authorities, with specific responsibilities for e.g. the deposit guarantee scheme or resolution planning versus execution.

In practice, these differences are not clear-cut due to cooperation and coordination between central banks and other authorities. In countries with an independent regulator, central banks often provide operational and analytical support through data collection, performing off-site analyses and participating in on-site inspections. In countries where macroprudential instruments are set by the regulator, central banks often have an advisory role and publish financial stability reports. Cooperation and coordination are also promoted by international bodies in which central banks, regulators and other authorities are represented. Examples at the global level are the Financial Stability Board and standard setters such as the Basel Committee for Banking Supervision, and at

Table 7.1   *Monetary and non-monetary authorities by jurisdiction*

| Country | Monetary/LOLR | Microprudential | | Macroprudential | Resolution |
		2020	2007		
Euro area					
Austria	Central bank	Regulator	Regulator	Regulator[a]	Regulator
Belgium	Central bank	Central bank	Regulator	Central bank	Central bank
Cyprus	Central bank	Central bank	Central bank	Central bank	Central bank
Estonia	Central bank	Regulator	Regulator	Central bank	Regulator
Finland	Central bank	Regulator	Regulator	Regulator	Resolution Authority
France	Central bank	Regulator	Regulator	Committee	Regulator
Germany	Central bank	Regulator	Regulator	Regulator[a]	Regulator
Greece	Central bank	Central bank	Central bank	Central bank	Central bank
Ireland	Central bank	Central bank	Regulator	Central bank	Central bank
Italy	Central bank	Central bank	Central bank	Central bank	Central bank
Latvia	Central bank	Regulator	Regulator	Central bank[a]	Regulator
Lithuania	Central bank	Central bank	Central bank	Central bank	Central bank
Luxembourg	Central bank	Regulator	Regulator	Regulator[a]	Regulator
Malta	Central bank	Regulator	Regulator	Central bank	Regulator
Netherlands	Central bank	Central bank	Central bank	Central bank[a]	Central bank
Portugal	Central bank	Central bank	Central bank	Central bank	Central bank
Slovakia	Central bank	Central bank	Central bank	Central bank	Resolution Authority
Slovenia	Central bank	Central bank	Central bank	Central bank[a]	Central bank
Spain	Central bank	Central bank	Central bank	Central bank	Multiple[b]
Euro area	Central bank	Central bank	–	Central bank	Resolution Authority
Other EU					
Bulgaria	Central bank	Central bank	Central bank	Central bank[a]	Central bank
Croatia	Central bank	Central bank	Central bank	Central bank[a]	Multiple[b]
Czech Republic	Central bank	Central bank	Central bank	Central bank	Central bank
Denmark	Central bank	Regulator	Regulator	Ministry of Finance[a]	Multiple[b]
Hungary	Central bank	Central bank	Regulator	Central bank[a]	Central bank
Poland	Central bank	Regulator	Regulator	Committee	Resolution Authority
Romania	Central bank	Central bank	Central bank	Committee	Multiple[b]

| Country | Monetary/LOLR | Microprudential | | Macroprudential | Resolution |
		2020	2007		
Sweden	Central bank	Regulator	Regulator	Regulator	National Debt Office
Non-EU					
UK	Central bank	Central bank	Regulator	Central bank	Central bank
US	Central bank	Other	Other	Central bank	Resolution authority
Japan	Central bank	Regulator	Regulator	Regulator	Regulator

Note: [a] Designated authority as indicated, but committee as macroprudential authority; [b] Several authorities responsible for resolution. In Spain and Croatia, these are the central bank and a resolution authority; in Romania the central bank and the regulator; in Denmark the regulator and a resolution authority.
Source: EBA, ESRB, World Bank Bank Regulation and Supervision Survey.

the regional level the ESRB. Finally, with the launch of the Banking Union in Europe, the ECB has been given responsibilities as a microprudential supervisor as well as a macroprudential authority. The ECB performs these tasks in close cooperation with national authorities, thereby ensuring a significant degree of central bank involvement in these non-monetary areas.

3.   HOW DO POLICIES INTERACT?

The different monetary and financial sector policy areas tend to be aligned in normal times but may work against each other in specific circumstances. Monetary policy promotes stable and non-inflationary economic growth; microprudential supervision increases financial institutions' resilience; and the lender of last resort function provides a safety net to contain a financial crisis. When asset prices, economic growth and inflationary pressures move in the same direction, these policy fields tend to be closely aligned. There are circumstances, however, in which policy goals may be contradictory. For instance, when consumer price inflation is low while financial imbalances are growing, monetary policy aimed at price stability may further exacerbate these imbalances. In such circumstances, pursuing different policy goals involves trade-offs and some goals may be compromised.

The extension of policy instruments, however, has enhanced the scope to pursue different policy goals simultaneously. According to the Tinbergen rule, policymakers need to control at least as many instruments as they have different policy goals. In this context, macroprudential policies can help counter imbalances and increase the financial system's resilience, especially in situations where monetary and microprudential instruments cannot be fully deployed for that goal. On top of that, resolution can help to deal with a crisis

Table 7.2   *Pros and cons of central bank involvement with non-monetary tasks*

	Advantages	Disadvantages
Microprudential supervision	Better understanding of bank lending channel (monetary policy) Better understanding of funding needs (LOLR)	Conflict of interests Reputation risk
Macroprudential policy	Macro-orientation Independence and long-term orientation Coordination with monetary stance	Conflict of interests
Resolution	More effective crisis management (LOLR)	Conflict of interest (LOLR)
Bundling of all tasks	*Operational synergies, better oversight and scope for policy coordination*	*Conflicts of interests Concentration of power Reputation risk*

Source: Authors assessment based on Calvo et al. (2018), Goodhart (2000), Kremers et al. (2003) and Llewellyn (2006).

in situations where prudential policies and the LOLR function are insufficient to safeguard financial stability.

Central bank involvement with new policy fields facilitates oversight and coordination but may also have disadvantages (Table 7.2). Combining tasks in a single institution makes it easier to exploit synergies, for instance through more efficient use of resources and more effective coordination. Central banks' relatively independent position and long-term system-wide orientation provides a view that is less biased by short-term considerations. Potential disadvantages of combining tasks are conflicts of interest, concentration of power and greater reputation risks. To weigh these trade-offs, the remainder of this section discusses how monetary policy and the LOLR function interact with the non-monetary tasks.

3.1   Interaction Between Monetary and Prudential Policies

Monetary policy can be used to pursue financial stability, but this must be weighed against the overriding goal of price stability. More than other policy tools, such as macroprudential instruments, monetary policy 'gets into all the cracks' of the financial system. In that regard, using monetary policy to contain financial imbalances alleviates the microprudential and macroprudential tasks. Several authors have therefore argued that monetary policy should explicitly incorporate financial stability considerations, or even be deployed to 'lean against the wind'.[3] In this manner, policy rates may be set higher or lower for financial stability purposes than would be justified by inflation targeting alone. Leaning against the wind policies are, however, controversial and the literature has not reached a consensus about the balance between costs (reduced scope to pursue price stability and support economic activity) and benefits (reducing the probability of a crisis).[4]

In the ECB's recent strategy review, the importance of macro-financial amplification channels in the monetary transmission process has been recognized more explicitly. Previously, the ECB used a two-pillar framework comprising an economic analysis, which increasingly relied on macroeconomic projections, and the monetary analysis, which increasingly focused on the assessment of monetary policy transmission. The new monetary strategy entails a more integrated framework, in which the economic and monetary analyses are retained as two specialized branches of analysis. But the focus has shifted towards longer-term developments and financial stability, with a more explicit weighting of side effects through a proportionality assessment to pursue an optimal instrument mix and minimize potential side-effects. Hence, although macroprudential policy and microprudential supervision remain the first line of defence against financial imbalances, financial stability considerations have received a more formal place in the decision-making process in view of their relevance for price stability.

Macroprudential policy instruments may then supplement monetary policy by focusing on financial resilience at the national level. Macroprudential instruments are typically aimed at strengthening the resilience of the financial and household sectors. Examples are systemic and countercyclical capital buffers that are imposed as an add-on to microprudential requirements, and loan-to-value and loan-to-income limits for residential mortgages. Even though such macroprudential instruments may not fully counter the build-up of macro-financial imbalances, the accumulation of additional capital buffers will contribute to greater resilience in the targeted parts of the financial sector.[5] In this respect, macroprudential policy is close to central banking with its traditional systemic orientation and focus on financial cycles.[6] Finally, macroprudential policy tools are set at the national level, which is particularly relevant in a currency union where monetary policy cannot take into account differences between national financial cycles and country-specific vulnerabilities. Macroprudential policy may then mitigate a country's vulnerability to imbalances and thereby improve the functioning of the currency union.[7]

Combining monetary policy and microprudential supervision within the central bank may enhance the understanding of monetary transmission but also brings potential conflicts of interests. With more information on the banking sector, the central bank will have a better insight in the way its policies are transmitted through the bank lending channel. This is particularly important for European economies, which have predominantly bank-oriented financial structures. Simultaneously, however, conflicts of interest may arise as supervisory considerations may affect incentives for the monetary policymaker. In particular, the central bank may be inclined to let its decision on monetary stance be influenced by the impact on banks' financial positions. Related to this point, bank failures may have adverse consequences for the central bank's reputation, which would also affect the central bank's credibility in conducting effective monetary policy.

3.2 Interaction Between LOLR Financing and Microprudential Supervision and Resolution

The LOLR function involves a trade-off between providing a safety net for banks and moral hazard. In periods of systemic liquidity stress, an increasing intermediary role of the central bank as LOLR is generally warranted.[8] Simultaneously, the availability of this safety net may stimulate moral hazard behaviour and undermine market discipline. Traditionally, therefore, LOLR support is provided only temporarily to illiquid but solvent banks against backstop rates and good collateral. As part of the Eurosystem's unconventional measures, however, bank refinancing operations have expanded in terms of volumes and duration with attractive pricing and a loosening of collateral requirements. A relevant question, in this context, is to what extent central bank liquidity provision should be arranged ex ante (which may prevent market stress) or ex post (to contain moral hazard).

Central bank involvement with non-monetary tasks helps to exploit synergies but may have adverse consequences for market discipline and may create conflicts of interest. Assessments of a bank's soundness and viability are facilitated by close cooperation between the central bank, the supervisor and the resolution authority. This is particularly the case when a bank's financial position significantly deteriorates and regular liquidity provision may have to be suspended or replaced by Emergency Liquidity Assistance (ELA). Indeed, the trade-offs surrounding a central bank's role as LOLR liquidity provider (safety net vs. moral hazard) become increasingly complex if these also involve the considerations of the resolution authority (resolving a bank as soon as it is no longer considered viable) and a potential supervisory preference to allow forbearance (to buy time for a bank to recover). In all, the trade-off may be summarized as, on the one hand, improving information flows and allowing inclusive decision-making (by combining tasks) and, on the other hand, avoiding potential conflicts of interests (by separating tasks).

4.   DETERMINANTS OF CENTRAL BANK INVOLVEMENT

In the wake of the GFC, decisions on non-monetary tasks have shown path dependence and a growing role of central banks. Most jurisdictions avoided an institutional overhaul and built on their existing approaches with supervision either inside or outside the central bank (Table 7.1).[9] However, four jurisdictions (Belgium, Hungary, Ireland and the UK) moved microprudential banking supervision to the central bank while there was no move in the opposite direction. For the new tasks – macroprudential policy and resolution – most euro area jurisdictions have followed a pragmatic approach by combining them within existing entities. The microprudential supervisor – either the central bank or an independent supervisor – has been made responsible for macroprudential policy in all but four jurisdictions and for resolution in all but also four cases.[10] Outside the euro area, new tasks – particularly resolution – have often been given to other institutions than central banks or regulators, such as independent resolution authorities. The latter also reflects path dependency, as some institutions that were already responsible for specific resolution tasks – such as running the deposit guarantee scheme – had their responsibilities extended to also include resolution planning.[11]

   Another determinant of the institutional set-up may be the size and concentration of the financial sector. Systemic risk is particularly relevant in the euro area, as bank-based financial systems are often associated with higher systemic risk than market-based systems (Bats and Houben, 2020). Especially in jurisdictions with a large and concentrated banking sector, there is a strong case for a prominent role of central banks in banking supervision, to ensure a macro-financial perspective. Indeed, in some of the European jurisdictions with the largest (UK) and most concentrated (Greece, Netherlands) banking systems, the central bank is also responsible for prudential policies and resolution. The institutional structures in the UK and the Netherlands were explicitly motivated by their concentrated banking systems.[12] Size and concentration are not always decisive arguments for a central bank supervisor, however, as there are jurisdictions with large (Germany) or concentrated (Estonia, Latvia) banking systems that have an integrated supervisor outside the central bank.

   A further consideration is that authorities should be able to effectively respond to structural changes. The financial system continuously evolves, driven by macro trends (internationalization, demographics, etc.) and innovation. Authorities need to be aware of such trends and implications for their tasks, which also involves the interaction with other authorities. An example in recent years is the emergence of non-banks on credit markets, which has implications for the design of bank and non-bank regulation but also for monetary transmission and the design of monetary operations. An integrated supervisor is more likely to incorporate cross-sector trends in its supervisory practices, whereas a central bank is more likely to oversee broader systemic aspects.

Finally, a role for the central bank in macroprudential policy may contribute to dealing with inaction bias when financial vulnerabilities are building up. Inaction bias is the tendency to postpone desirable policy action when this involves accepting certain, visible, short-term costs on account of uncertain, invisible long-term benefits. Given the length of financial cycles and the low frequency of financial crisis, inaction bias seems particularly relevant for macroprudential policy. This raises the question of whether central banks, which are designated as macroprudential authorities in most jurisdictions, are better able to deal with inaction bias than other institutions. Although it is premature to draw strong conclusions at this stage, Figure 7.1 (left) presents some preliminary evidence that central banks seem to have implemented macroprudential tools earlier than non-central bank authorities. The ECB's macroprudential mandate has been specifically tailored to counter inaction bias. In particular, the ECB has top-up power to tighten (i.e. not to loosen) certain national macroprudential measures.[13] This reflects the presumption that national authorities will not delay when loosening their macroprudential policy stance, but may tend to postpone any tightening.

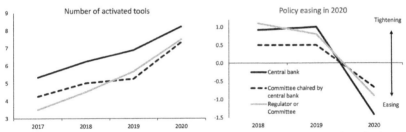

Note: Both graphs present averages in jurisdictions per category. In the right-hand graph, the net macroprudential policy stance is based on the ESRB's assessment for five categories of tools: countercyclical buffers, systemic risk buffers, buffers for systemically important banks, real estate and a category of remaining instruments. The graph is based on the net overall score by country, where easing is -1, tightening is +1 and neutral is 0, and presents country averages grouped by the degree of central bank involvement with macroprudential policy. The graph should be interpreted cautiously because of (1) the limited number of observations and (2) not all measures are equally important.
Source: Chart based on ESRB (2021), ESRB (2020), ESRB (2019) and ESRB (2018).

Figure 7.1   Implementation of macroprudential policy in the euro area

5.   THE COVID-19 POLICY RESPONSE

The COVID crisis may be considered a first test for institutional arrangement since the GFC. Although it is too early to draw definitive lessons, some initial observations can be made about policy interventions and the interaction between policy areas. First of all, policy measures across the board have been swift and powerful and the policy response has clearly incorporated lessons learnt from the GFC.[14] Central banks aggressively eased monetary policy, using unconventional tools such as asset purchases, long-term lending operations and forward guidance.[15] Macro- and microprudential policies have been relaxed, for instance by temporarily reducing buffer requirements. As a result, financial markets recovered fairly quickly and surged ahead once a vaccine had been found. A second observation is that different policies have reinforced each other. For instance, dividend restrictions and the release of macroprudential capital buffers have made it easier for banks to absorb losses. And banks' holdings of central bank reserves, which increased as a direct effect of monetary interventions, have temporarily been exempted from the calculation of the leverage ratio.

Preliminary evidence suggests that the easing of macroprudential policy was slightly more pronounced in jurisdictions with a prominent central bank role. Macroprudential tools can be used to address country-specific imbalances which, as already discussed, may be particularly relevant in a currency area. While macroprudential policy was relaxed across the euro area, macroprudential authorities with a prominent role of central banks have been eased somewhat more than others (Figure 7.1, right). The latter may reflect that these jurisdictions had more policy space as they started implementing macroprudential instruments relatively early.

6.   CONCLUDING REMARKS

Central bank involvement with non-monetary tasks differs across jurisdictions but has increased since the Global Financial Crisis. Central banks play a prominent role in macroprudential policy, but their involvement with microprudential supervision and crisis resolution has also grown. At the same time, differences across Europe remain substantial as most jurisdictions have chosen to build on their pre-crisis institutional frameworks. Most jurisdictions stuck to their initial choices to have the banking supervisor either inside or outside the central bank, and designated new policies to that supervisor. But the exceptions generally moved more regulatory powers to central banks.

Combining monetary and regulatory tasks improves operational synergies, oversight and policy coordination but may also involve conflicts of interests, concentration of power and reputation risk. The extension of policy instruments has increased the scope to pursue different policy goals simultaneously. Moreover, macroprudential policies in Europe are set at the national level, which increases the scope to address country-specific financial imbalances and improve the functioning of the internal market. The benefits of better policy coordination and oversight can be best exploited by bundling all regulatory policies and monetary instruments into the central bank. Preliminary evidence suggests this may increase the strength and speed of policy action. In practice, however, this means that the central bank may have to deal with conflicts of interest between different policies and reputation risk. In addition, the combination of many policies in one institution leads to a significant concentration of power.

NOTES

1. The views expressed in this chapter are those of the authors and do not necessarily reflect the position of De Nederlandsche Bank.
2. This article focuses on microprudential banking supervision and does not discuss conduct of business supervision. Both are sometimes combined (integrated supervision model) or explicitly separated (twin peaks model).
3. See Borio and White (2004), Borio (2014).
4. See Galati and Moessner (2013).
5. However, the almost exclusive focus of macroprudential instruments on banks implies a potential for risk-shifting beyond the banking sector (Cizel et al., 2019).
6. See BIS (2011), De Haan et al. (2012).
7. Houben and Kakes (2013).
8. See Bats et al. (2018) for an extensive analysis of the LOLR function in the context of the GFC and its aftermath.
9. Calvo et al. (2018) find a similar trend in a survey on institutional changes in 82 jurisdictions.
10. This follows the ESRB (2011) recommendation that central banks should play a leading role in macroprudential policy, particularly if they are also responsible for microprudential supervision.
11. Examples include the Canadian Deposit Insurance Corporation (CDIC) and the Federal Deposit Insurance Corporation (FDIC) in the United States. See FSB (2019) for an overview of resolution authorities in major economies.
12. See Osborne (2010) and Kremers and Schoenmaker (2010).
13. More specifically, the ECB has top-up power for macroprudential instruments that are included in the Capital Requirements Directive (CRD-IV) and the Capital Requirement Regulations, such as countercyclical and systemic capital buffers and specific liquidity requirements for banks. Other macroprudential tools that some jurisdictions may use, such as Loan-to-Value ratios for mortgages, cannot be changed by the ECB.
14. See Financial Stability Board (2021), Cavallino and De Fiore (2020).
15. In the case of the Eurosystem, the main COVID-19-related operations are the Pandemic Emergency Purchase Programme (PEPP) and attractive lending conditions through the Targeted Longer-Term Refinancing Operations (TLTROs).

REFERENCES

Bats, Joost and Aerdt Houben (2020), Bank-based versus market-based financing: implications for systemic risk. *Journal of Banking & Finance*, 114, 105776.

Bats, Joost, Jan Willem van den End and John Thoolen (2018), Revisiting the central bank's lender of last resort function, *DNB Occasional Studies* 16(4).

BIS (2011), Central bank governance and financial stability. A report by a Study Group chaired by Stefan Ingves.

Borio, Claudio (2014), Monetary policy and financial stability: what role in prevention and recovery? BIS Working Papers, No. 440.

Borio, Claudio and William White (2004), Whither monetary and financial stability? The implications of evolving policy regimes. BIS Working Papers, No. 147.

Calvo, Daniel, Juan Carlos Crisanto, Stefan Hohl and Oscar Pascual Gutiérrez (2018), Financial supervisory architecture: what has changed after the crisis? FSI Insights on Policy Implementation, No. 8, Bank for International Settlements.

Cavallino, Paolo and Fiorella De Fiore (2020), Central banks' response to COVID-19 in advanced economies, BIS Bulletin, No. 21.

Cizel, J., J. Frost, A. Houben and P. Wierts (2019), Effective macroprudential policy: cross-sector substitution from price and quantity measures. *Journal of Money, Credit and Banking*, 51(5), 1209–1235.

De Haan, Jakob, Aerdt Houben and Remco van der Molen (2012), Governance of macroprudential policy. *Zeitschrift für Öffentliches Recht* 67(2), 283–302.

ESRB (2021), A Review of Macroprudential Policy in the EU in 2020, 1 July 2021.

ESRB (2020), A Review of Macroprudential Policy in the EU in 2019, 29 April 2020.

ESRB (2019), A Review of Macroprudential Policy in the EU in 2018, 30 April 2019

ESRB (2018), A Review of Macroprudential Policy in the EU in 2017, 25 April 2018.

European Systemic Risk Board (2011), Recommendation of the European Systemic Risk Board of 22 December 2011 on the macro-prudential mandate of national authorities, *Official Journal of the European Union*, ESRB/2011/3.

Financial Stability Board (2019), *Thematic Review on Bank Resolution Planning*, Basel.

Financial Stability Board (2021), *Lessons Learnt from the COVID-19 Pandemic from a Financial Stability Perspective*, Basel.

Galati, Gabriele and Richhild Moessner (2013), Macroprudential policy – a literature review. *Journal of Economic Surveys*, 27(5), 846–878.

Goodhart, Charles (2000), The Organisational Structure of Banking Supervision, FSI Occasional Papers, No. 1, Bank for International Settlements.

Houben, Aerdt and Jan Kakes (2013), Financial imbalances and macroprudential policy in a currency union, *DNB Occasional Studies* 11(5).

Kremers, Jeroen and Dirk Schoenmaker (2010), Twin Peaks: Experiences in the Netherlands, LSE Financial Markets Group Paper Series, Special Paper No. 196.

Kremers, Jeroen, Dirk Schoenmaker and Peter Wierts (2003), Cross-sector supervision: which model? In R. Herring and R. Litan (eds), *Brookings-Wharton Papers on Financial Services*, Brookings Institution, Washington DC.

Llewellyn, David (2006), Institutional structure of financial regulation and supervision: the basic issues. In A Fleming, D Llewellyn and J Carmichael (eds), *Aligning Financial Supervision Structures with Country Needs*, World Bank, Washington DC.

Osborne, George (2010), Speech by the Chancellor of the Exchequer at the Lord Mayor's dinner for bankers and merchants of the City of London, Mansion House.

8. Monetary and macroprudential policies: a troubled marriage

Phurichai Rungcharoenkitkul[1]

1. INTRODUCTION

The last decade has brought financial stability into focus following a two-decade long belief in a Great Moderation. The Great Financial Crisis (GFC) in 2008 decisively pivoted attention towards the importance of financial stability as a pillar of macroeconomic stability and brought a renewed sense of urgency to the debate. The question was no longer *whether* central banks should play an active role in preserving financial stability, but *how* the task may be accomplished and with what policy tools. What quickly emerged as a new consensus, at least among major central banks, was a separation principle: two tools for two purposes. Macroprudential policy (MaPP) was embraced and tasked with ensuring financial stability, generally defined as conditions in the credit and financial markets that are conducive to sustainable macroeconomic outcomes in the medium term. Monetary policy, meanwhile, would maintain its primary focus on price stability. It is a marriage of two tools, whose key feature is ironically a separation.

Time is now ripe to reflect and ask how well the separation framework has worked. Has MaPP succeeded in preserving financial stability as promised? What have been the outcomes of dedicating monetary policy solely/largely to the price stability objective? What have we learned about the virtues or pitfalls of 'lean-against-the-wind' monetary policies? This chapter looks back at the experience over the last decade to provide a critical assessment and tentative answers to these questions.

2. A DECADE OF SEPARATION: HAS IT DELIVERED?

The post-GFC paradigm shift towards MaPP is unmistakable. Prior to 2008, it was predominantly the emerging market economies (EMEs) that made use of MaPP, while the advanced economies (AEs) stayed on the sidelines (Figure

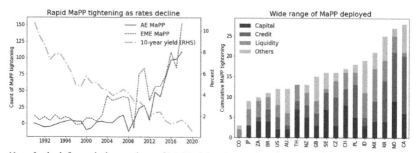

Note: In the left panel, the numbers of MaPP tightening are based on all available countries, while the *ten*-year yield is the cross-country median of 19 advanced economies from Borio et al. (2017). The right panel shows the cumulative numbers of MaPP tightening by types and countries, between 2009 and 2018.
Source: iMaPP database (Alam et al., 2019); Borio et al. (2017).

Figure 8.1   The rise of macroprudential policy

8.1, left panel). After the crisis, MaPP uses were widespread in both AEs and EMEs, as the tool quickly became part of global best practice. Policy adjustments have overwhelmingly been on the tightening side. In cumulative terms, MaPP was tightened by more than 1,200 times across 161 countries between 2009 and 2018. In Canada, Norway and Korea, where financial overheating caused greater concerns, MaPP tightenings totalled more than four times those of an average country (right panel). Globally, measures were broad in scope and objectives: countries have sought to strengthen financial resilience via capital and liquidity requirements, as well as to curb financial booms through limits on leverage and credit extension.

Active deployment of MaPP provides fertile ground for research on its effectiveness. Studies have generally found MaPP to exert a statistically significant dampening effect on financial imbalances. In a systematic summary of this literature, Araujo et al. (2020) conducted a meta-analysis of 58 empirical studies and find that each MaPP tightening reduces credit by about 0.04–0.12 standard deviations. Liquidity measures, such as liquidity coverage ratios or reserve requirements, have the strongest effect on credit. At the same time, housing-targeted MaPP such as limits to loan-to-value (LTV) or debt-service-to-income (DSTI) ratios have only insignificant effects on house prices.[2]

The effectiveness of MaPP *at the margin* is encouraging but does not imply that MaPP can single-handedly achieve financial stability. One reason is efficiency – to have traction on financial boom on its own, MaPP tightening may need to be so substantial that the macroeconomic costs become prohibitive.[3] This trade-off blurs the distinction between MaPP and monetary policy.[4] To compound the challenge, MaPP has had to operate in the context of extraordinary monetary policy accommodation and a sharp decline in the nominal interest rates to a historic low (Figure 8.1, left panel). All these provide a tough test for MaPP.

With the two policy tools pulling sharply in opposite directions, one must ask if the separation approach, on net, has delivered in terms of financial stability. The absence of a major systemic event so far may be one metric of success. Standard vulnerability indicators also suggest the approach has worked in containing financial imbalances, up to a point. The credit gap measure has moderated and remained stable since the crisis up until the pandemic hit (Figure 8.2, left panel), thanks to MaPP as well as post-crisis regulatory reforms. But risk levels are far from uniform, and many countries experience large sector-specific credit booms. In Norway, Korea and Thailand, high household debts remain key areas of concerns. In the United States and Europe, risks have migrated outside of the banking system, e.g. to the leveraged loans segment. The overall dashboard is flashing amber, if not red.

Asset prices provide another gauge of post-GFC financial risk taking, and point to vulnerabilities. While real house prices have been expanding at a steady pace of about 2.7% after recovering from the GFC trough, they rose much more rapidly in some countries (Figure 8.2, right panel). The pandemic has spurred further increases in housing demand globally: in New Zealand and Canada, real house prices grew by 14.4% and 7.5% respectively at the end of 2020. These rapid price increases took place despite an active use of MaPP targeted at the housing market. Abrupt price reversals could have severe macro-financial implications, especially if they expose other vulnerabilities.[5]

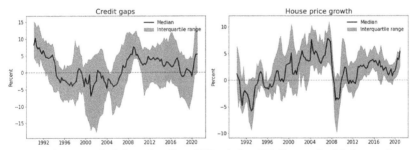

Note: Credit gaps are deviations of credit-to-GDP ratio from HP-filter trend, while house price growth is year-on-year percentage changes in real residential house prices. Sample includes United States, the euro area, the United Kingdom, Japan, Canada, Norway, Sweden, Switzerland, Australia, New Zealand, Czech Republic, Poland, South Africa, Indonesia, Korea, Thailand, Brazil, Colombia, Chile and Mexico.
Source: BIS; author's calculations.

Figure 8.2   *Financial cycles dormant but risks are emerging*

Active financial risk-taking and search-for-yield behaviour are also evident in the equity market valuations, which have become increasingly stretched over the last decade, even as output slumped during the pandemic. The cyclically adjusted price-earning ratio for S&P 500 is 39 times as of September 2021, more than double the historical average of 17. Total market capitalisation is almost twice the size of GDP, surpassing the previous dotcom-high of 1.4. In the debt market, low-rated corporate bond spreads are at the lower end of their historical distributions. Buoyant IPO activities in special purpose acquisition companies (SPACs) and active corporate bond issuance corroborate the notion that risk appetite is elevated (see BIS, 2021).

The general picture points to a significant residual effect of low interest rates on financial risk-taking which MaPP could not mop up. Simply having a dedicated tool for financial stability does not guarantee its attainment. It is critical to internalise the tight connections between the two policy objectives and the two instruments. Indeed, financial stability broadly defined is nothing but macroeconomic stability at a longer horizon. How the tools transmit to objectives is also similar and interdependent. Monetary policy stimulates output in part through risk-taking and credit channels, which can have side effects on financial stability. MaPP keeps the financial system safe by restraining risk-taking and leverage, which can entail output costs. Combining the tools does not eliminate the underlying policy trade-off, which transcends the use of tools and is intertemporal in nature.

3.   TIME FOR A RENEWED VOW?

In an influential review, Smets (2014) argued: '… if macroprudential tools are ineffective in managing the financial cycle, it may be more appropriate for monetary policy instruments to also pursue a financial stability objective'.[6] Evidence since then confirms that MaPP has struggled on its own in dampening the financial cycle. A reorientation of the policy framework has not been forthcoming, however – as noted, monetary policy has in general been pushing in the accommodative direction. There may be several reasons for this. First, using monetary policy to promote financial stability remains a contested issue. Second, concerns about persistently low inflation and target credibility have dominated the attention of monetary policy. Finally, institutional constraints may prohibit monetary policy from taking a broader responsibility. We examine each in turn.

3.1   The Economics of Leaning Against the Wind

Whether monetary policy should play a role in leaning against the wind (LAW) of financial booms and busts is a timeless unsettled debate.[7] The traditional view is that assigning monetary policy with too many goals could compromise a core objective of price stability, justifying a strict separation approach. Another view is that, because it is difficult to assess financial stability risk with precision, monetary policy should weigh in only when the danger is imminent – a separation approach with an escape clause.[8] Yet another view is that maintaining financial stability requires a systematic involvement of monetary policy, possible only under an integrated framework that deploy all policy tools flexibly to achieve the 'optimal' outcome for the society.

The fuzziness of what it means to lean against the wind partly explains these disagreements. One definition is a temporary and ad hoc increase of the interest rate intended to defuse financial booms, a strategy which we shall refer to as a *discretionary* LAW *(DLAW)*. One common criticism of DLAW policies, which is sometimes confused to be a critique of LAW policies in general, is that they can worsen or precipitate a financial crisis instead of preventing it – e.g. Svensson (2017) and Schularick et al. (2021). The reason for this is that a discretionary tightening comes too late almost by construction. By the time imbalances are large and conspicuous enough to warrant exceptional discretionary intervention, a disruptive bust is all but certain.

Many proponents of LAW instead emphasise the need to take a *systematic* rule-based approach and always internalise the impact of monetary policy on financial stability. By 'keeping the financial side of the economy on an even keel (Borio, 2016)', this *SLAW* strategy is likely to be more effective than DLAW in pre-empting financial booms. When credible, SLAW need not require much higher interest rate to be effective. By stating its intention to limit financial imbalances, SLAW could weaken speculative incentives ex ante, lessening the likelihood of a boom and the need for a higher interest rate ex post (see Filardo et al. (2022) for evidence of this 'reaction function' channel, and Boissay et al. (2021) for theoretical results). SLAW can in principle yield greater benefits at lower costs than DLAW.

Deeper controversies about LAW owe to different models of the economy and assumptions about how monetary policy interacts with financial imbalances. To shed light on sources of disagreements, it may be helpful to conjecture a set of sufficient conditions for (S)LAW to be desirable.[9]

1. A tighter monetary policy can restrain financial booms.
2. There are recurrent financial boom-bust cycles. By this we mean (1) financial imbalances tend to increase over time when interest rates are too low, and (2) financial busts are endogenous outcomes of preceding booms.
3. A financial bust has macroeconomic costs, which policies cannot fully offset ex post. Cleaning up is not perfect.

The first condition postulates that a tighter monetary policy can (with some lag) reduce financial imbalances, hence forestall or mitigate financial booms. The second condition establishes a causal link between the boom and the subsequent costly bust. The last condition puts a lower bound on this cost, thus assigning a positive value to pre-emptive action during the boom.

When the models satisfy the sufficient conditions, the analyses invariably lend support to SLAW. Recent examples include Filardo and Rungcharoenkitkul (2016), Juselius et al. (2017), Rungcharoenkitkul et al. (2019), Boissay et al. (2021) and Van der Ghote (2021) (Table 8.1). These models differ in structures and frictions that generate the financial boom-bust cycle. But SLAW has a stabilising effect for the same reason – it mitigates the boom and hence lowers the cost associated with the bust.

Some models do not strictly meet these sufficient conditions, but still share sufficiently similar elements for LAW to remain desirable. In Adrian et al. (2020), there is no endogenous financial boom-bust as such, but their 'price of risk' process can behave in a cycle-like fashion as it follows an AR(2) process. In Ajello et al. (2019) and Gourio et al. (2018), there is no internal mechanism generating boom-bust cycles, and the policy problem is whether it is worth sacrificing some output today to lower the crisis probability and avoid the associated costs tomorrow. The answer is yes in general, though the optimal degree of leaning tends to be small as the benefits of pre-emptively mitigating the boom are not being captured.

Other models that find LAW to be counterproductive altogether violate the sufficient conditions more fundamentally. The influential cost-benefit framework of Svensson (2017) implies that the policymaker can 'front run' an impending crisis by leaning *with* the wind and running the economy hot. This strategy in principle can fully offset the impact of a crisis on output, violating the third sufficient condition. If one can completely nullify the crisis impact, there is no value in preventive measures.[10] In Cairo and Sim (2020), a monetary tightening boosts credit as agents borrow more to smooth consumption while output contracts. Leaning worsens financial imbalances as a result, violating the first condition. In a similar vein, DLAW in Gelain et al. (2018) increases debt-to-GDP because long-term debt responds less to interest rate increases than GDP does. For this reason, SLAW in their model exacerbates rather than mitigates financial instability.

Further research could help bridge these differences and forge greater consensus. One empirical agenda is to investigate if and when the sufficient conditions for LAW are met. Theoretical works could benefit from further exploring the intertemporal dimension of the policy problem. Financial stability is not an independent goal but a means to an end, and the problem is one of macroeconomic stabilisation over a long timeframe. The LAW debate is in

Table 8.1   *Recent research on leaning against the wind and assumptions*

Papers	Model assumptions			Types of LAW	Presence of MaPP	LAW is desirable
	MP mitigates financial boom	Endogenous financial boom-busts	Cleaning after bust is imperfect			
Filardo and Rungcharoenkitkul (2016)	Yes	Yes	Yes	SLAW	No	Yes
Juselius et al. (2017)	Yes	Yes	Yes	SLAW	No	Yes
Rungcharoenkitkul et al. (2019)	Yes	Yes	Yes	SLAW	No	Yes
Van der Ghote (2021)	Yes	Yes	Yes	SLAW	Yes	Yes
Boissay et al. (2021)	Yes	Yes	Yes	DLAW and SLAW	No	Only SLAW
Adrian et al. (2020)	Yes	Partial	Yes	SLAW	No	Yes
Ajello et al. (2019)	Yes	Partial (crisis module)	Yes	DLAW	No	Yes
Gourio et al. (2018)	Yes	Partial (crisis module)	Yes	SLAW	No	Yes
Svensson (2017)	Yes	Partial (crisis module)	No	DLAW	No	No
Cairo and Sim (2020)	No	Partial	Yes (under ZLB)	DLAW and SLAW	No	Neither
Gelain et al. (2018)	No	No	N / A	DLAW & SLAW	No	Neither

Source: Author's summary.

essence a question of whether there is a divine coincidence between short- and long-term macroeconomic stability.

3.2   Inflation Credibility Under Threat?

A key concern of practising LAW is that it may undermine the credibility of the inflation targeting regime and risk de-anchoring inflation expectations. The severity of this risk is ultimately an empirical issue, a challenging task given the small treatment group of countries that have pursued SLAW for an extended period. An easier test may be, how much does average monetary policy stance matter for average inflation? In an illustrative exercise shown in Figure 8.3, countries that have set higher interest rates relative to the Taylor

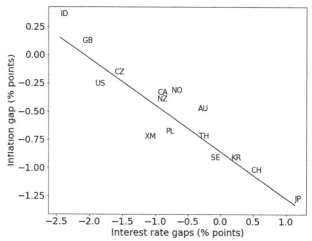

Note: 'Inflation gaps' are post-GFC average inflation as deviations from central bank targets while 'Interest rate gaps' are deviations of nominal interest rates from the Taylor rule. For all countries, the Taylor rule is: $i(t) = i^*(t) + 1.5(\pi(t) - \pi^*(t)) + (y(t) - y^*(t))$, where the natural interest rate $i^*(t)$ is proxied by the 5-year, 5-year forward rate from the government bond yield curve, and the potential output $y^*(t)$ is computed using the HP-filter. Alternative policy rules and filtering methods produce similar results.
Source: Author's calculations.

Figure 8.3   Average monetary policy stances and inflation outcomes

rule benchmarks after the GFC indeed tend to experience lower inflation. But the trade-off is not steep: a full percentage point higher nominal interest rate is associated with about 40 basis points lower inflation, well within the tolerance zone of many central banks. And, as argued above, SLAW need not imply much higher interest rates to be effective. Norway, whose policy framework includes financial imbalances as an explicit consideration, maintains an average monetary policy stance close to the group median with superior inflation outcomes compared to most.

In principle, downside risks to inflation could rise more distinctly if the effective lower bound (ELB) were to bind more frequently for structural reasons related to a falling natural interest rate (e.g. Summers, 2020). In the canonical macroeconomic model, this would narrow the room for monetary policy to manoeuvre and, in the absence of countermeasures, lead to unanchored inflation expectations. The fact that post-GFC inflation has generally undershot its target fuels this concern (see Figure 8.3). Partly to allay it, the Federal Reserve and the European Central Bank have recently taken steps to revise their policy frameworks and strengthen commitment to price stability.

Should concerns about inflation target credibility preclude monetary policy from financial stability duties? The answer depends in part on how strictly realised inflation must adhere to a numerical target to successfully anchor expectations. The pervasive inattention on the part of households and firms in a low inflation environment (Coibion et al., 2020) implies less risk of de-anchoring than rational-expectations models suggest. Recent survey evidence in fact highlights the upside de-anchoring risks as more relevant (Galati et al., 2021; Coleman and Nautz, 2021), pointing to other factors at work such as trust (Christelis et al., 2020). On the flip side, central banks' ability to fine-tune inflation outcomes may be limited to begin with. Globalisation and trade competition have exerted downward pressures on prices globally (Forbes, 2019), while the growing prominence of relative prices has weakened the link between inflation and aggregate demand (Borio et al., 2021). In the context of low and stable inflation, nudging inflation up by a relatively small margin may be both difficult and unnecessary.

Another question is whether a secular decline in the natural interest rate constitutes a persistent deflationary force that leaves no room for LAW. Goodhart and Pradhan (2020) argue that some of the structural factors, e.g. demographics, could soon reverse and ease the pressure on the natural rate. Financial busts themselves, which LAW seeks to prevent, are historically a powerful cause of deflation. A recent strand of literature has indeed raised the possibility that the trend decline in real interest rates may be related to financial factors endogenous to monetary policy.[11] These mechanisms suggest that aggressive monetary policy accommodation designed to avert deflation could potentially contribute to it.[12]

3.3   Institutional Constraints

Legal remit and political economy factors play a role in defining the boundary of policy objectives and instruments. Society's demand for accountability and transparency may favour a narrow and easily verifiable goal, e.g. a strict inflation targeting regime.[13] Sticking to a narrow objective could help shield the central bank from outside challenges, preserving its independence. At the same time, public support for a broad mandate would allow the central bank to flexibly manage multiple goals and internalise its interdependence, potentially improving macroeconomic outcomes. A certain degree of public trust in the central bank may be necessary in this case.

Institutional constraints present additional challenges to the integration of financial stability into monetary policy strategy. Pursuing financial stability as a secondary objective may be one compromise, a way to maintain a narrow price stability focus without ignoring financial stability. Whether this would be adequate to stabilise the financial cycle is a key issue (as discussed, a last-resort DLAW measure may be too late). Another option is to proactively build public support for a broader mandate and toolset to robustly tackle financial stability risks. This approach requires more open engagements with the public and stakeholders, possibly exposing central bank policies to greater public scrutiny. But if successful in preventing financial crises, the approach could strengthen central bank credibility and independence in the long run.[14]

4.   CONCLUSION

This chapter reviews the experience over the last decade of applying the separation approach of one tool for one purpose. I argue that this arrangement overburdens macroprudential policy and leaves a gap in effectively safeguarding financial stability. And despite low inflation concerns[15] and institutional limitations, there appear to be valid economic grounds for monetary policy to play a greater role in this pursuit. Indeed, the consensus may be shifting. In their recent reviews of monetary policy strategy, both the Federal Reserve and the European Central Bank now explicitly acknowledge financial stability as a relevant consideration. Steps in this direction would help fortify macroeconomic stability by making economic expansion more durable and sustainable.

Monetary policy framework will need to continue evolving and adapting to new challenges. Financial instability is an old enemy but can take new unfamiliar forms as the macro-financial landscape changes. The rapidly rising popularity of digital speculative assets is one example of modern-day financial exuberance. But technology may also bring new solutions, by offering better ways of monitoring macro-financial developments and conducting monetary policy. It is up to central banks to keep pace with these new risks and opportunities. And the monetary policy framework needs to be flexible enough to accommodate them.

NOTES

1.   I thank Frederic Boissay, Claudio Borio, Stijn Claessens, Fiorella De Fiore, Deniz Igan, Aaron Mehrotra, Richhild Moessner and Benoît Mojon for helpful comments. The views expressed are my own and do not reflect those of the Bank for International Settlements nor my colleagues.
2.   See also Claessens (2015) and Galati and Moessner (2018) for broad literature reviews on MaPP, and Duca et al. (2021) for measures specific to the housing market.
3.   Assuming each MaPP tightening reduces credit by 0.12 standard deviations (the upper bound estimate of Araujo et al., 2020), it would take as many as 17 MaPP tightenings to offset a pre-GFC-type credit boom (about 2 standard deviations above trend). Such adjustments would likely involve substantial macroeconomic costs. Richter et al. (2019) find that a 10-percentage-point decrease in LTV cap reduces output by 1.1%, while Kim and Mehrotra (2018) find that MaPP and

monetary policy, expressed in standardised shocks, induce a similar impact on credit and output.

4. Like monetary policy, MaPP could have unintended effects on credit allocation, e.g. Acharya et al. (2020) find that MaPP reallocates mortgage credit from low to high-income households, and away from urban areas. Political economy implications of MaPP are additional costs that could limit its uses.

5. The recent debt crisis of Evergrande in China illustrates how the problems of one systemic property developer could have serious global repercussions.

6. See also IMF (2013a, 2013b).

7. Incidentally, easing MaPP to allay a recession is hardly controversial, despite violating the separation principle no less than LAW monetary policies. The debate is whether the duties should also be shared more symmetrically during the prevention.

8. Smets (2014) is a notable advocate of this approach.

9. These conditions are based on Filardo and Rungcharoenkitkul (2016). An implicit assumption here is that MaPP, if available, does not fully eliminate financial stability risks.

10. Svensson (2017) also analyses the benefits of DLAW in terms of reducing the crisis probability, and does not capture the cumulative effects of SLAW on financial booms.

11. In Rungcharoenkitkul et al. (2019), a short-term-focused monetary policy rule exacerbates the financial boom-bust cycle, requiring interest rates to stay lower for longer to deal with more frequent crises. In Mian et al. (2020) and Beaudry and Meh (2021), aggressive monetary accommodation can entrench the low-rate equilibrium due to a backward-bending saving function in the presence of bequest motives. In Rungcharoenkitkul and Winkler (2021), excessive monetary accommodation can cause an endogenous decline in the natural interest rate by influencing the expectations of boundedly-rational agents. See Borio (2021) and Rungcharoenkitkul (2019) for a discussion of this literature.

12. The decline in the natural interest rate has recently been used to justify elevated asset prices and financial risk taking as sustainable. This conclusion loses force if the natural interest rate is in fact endogenous to monetary policy.

13. This demand tends to be higher in economies plagued by macroeconomic instability. But even with stable macroeconomic track records, there may still be a high premium on a transparent and simple policy reaction function, e.g. due to the importance of monetary policy for financial markets.

14. See Borio (2019) for a discussion on central bank independence and its determinants.

15. These concerns have recently dissipated as supply constraints in the wake of the COVID-19 pandemic pivoted attention to the opposite risks of higher inflation.

REFERENCES

Acharya, V., K. Bergant, M. Crosignani, T. Eisert and F. McCann (2020): 'The anatomy of the transmission of macroprudential policies', NBER Working Paper 27292.

Adrian, T., F. Duarte, N. Liang and P. Zabczyk (2020): 'NKV: A New Keynesian model with vulnerability', *AEA Papers and Proceedings*, 110, 470–476.

Ajello, A., T. Laubach, D. Lopez-Salido and R. Nakata (2019): 'Financial stability and optimal interest rate policy', *International Journal of Central Banking*, 15(1), 279–326.

Alam, Z., A. Alter, J. Eiseman, G. Gelos, H. Kang, M. Narita, E. Nier and N. Wang (2019): 'Digging deeper – evidence on the effects of macroprudential policies from a new database', IMF Working Paper WP/19/66.

Araujo, J., M. Patnam, A. Popescu, F. Valencia and W. Yao (2020): 'Effects of macroprudential policy: Evidence from over 6000 estimates', IMF Working Paper WP/20/67.

Bank for International Settlements (BIS) (2021): *BIS Quarterly Review*, March, 1–16.

Beaudry, P. and C. Meh (2021): 'Monetary policy, trends in real interest rates and depressed demand', Staff Working Paper 2021-27, Bank of Canada.

Boissay, F., F. Collard, J. Gali and C. Manea (2021): 'Monetary policy and endogenous financial crises', mimeo.

Borio, C. (2016): 'Towards a financial stability-oriented monetary policy framework?', Speech at the 'Central banking in times of change' conference on the occasion of the 200th anniversary of the Central Bank of the Republic of Austria.

Borio, C. (2019): 'Central banking in challenging times', SUERF Annual Lecture, SUERF/BAFFI CAREFIN Centre Conference on 'Populism, economic policies and central banking', Milan.

Borio, C. (2021): 'Back to the future: Intellectual challenges for monetary policy', David Finch Lecture, University of Melbourne.

Borio, C., P. Disyatat, M. Juselius and P. Rungcharoenkitkul (2017): 'Why so low for so long? A long-term view of real interest rates', BIS Working Papers No. 685.

Borio, C., P. Disyatat, D. Xia and E. Zakrajšek (2021): 'Monetary policy, relative prices and inflation control: Flexibility born out of success', *BIS Quarterly Review*, September.

Cairo, I. and J. Sim (2020): 'Monetary policy and financial stability', Finance and Economics Discussion Series 2020-101, Washington: Board of Governors of the Federal Reserve System.

Christelis, D., D. Georgarakos, T. Jappelli and M. Van Rooij (2020): 'Trust in the central bank and inflation expectations', *International Journal of Central Banking*, 16(6), 1–37.

Claessens, S. (2015): 'An overview of macroprudential policy tools', *Annual Review of Financial Economics*, 7, 397–422.

Coibion, O., Y. Gorodnichenko, S. Kumar and M. Pedemonte (2020): 'Inflation expectations as a policy tool?', *Journal of International Economics* 124, 103297.

Coleman, W. and D. Nautz (2021): 'Inflation expectations, inflation target credibility and the Covid-19 pandemic: New evidence from Germany', Discussion Paper No. 2021/12, Freie University, Berlin.

Duca, J., J. Muellbauer and A. Murphy (2021): 'What drives house price cycles? International experience and policy issues', *Journal of Economic Literature*, 59(3), 773–864.

Filardo, F. and P. Rungcharoenkitkul (2016): 'A quantitative case for leaning against the wind', BIS Working Papers No. 594.

Filardo, F., P. Hubert and P. Rungcharoenkitkul (2022): 'Monetary policy reaction function and the financial cycle', *Journal of Banking and Finance*, 142, 106536.

Forbes, K. (2019): 'Has globalisation changed the inflation process?', BIS Working Papers No. 791.

Galati, G. and R. Moessner (2018): 'What do we know about the effects of macroprudential policy?', *Economica*, 85(340), 735–770.

Galati, G., R. Moessner and M. van Rooij (2021): 'The anchoring of long-term inflation
expectations of consumers: Insights from a new survey', BIS Working Papers No.
936.

Gelain, P., K. Lansing and G. Natvik (2018): 'Leaning against the credit cycle', *Journal
of the European Economic Association*, 16(5), 1350–1393.

Goodhart, C. And M. Pradhan (2020): *The great demographic reversal: Ageing societies, waning inequality and an inflation revival*, Palgrave Macmillan, London.

Gourio, F., A. Kashyap and J. Sim (2018): 'The trade-offs in leaning against the wind',
IMF Economic Review, 66, 70–115.

International Monetary Fund (IMF) (2013a): 'The interaction of monetary and macroprudential policies', Washington.

International Monetary Fund (IMF) (2013b): 'The interaction of monetary and macroprudential policies—background paper', Washington.

Juselius, M., C. Borio, P. Disyatat and M. Drehmann (2017): 'Monetary policy, the
financial cycle, and ultra-low interest rates', *International Journal of Central
Banking*, 13(3), 55–89.

Kim, S. and A. Mehrotra (2018): 'Effects of monetary and macroprudential policies –
Evidence from four inflation targeting economies', *Journal of Money, Credit and
Banking*, 50(5), 967–992.

Mian, A., L. Straub and A. Sufi (2020): 'Indebted demand', NBER Working Paper
26941.

Richter, B., M. Schularick and I. Shim (2019): 'The costs of macroprudential policy',
Journal of International Economics, 118, 263–282.

Rungcharoenkitkul, P. (2019): 'An integrated macroprudential framework in the
post-pandemic world', Proceedings of 22nd OeNB Workshop 'How do monetary,
micro- and macroprudential policies interact?', Vienna.

Rungcharoenkitkul, P. and F. Winkler (2021): 'Natural interest rate through the hall of
mirrors', mimeo.

Rungcharoenkitkul, P., C. Borio and P. Disyatat (2019): 'Monetary policy hysteresis
and the financial cycle', BIS Working Paper No. 817.

Schularick, M., L. Ter Steege and F. Ward (2021): 'Leaning against the wind and crisis
risk', *American Economic Review: Insights*, 3(2), 199–214.

Smets, F. (2014): 'Financial stability and monetary policy: How closely interlinked?',
International Journal of Central Banking, 10(2), 263–300.

Summers, L. (2020): 'Accepting the reality of secular stagnation', *Finance and
Development*, 57(1), 17–19.

Svensson, L. (2017): 'Cost-benefit analysis of leaning against the wind', *Journal of
Monetary Economics*, 90, 193–213.

Van der Ghote, A. (2021): 'Interactions and coordination between monetary and macroprudential policies', *American Economic Journal: Macroeconomics*, 13(1), 1–34.

9. The architecture of macroprudential policy: delegation and coordination

Charles Bean

1. INTRODUCTION

The great financial crisis of 2007–8 not only resulted in a recasting and tightening of the regulation of financial intermediaries, but also the introduction of a new arrow into the policy makers' armoury in the shape of macroprudential policies. The purpose of such policies is to moderate building financial stability risks during normal economic times so as to reduce their likelihood and impact in the event of crystallization. It therefore constitutes a preventative counterpart to central banks' long-standing role as the lender of last resort during a financial crisis.

Many of the instruments of macroprudential policy are not new. Lender-focused instruments such as bank capital requirements have long been part of the prudential framework but varying them with a view to managing systemic financial risk is novel. By the same token, borrower-focused instruments such as restrictions on the terms of household borrowing have been deployed historically as a tool to control aggregate demand, though in recent years they have been displaced by variations in interest rates. But exploiting their potential to moderate systemic financial risks represents a new direction.

Alongside the introduction of this new armoury is the issue of how macroprudential policies should be decided, and by whom. Present arrangements differ across jurisdictions, often building on existing institutional arrangements, though in most cases the central bank is assigned a central role. In this chapter, I therefore consider three questions:

- Should macroprudential policies be delegated and if so to whom?
- Do macroprudential policies need to be coordinated with monetary policy?
- What light does the COVID-19 pandemic shed on present arrangements?

2.   SHOULD MACROPRUDENTIAL POLICIES BE DELEGATED?

I begin by reviewing the circumstances under which it makes sense for a principal – in this case the government – to delegate a function to an independent agent. Doing so also helps to shed light on some of the potential difficulties.

2.1   Principles for Delegation

Broadly speaking, there are three main considerations (for a fuller discussion of the issues, see Tucker, 2018). In the first place, there should be a good *reason* for someone other than the principal to take the decision. That could be because of its specialized nature or technical complexity – this is the case for banking supervision and the authorization of vaccines, for instance. Even then, the principal could retain ultimate decision-making responsibility, basing it on the advice provided by a suitably expert body or committee.

A more powerful argument for delegation applies when the principal cannot be trusted to take appropriate decisions, for instance because they may favour particular individuals or constituencies or because they place too much weight on short-term objectives relative to the long term. This is the classic argument for separating the impartial administration of the law by the judiciary from its formulation by the legislature and from the executive. It is also the basis for the standard argument for the delegation of monetary policy, where there is a temptation to exploit the short-run Phillips Curve in order to generate higher activity, even though in a rational expectations equilibrium it just results in higher inflation and no gain in output.

Second, if the task is delegated, democratic legitimacy requires that the agent is held *accountable* for delivery of its mandated objective. It thus requires both a well-defined goal against which performance can be assessed and appropriate mechanisms for public accountability, such as appearances before the appropriate representatives of parliament.

Third, the execution of the task ideally should have only *limited impact* on the principal's other objectives or else be open to mitigating actions by the principal. If that is not the case, then it may be necessary either to re-cast the agent's mandate to take such considerations into account or for the principal to have some other way of ensuring that these other objectives carry appropriate weight in the agent's decisions.

An example of the problems that can arise is again provided by recent monetary policies. Large-scale asset purchases by central banks in the aftermath of the financial crisis and again during the COVID-19 pandemic have led to criticism that by raising asset prices they are benefiting older and wealthier individuals at the expense of the young (e.g. Coibion et al., 2017), as well as altering the fiscal risks that governments are exposed to (Office for Budget Responsibility, 2021). Questions of distribution are inherently political in nature and ideally should not be left in the lap of technocrats.

2.2   Should Macroprudential Policies be Delegated?

In light of these principles, should macroprudential policies be delegated? And if they are, where might tensions arise? First, it is worth noting the case for delegating macroprudential policy is weaker – or at least more complex – than for monetary policy. With respect to the first of the three criteria, there is certainly a good reason for delegating macroprudential policy to an independent agent. There are high technical demands placed on decision makers. Moreover, during the upswing of a financial cycle, risks tend to appear low and financial institutions and investors are prone to claim that 'this time is different'. There is little incentive for a government to take the punch bowl away just as the party is getting lively, especially if an election is in the offing. Delegation to an agency hard-wired to take a long view of the risks to financial stability therefore makes sense. So far, this is like the argument for delegating the operational responsibility for monetary policy.

Meeting the other criteria for effective and legitimate delegation is trickier. For monetary policy, we have a widely accepted and regularly and objectively measured yardstick in the form of inflation. To be sure, the appropriate inflation target and how quickly to meet it are open to debate. But nevertheless, we know broadly what the objective of monetary policy should be; namely, to stabilize inflation (or perhaps the price level). In contrast, the objective of macroprudential policy is to limit the build-up of systemic financial risks but we have no objective and regularly observed indicator of systemic risks analogous to the monetary policy objective. Adrian, Boyarchenko and Giannone (2019) have adopted the approach from finance of estimating the 'value at risk' on a portfolio and applied it at an aggregate level to derive an analogous measure of 'Gross Domestic Product (GDP) at risk'. The International Monetary Fund (2017) has also used this approach to quantifying and tracking countries' risk exposure. While useful, however, this approach relies on lots of potentially debatable underlying assumptions, rendering it less suitable for the purposes of justifying policy decisions and holding decision makers to account.

In practice, most macroprudential policy committees rely instead on tracking a dashboard of indicators, supplemented by additional indicators as appropriate, to inform and explain their decisions. Inevitably judgement plays an important role as to their significance and there is often likely to be disagreement on whether action is necessary. This disagreement is likely to become more pronounced during the upswing of a financial cycle. So effective monitoring and accountability of decision makers is bound to be more elusive than for monetary policy.

Finally, some macroprudential actions, by their very nature, are likely to impact on particular individuals and businesses. That may be less of an issue with lender-focused instruments, such as the countercyclical capital buffer and risk weights, which have a generalized impact on the supply of credit. Measures designed to increase the resilience of banks may have the effect of reducing the supply of credit but that will not be immediately obvious to the general public. In contrast, borrower-focused instruments, such as limits on loan-to-income or loan-to-value ratios, directly restrict the availability of credit to particular borrowers. Consequently, they may prove contentious unless there is clear public support for the delegation of such powers.

Balls, Howat and Stansbury (2016) suggest that a potential solution lies in introducing an additional layer of political oversight in order to bolster political legitimacy, while retaining operational independence. The open question is whether that also creates a re-entry route for the time-inconsistency problem.

2.3   Delegation in Practice

Figure 9.1 shows how responsibility for macroprudential policy-making varies across 47 selected jurisdictions. The diversity of arrangements is striking and to a large extent an historical accident, with each country usually building on existing institutional arrangements, rather than the outcome of deliberate institutional design. Delegation to a technocratic agency is the norm though, with the finance ministry (i.e. the executive branch of government) in the lead in only five instances, although finance ministries will often have a voice in other set-ups, particularly where there is a committee composed of representatives of several agencies.

Where the central bank is responsible for banking regulation and supervision, it is often in the lead for macroprudential policies, and indeed in 40 per cent of the jurisdictions the central bank is the agency with prime responsibility. And there are a handful of countries where another regulatory agency takes lead responsibility. But in 20 per cent of cases, policy-making is the responsibility of a committee or council, with representatives drawn from several bodies or agencies.

This is notably the case in both the United States (the Financial Stability Oversight Council, chaired by the Treasury and comprising the federal supervisory agencies and securities regulators) and the European Union (the European Systemic Risk Board, comprising the European Central Bank and constituent national central banks, the European authorities on banking, insurance and securities, the European Commission, and the Economic and Financial Committee). In both cases, the fragmentary structure of the regula-

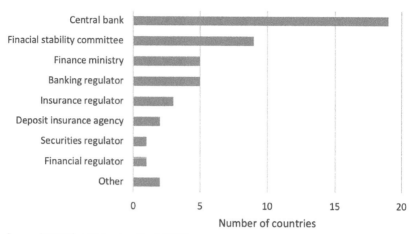

Source: International Monetary Fund (2011).

Figure 9.1   Macroprudential responsibility across 47 jurisdictions

tory landscape makes a committee approach almost unavoidable. However, the cost is that such arrangements tend to inhibit nimble and decisive policy action, especially if there is a focus on trying to act by consensus.

This structural bias towards delay can, though, be mitigated if there is one or more actors that can enforce system-wide action. For instance, the European Systemic Risk Board lacks direct executive powers and can only issue recommendations for action to the relevant regulatory or supervisory bodies, which will often be located at the national rather than supra-national level. However, the European Central Bank, which under the Single Supervisory Mechanism has direct supervisory responsibility for only the larger European banks and relies on national agencies to supervise smaller banks, can impose higher bank capital requirements across the system if it judges that is necessary to contain the risks to financial stability.

3.   THE INTERACTION OF MACROPRUDENTIAL AND MONETARY POLICIES

Although the central bank is often the natural agency to carry the responsibility of macroprudential policy, especially if it is also the banking regulator, an additional argument that is sometimes heard is that it facilitates co-ordination with monetary policy. In this section I therefore explore the issue of the co-ordination of monetary and macroprudential policies in a little more depth.

3.1   Theory

To see how monetary and macroprudential policies interact, rather than develop a formal model with micro-foundations, I instead adopt a simple schematic approach (see Figure 9.2) which I believe captures the key features present in most such formal models; for a fuller description, see Bean (2014).

The twin objectives of policy are to meet a given inflation target and to keep financial stability risks below some specified level (as captured by the level of GDP at risk, for instance). For simplicity, I assume there are just two policy instruments: the nominal policy rate, R, and a minimum bank capital ratio, K. Importantly, each instrument affects the likelihood of meeting both objectives.

Starting with the market for goods and services, aggregate demand is assumed to be a decreasing function of the real interest rate and thus also of R. In addition, because a higher bank capital requirement reduces the volume of credit and increases its price (see below), aggregate demand is also assumed to be a decreasing function of K.[1] The inflation target can then be achieved by the set of pairs of R and K along the downward sloping schedule PS (for Price Stability) in the left-hand panel of Figure 9.2. An increase in demand resulting from, say, an increase in the propensity to invest, would shift this schedule out to the right.

Turn now to the credit market. The demand for credit decreases with the rate banks charge on their loans, while the supply of funds to banks increases with the rate offered on banks' debt (including deposits), which I assume moves with the policy rate R. In a competitive market, the spread between the rate charged on bank loans and the rate paid on bank debt then reflects

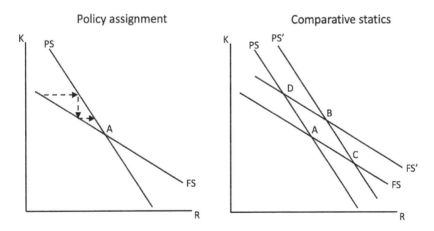

Figure 9.2   Monetary-macroprudential policy interaction

the likelihood of default not only by end borrowers but also by the bank (as well as all the other costs of intermediation). In credit booms, this spread is unsustainably compressed, while during credit crunches it widens sharply. Higher bank capital requirements, K, reduce the supply of credit and increase the spread between the loan rate and the rate on bank debt. It thus lowers the risks of future financial instability. Because a higher level of the policy rate R reduces the volume of funds supplied to banks, it too lowers the quantity of credit. A higher policy rate therefore also reduces the risks of future financial instability.

We can now construct a second downward-sloping relationship FS (for Financial Stability) that shows the minimum acceptable level of the policy rate for any given setting of the bank capital requirement; see the left-hand panel of Figure 9.2. A reduction in perceived risk leading to excessive exuberance on the part of investors or borrowers would shift this frontier to the right.

The respective slopes of the PS and FS schedules depend on the *relative* impact of the policy rate and the bank capital requirement on aggregate demand and on the quantity of credit. A well-chosen and well-designed macropruden-tial tool is one that has a relatively large effect on the quantity of credit and thus on financial stability risks but only a modest impact on aggregate demand and inflation. That would generate a relatively flat FS frontier. Moreover, since changes in policy rates also affect aggregate demand through routes other than the credit channel (such as the exchange rate), it seems reasonable to assume that the PS schedule is relatively steep. That is the configuration of relative slopes shown in the left-hand panel of Figure 9.2. Provided the two schedules do not coincide, both price and financial stability objectives can be achieved simultaneously – a simple application of the Tinbergen principle.

With this configuration, it is also natural to assign instruments according to their comparative advantage in meeting the respective objectives: the policy rate to the pursuit of price stability; and the bank capital requirement to the pursuit of financial stability. This is just an application of Mundell's (1962) principle that policies should be paired with the objectives on which they have the most relative influence.

Furthermore, with these slopes and this assignment, no active co-ordination in the setting of the instruments is strictly necessary: a process whereby each instrument is set independently, taking the other as given would converge on the point A (i.e. the Nash equilibrium), as shown by the dashed lines. Under these circumstances, the two policies can be delegated to two different agents or committees, in principle operating quite independently.

This analysis also suggests that if more than two instruments are available – say, large-scale asset purchases and limits on loan-to-income (or value) ratios are also available – those instruments with a large impact on aggregate demand relative to their impact on financial stability risks should be assigned to the agent/committee responsible for achieving price stability, while those with a relatively large impact on financial stability risks relative to aggregate demand should be assigned to the agent/committee responsible for managing the risks to financial stability.

Finally, the right-hand panel of Figure 9.2 illustrates some simple comparative static results. For instance, a bout of 'irrational exuberance' on the part of households, businesses and investors could be expected to be associated with an increase in the demand for goods and services from households and businesses, together with increased demand for credit and a reduction in the credit spread. In that case, both PS and FS would shift out, taking us from A to B with a tightening in both instruments.

On the other hand, a beneficial supply shock will shift the price stability schedule in (say, from PS' to PS) but may also encourage increased borrowing and a compression in spreads, leading the financial stability frontier to shift out. In this case we move from C to D, with monetary policy being loosened at the same time as macroprudential policy is tightened. Superficially this looks as if monetary and macroprudential policies are at odds with each other, though such a rebalancing of the policy mix is in fact entirely appropriate.

3.2   Practice

While macroprudential and monetary policies could, then, in theory be delegated to entirely separate agents or agencies, in practice there is much to be said for them to be at least closely connected, acting on a common basis of information and well informed about each other's thinking. At a minimum, it ensures co-ordination is smoother and there are less likely to be differences in view about appropriate policy setting. Certainly, in my time at the Bank of England, it was immensely helpful that the Monetary Policy Committee (MPC) and Financial Policy Committee (FPC) were in the same institution, with overlapping memberships, received briefing in common and had the scope to meet jointly if required. But distinct committees also allowed for some members that have specialist knowledge relevant to monetary policy but not financial policy (such as labour market experts) and vice versa (such as financial market practitioners). It also makes the lines of accountability clearer: the monetary policy committee has prime responsibility for maintaining macroeconomic (price) stability, while the macroprudential policy committee has prime responsibility for the prevention of harmful episodes of financial instability.

The case for architectural closeness – or even a single agent/committee being responsible for both tasks – becomes even stronger when there are the limits on the ability of one of the agents/committees to achieve its objective with its own instruments. In that case, we may want the other agent/committee to seek to achieve an appropriate balance across between achieving both monetary and financial stability.

Ahead of the financial crisis, and even more so subsequently, there was a lively debate as to whether monetary policy should be tightened during the upswing of a putative financial cycle so as to restrain a dangerous build-up of leverage, even though such a policy might involve slower output growth and inflation undershooting its target. Notable advocates of such 'leaning against the wind' (LATW) include White (2009) and Bank for International Settlements (2014, 2016), while a prominent counter view is provided by Svensson (2017).

In line with my earlier theoretical discussion, most policy makers accept that macroprudential instruments should be the first line of defence against such incipient risks to financial stability. But there may be times when those instruments are ineffective, for instance if they have insufficient traction or the financial stability risks are building outside of the regulatory perimeter. In that case, tightening monetary policy may be the only viable option; monetary policy may be a blunt tool for addressing financial stability risks, but it does have the virtue that it 'gets in all of the cracks' (Stein, 2013).

The policy-making architecture needs to accommodate this possibility. Clearly that is not a problem if a single committee has charge of both policy toolkits and is responsible for achieving both objectives. But what about when there are two committees with distinct toolkits and objectives?

The arrangements adopted in the UK offer, I believe, a viable approach. Since 2013, the remit for the MPC has contained an instruction along the following lines:

> Circumstances may also arise in which attempts to keep inflation at the inflation target could exacerbate the development of imbalances that the FPC may judge to represent a potential risk to financial stability. The FPC's macroprudential tools are the first line of defence against such risks, but in these circumstances the MPC may wish to allow inflation to deviate from the target temporarily, consistent with its need to have regard to the policy actions of the FPC. (Remit for the MPC, March 2021)

This allows the MPC to undertake an LATW-type response when the FPC believes its own instruments are not up to the task. Importantly, this rubric does not *force* the MPC to respond to these concerns; it is only permissive. For instance, it may well be the case that the MPC (potentially in conjunction with the FPC) takes the view that monetary policy tightening would also prove ineffective or that the cost-benefit calculus does not warrant taking such action (Svensson, 2017).

It is worth noting that with two committees, the set-up should really be symmetric. Policy rates are now at or close to their effective lower bound, while the very flat yield curve potentially renders quantitative easing through large-scale bond purchases of limited effectiveness in boosting aggregate demand. In such circumstances, fiscal policy really ought to be the first line of defence in sustaining demand. But if for some reason that is unavailable, there is at least an argument that some loosening of macroprudential policy in order to boost aggregate demand by expanding the supply of credit is warranted. While LATW has received a lot of recent attention, few seem to have appreciated that there is a parallel argument that there may be times when macroprudential policy should be directed to sustaining aggregate demand even at the cost of increasing the risk of future financial instability. The corresponding remit for the FPC also enjoins it to have regard for the actions of the MPC, so allowing for this possibility.

4.   LESSONS FROM THE PANDEMIC

To close, I shall briefly consider what the COVID-19 pandemic tells us about the effectiveness of the macroprudential architecture. Of course, the heavy lifting in response to the pandemic came through the health response and various fiscal measures to support households and businesses while activity was constrained. But the early stages of the pandemic during the spring of 2020 were also marked by substantial turbulence in financial markets. That necessitated significant intervention by central banks both as a lender of last resort and as a market maker of last resort, as liquidity disappeared in many market segments, including the market for US Treasuries, normally seen as a go-to asset during times of stress. Subsequently, central banks acted along-side fiscal authorities to keep the supply of credit flowing.

Macroprudential policies were simultaneously loosened in many jurisdictions. Edge and Liaing (2021) record one or more such interventions in 41 out of 56 jurisdictions, most notably including reducing bank capital requirements but also introducing forms of non-capital relief and loan forbearance programmes. But it is an open question whether the authorities could have done more before the event to moderate the risks.

That this period of market stress did not result in major institutional failures in part reflected the fact that banks were generally better capitalized following the tightening in regulation after the global financial crisis. But it surely also reflected the shock being a truly exogenous tail event, as well as the extensive fiscal support, which effectively transferred some of the prospective loan losses onto the public sector balance sheet.

What the episode did highlight, however, is that episodes of financial instability are as likely to arise from market illiquidity and affect players outside the banking sector, as they are to be located within the core of the banking system. Macroprudential authorities were already aware of the incentives for activities to migrate outside the regulatory perimeter, and rapid advances in the application of information technology to finance is also generating new sources of instability. But the market stress of spring 2000 reinforced the importance of keeping such new threats under surveillance and, if necessary, acting to contain them.

From an architectural point of view, that makes it all the more important that the macroprudential authorities have access to good information on such emerging threats, as well as a sufficiently wide representation to understand them properly. Hubbard et al. (2021) provide a comprehensive assessment of the limitations of the US arrangements exposed by the pandemic and make several practical proposals for improvement. Authorities elsewhere would be wise to use the opportunity afforded by the pandemic to identify and address similar shortcomings, for (to mis-quote Thomas Jefferson) 'eternal vigilance is the price of stability'.

NOTE

1. Credit frictions and higher bank capital requirements could also restrict the supply of output (as in Cúrdia and Woodford, 2010, for instance) but, if so, I assume that the net effect of a higher bank capital requirement is to reduce the demand for goods and services more than its supply.

REFERENCES

Adrian, Tobias, Nina Boyarchenko and Domenico Giannone (2019) 'Vulnerable growth'. *American Economic Review*, 109 (4): 1263–89.

Balls, Edward, James Howat and Anna Stansbury (2016) 'Central bank independence revisited: After the financial crisis, what should a model central bank look like?' Mossavar-Rahmani Center for Business and Government, Harvard University Associate Working Paper No. 67.

Bank for International Settlements (2014) *84th Annual Report*, Basel.

Bank for International Settlements (2016) *86th Annual Report*, Basel.

Bean, Charles R. (2014) 'The future of monetary policy'. Speech at the London School of Economics, 20 May.

Coibion, Olivier, Yuriy Gorodnichenko, Lorenz Kueng and John Silvia (2017) 'Innocent bystanders? Monetary policy and inequality'. *Journal of Monetary Economics*, 88: 70–89.

Cúrdia, Vasco and Michael Woodford (2010) 'Credit spreads and monetary policy'. *Journal of Money, Credit and Banking*, 42 (S1): 3–35.

Edge, Rochelle M. and J. Nellie Liang (2021) 'Macroprudential bank capital actions in response to the 2020 pandemic', in *Monetary Policy and Central Banking in the Covid Era*, eds William English, Kristin Forbes and Angel Ubide, Centre for Economic Policy Research, London.

Hubbard, Glenn, Donald Kohn, Laurie Goodman, Kathryn Judge, Anil Kashyap, Ralph Koijen, Blythe Masters, Sandie O'Connor and Kara Stein (2021) *Task Force on*

Financial Stability, Hutchins Center on Fiscal & Monetary Policy and the University of Chicago Booth School of Business Report.

International Monetary Fund (2011) *Macroprudential Policy: An Organizing Framework*.

International Monetary Fund (2017) *Financial Conditions and Growth at Risk*, Global Financial Stability Report, October, chapter 3.

Mundell, Robert A. (1962) 'The appropriate use of monetary and fiscal policy for internal and external stability', *IMF Staff Papers*, 9 (1): 70–9.

Office for Budget Responsibility (2021) *Fiscal Risks Report*, chapter 4, London.

Stein, Jeremy (2013) 'Overheating in credit markets: Origins, measurement, and policy responses'. Speech at the Federal Reserve Bank of St. Louis, 7 February.

Svensson, Lars E. O. (2017) 'Cost–benefit analysis of leaning against the wind'. *Journal of Monetary Economics*, 90: 193–213.

Tucker, Paul (2018) *Unelected Power: The Quest for Legitimacy in Central Banking and the Regulatory State*, Princeton University Press.

White, William R. (2009) 'Should monetary policy "lean or clean"?' Federal Reserve Bank of Dallas Globalization and Monetary Policy Institute Working Paper 34.

10. Governance of financial sector policies in an era of climate change

Daniel C. Hardy

1.   INTRODUCTION

Climate change, how to limit its extent, and how to handle its consequences has become a central policy issue at the start of the 21st century. The financial sector, and the policies of central banks and supervisors, are deeply implicated.

When considering what financial sector policies should be adopted in response to the climate crisis, questions arise about what actions are consistent with the mandates of the responsible agencies; whether these actions may come into conflict with the attainment of other objectives; and how good governance practices can be maintained. These questions become more pressing when proposals are made for more radical action that going beyond the traditional areas of monetary stability, financial stability, and consumer protection.

The debate is far from resolved, especially in Europe. UN Environment Inquiry (2017) and Dikau and Volz (2021) present well-balanced arguments on cross-cutting issues. The specific situation in Europe is informed by the functioning of supranational structures and institutions, such as the European Central Bank (ECB), and the hard-won independence of the central banks and supervisors.

This chapter provides an expressly European angle on the questions posed above, emphasizing the linkages across policy areas and political economy factors that influence the functioning of the supervisory architecture. The European monetary authorities, the micro- and macroprudential authorities, and the market conduct and consumer protection authorities all have roles to play and instruments to use. It will be emphasized, however, that any action taken must be justifiable and justified, not least in order to avoid a reaction to perceived "over-reach."

The next section provides background material on governance and institutional architecture related to financial sector policies, and on some relevant aspects of the economic implications of climate change. The subsequent section considers first the governance implications of central banks and supervisors extending existing policies to ensure that the financial system is more robust in the face of the adverse consequences of climate change and can contribute to the mitigation of those consequences. The section then considers whether the institutional architecture could support a more active approach, using financial sector policies dedicated to promoting the transition to a sustainable economy. The final section concludes.

2.   BACKGROUND

2.1   Governance of Financial Sector Policies

The rules, structures, and practices by which decisions are made and implementation overseen constitute the main elements of a governance structure.[1] Good governance helps ensure that decisions are reliably taken and effectively carried out in a deliberate manner, based on adequate information, in pursuit of the agency's mandate.

Governance in the public sector, and in particular for agencies responsible for financial sector policies, has to cope with certain distinct challenges.[2] One challenge is that the set of stakeholders of a public sector institution is wider and more diffuse than that of a private institution. The boundaries are not well defined: do stakeholders include just current citizens, or also future generations—especially when long-term policies and the prevention of future climate catastrophes are at stake? Arguably, regional partners and even the global community are stakeholders, notably when policy relates to global phenomenon such as climate change.

Various stakeholders will differ in their incentives and ability to attempt regulatory capture. Capture in the narrow sense refers to a financial policy agency being "captured" by the entities that it is meant to oversee and therefore to act sometimes in their interest rather than the public interest.[3] Regulatory capture in the wider sense refers to undue influence exercised by different special interest group on the design and implementation of polices. "Capture" is thus a matter of degree, and complicated by competition between interest groups. The government of the day is itself an influential stakeholder that may, for example, have a shorter planning horizon than does the financial policy agency concerned.

Two other relevant challenges affecting governance in the public sector relate to (1) difficulties in measuring effectiveness and linking outcomes to particular actions; and (2) the need to balance incommensurate objectives. The ultimate purpose of a public institution is to promote general welfare over the medium term, which is not readily measurable or closely linked to specific decisions. Moreover, welfare is affected by many factors (e.g., the level and distribution of income and environmental conditions). There is no obvious measure that can be used to capture, say, the value of both price stability and preservation of the natural world. It is worth noting that inflation targets are easier to define, and their achievement easier to measure on a timely basis, than objectives related to financial stability or indeed climate change.

Because of these considerations, the public sector typically establishes inter-mediary goals, and a hierarchy of intermediary goals. Article 2 of the Statute of the European System of Central Banks and of the European Central Bank states that:

> The primary objective of the ESCB shall be to maintain price stability. Without prejudice to the objective of price stability, it shall support the general economic policies in the Union with a view to contributing to the achievement of the objectives of the Union as laid down in Article 3 of the Treaty on European Union.[4]

which in turn states that:

> The Union shall establish an internal market. It shall work for the sustainable development of Europe based on balanced economic growth and price stability, a highly competitive social market economy, aiming at full employment and social progress, and a high level of protection and improvement of the quality of the environment. It shall promote scientific and technological advance.
>
> It shall combat social exclusion and discrimination, and shall promote social justice and protection, equality between women and men, solidarity between generations and protection of the rights of the child.
>
> It shall promote economic, social and territorial cohesion, and solidarity among Member States.
>
> It shall respect its rich cultural and linguistic diversity, and shall ensure that Europe's cultural heritage is safeguarded and enhanced.

Accordingly, protection of the environment is one among several secondary objectives, subject to the overriding price stability objective. Financial agencies in Europe are further subject to EU commitments and common principles (ECB, 2021, explains the relevant elements applicable at the level of the ECB).

Financial sector supervision combines stability and market conduct/consumer protection objectives, without an explicit environmental protection mandate, as expressed for example in the statement:

> The main objective of the [European System of Financial Supervision] is to ensure that the rules applicable to the financial sector are adequately implemented across Member States in order to preserve financial stability, promote confidence and provide protection for consumers.[5]

2.2   Climate Change and Economic Risks

Economic effects and risks related to climate change are diverse; the term "climate change-related risks" will be used to cover this multitude when there is no need to be more specific. Climate change itself will have direct effects, for example, through more prolonged drought that leads to a shortage of water for agriculture and industry. Another set of effects will reflect technological changes, such as the development of carbon-neutral means of transportation and power generation. Policies to reduce greenhouse gas (GHG) emissions (e.g., through carbon taxes) and adapt to climate change (e.g., through modified infrastructure) will have effects that are decisive for the economic viability for many projects and even whole sectors.

These effects interact and will evolve over time in hard-to-predict ways. Regarding interaction, the slower countries reduce GHG emissions, the larger and faster will be climate change itself, but strong policies to discourage GHG emissions create incentives for more technological innovation. Thus, policy risk is pervasive. The risks are not all to the downside. For example: the transition to a sustainable economy may reduce pollution and its attendant costs. Certain climate change effects, such as sea level rise, may affects some countries greatly but not others, and in any case there is great uncertainty about when effects will become critical.

3.   FINANCIAL SECTOR POLICIES IN THE FACE OF CLIMATE CHANGE

Financial policy agencies have recognized that climate change-related risks impinge on their areas of responsibility and on society as a whole, and that they therefore have to consider what if anything they can usefully do. One approach, which is dominant so far, is to incorporate management of these risks into current frameworks: policies are extended and elaborated, but the objectives and time horizons remain as before, and the focus remains on the financial system. The second approach is to adopt policies that promote de-carbonization and mitigation of the effects of the climate crisis throughout the economy. The approaches place different demands on supervisory architecture and governance mechanisms.

3.1   Extending Current Policies

Some economic developments and risks related to climate change are clearly relevant to the existing mandates of financial policy agencies, but even here there are both technical and political economy challenges. To some extent, climate change-related risk can be seen as another risk factor, much like operational risk, or as contributing to familiar risk factors, such as credit and market risk (Pointner and Ritzberger-Grünwald, 2019, provide a summary). However, the diversity of and uncertainty about climate change-related risks need to be accommodated if financial sector policies are to remain fact-based and defensible. The accommodation can take the form of proportionality (action should concentrate on factors that, on a risk-adjusted basis, are likely to be most important) and respecting the time dimension (short-term action need not take into account long-term trends).

A non-exhaustive list of how climate change-related risks are being taken into account includes the following:[6]

- Microprudential regulation and supervision is mandated to ensure that financial institutions measure, price, and manage all material risks, which will include climate change-related risks. Thus, supervisors may use regulations (such as minimum risk weights for capitalization) that in effect require financial institutions to build buffers against the realization of these risks, once they are material.[7] Perhaps more importantly in the near term, supervisors may require financial institutions to collect and analyze the information they need to assess and manage climate change-related risks. Building such capacity involves a costly investment for a long-term gain; the supervisor can help ensure that financial institutions do not fall prey to "short-termism."

- Macroprudential policies may be evoked where systemic effects are possible. Climate change risks are often highly correlated across firms in a sector, the economy as a whole, and internationally. A regulation or risk management system calibrated for the risk faced by an individual financial institution may not take this correlation fully into account. For example, water shortage or flooding could reduce the value of real estate across a large region, weakening all mortgage lenders at once. A restricted credit supply could then feed back into lower house prices. Hence, incorporation of a "systemic climate risk premium" can be justified, if it is based on best-available estimates of the effect over the relevant time horizon.

- The regulation and supervision of market conduct and consumer protection are likewise mandated to address climate change-related risks and the financing of the transition to a sustainable economy. First, a financial institution itself is required to be transparent to investors about its risk profile, and that profile will be deeply affected by its exposures to climate change-related risks. Here is another incentive for a financial institution to gather and assess information on its exposures and those of its clients. Second, a financial institution needs to provide reliable information to clients on climate change-related risks in the products it sells. Information needs to cover not only underlying risks, but also governance and regulatory risks, and specifically the risk of "greenwashing." The European green bond standard, for example, aims to ensure that securities marketed as "green" genuinely finance sustainable projects.

- A link to monetary policy instruments and implementation exists, but is weaker, under current conditions and understanding of monetary policy goals. A central bank acting prudently should allow for climate change-related risks, for example, in the pricing of collateral eligible for refinancing. A security with a substantial exposure to such risks should, even under existing norms, be subject to a larger "haircut" than is an otherwise comparable security free of this exposure.[8] Whether an exposure is substantial depends on the time horizon; climate risks are negligible for short-term operations such as the ECB's one-week Main Refinance Operations. In addition, climate change and policies to combat it may have an effect on prices, and a central bank will have to decide how to respond. For example, an increase in a carbon tax will raise prices. If this uptick occurs when inflation is already above target, a central bank such as the ECB would be warranted in taking offsetting measures, ensuring that inflation expectations do not drift upwards. Finally, a prudent central bank would take climate change-related risk into account in allocating its non-monetary portfolio, including its international reserves, though most reserve assets are very short term and not materially exposed to these risks.

Financial policy agencies are taking action in these areas, devoting substantial resources and setting an example of engagement. Stress testing exercises now incorporate climate change-related risks. Doing so, and giving prominence to the results, has benefits in terms of micro- and macroprudential oversight, building capacity in financial institutions, and facilitating informed investment by savers. Financial policy agencies have contributed to the formulation and use of "green" standards, and have issued warnings about "greenwashing." The Network of Central Banks and Supervisors for Greening the Financial System, whose membership now includes almost all countries, is representative of this dynamism.[9]

Taking the sort of actions outlined above is technically difficult because understanding of climate change-related economic effects and especially the ability to quantify them are still limited. The financial policy agency in question will have difficulty calibrating any quantitative measure, or even in judging what constitutes a reasonable effort, for example, in a financial institution's management of climate change-related risks and associated disclosures. Moreover, the financial policy agency will have to reveal its reliance on very imperfect information and heroic assumptions when it is held to account by parliament and the public. The general problem of the difficulties attached to measuring the achievement of financial sector policy objectives is exacerbated when final outcomes are far in the future and subject to multi-dimensional uncertainty, as with climate change-related effects.

Taking these actions may be difficult in political economy terms because they affect the interests of powerful groups, who may attempt to "capture" financial policy and resist greater transparency. Suppose that the prudential authority has good evidence that a large region is subject to elevated flood risk. Therefore, real estate there is less valuable as collateral and lenders have to hold more capital against related financing. The owners of that real estate and existing lenders will lobby to have this evidence ignored, or to receive compensation in some form, which pushes to risk onto others. The financial policy governance system is meant to be robust against this sort of capture; awareness of the possibility is a precondition for such robustness.

The political economy challenge is greater in this area because many of the risks relate to government policy: the financial policy agencies may have to "speak truth to power," which is rarely welcome. Perhaps most important is uncertainty about polices aimed at de-carbonizing the economy through various taxes and regulations. The details of these policies cannot be predicted but will have large effects on the economic costs and benefits incurred, and their distribution. Also, the government's ability to commit to a given policy over a long period is open to question. Technological and infrastructure investments are largely "sunk" once initiated and can have planning horizons stretching over decades. One of the largest disincentives for such investment is the possibility that de-carbonization measures will be substantially revised or even reversed. Hence, if the financial policy authorities are to take major climate change-related risks into account, they must acknowledge the political risk generated by their own government (and international agreements and governments abroad). The financial policy authorities may have to say to the government of the day and to parliamentarians that promises to meet emissions reduction targets are not fully credible, and that financial institutions should plan accordingly. The same contingency planning is needed with regard to promised infrastructure investments aimed at adapting to the effects of climate change.

Relations with government may become even more delicate when the financial policy agencies are critical of the government's policies. For an emerging market economy, large external borrowing for infrastructure investment may be criticized as destabilizing even though individual projects are well-designed. For an investment-grade advanced economy, the financial conduct authority may be required by its mandate to criticize government claims that proceeds from the sale of a sovereign green bond will be spent on environmental projects; the fungibility of money implies that, in the author's opinion, such a claim amounts to false advertising.

3.2   Promotional Financial Sector Policies

The seriousness of climate change challenges has led some to suggest that the financial policy agencies adopt measures that actively promote projects to help mitigate climate change or adapt to its effects. The measures would not just take into account estimated climate change-related risk in the design of existing policies, as described above, but would try to contribute to the reduction of these risks for the economy as a whole. Proposals along these lines have been made by Bartholomew and Diggle (2001), for example. It has been suggested that "[i]n addition to risk management considerations, the Eurosystem could play a supportive catalytic function in financial markets with its monetary policy measures ... [by] using its own operational tools and leading by example with its own efforts" (ECB, op. cit., p. 146).

The financial policy agencies generally have as an objective supporting the government's policies, at least insofar as actions to this end do not impinge on first priority objectives such as price stability or financial sector stability.[10] The text of the ECB's mandate, reported above, includes the promotion of "a high level of protection and improvement of the quality of the environment." One could also argue that the attainment of "balanced economic growth and a highly competitive social market economy, aiming at full employment and social progress" and promoting "solidarity between generations" requires action on the climate. Hence, such promotional policies are consistent with the mandate.

Some possible policy actions include the following:

- Instituting central bank long-term refinancing operations based on lending for suitably "green" projects at favorable rates, modeled on the recent ECB Targeted Long-Term Refinance Operations. Banks—and perhaps others—could obtain cheap refinancing of loans going to investments that reduce GHG emissions or protect from effects such higher temperatures or flooding. The cost of such refinancing operations would be reflected in reduced central bank profits.
- Allocating a minimum share of an asset purchase program to "green" securities and other long-term, low-carbon securities.[11] Part of the quantitative easing quantum would be devoted to suitable securities, thus increasing demand for them from the central bank itself and increasing their "option value" to others. Hence, green financing would become cheaper. Much of the cost would be reflected in what the central bank pays for the securities. One drawback may be a reduced "free float" and thus liquidity of green securities.
- Favorable "haircuts" on "green" securities used as the basis of refinance operations. The "haircuts" to the value of a security used in refinancing

operations contain a substantial margin of error relative to the objectively
estimated probability of default and loss given default. Green bonds could
be favored, and demand for them increased, by reducing this margin of
error. The potential cost would never be realized unless the securities
involved defaulted and losses were more than projected.

- Prudential requirements such as risk weights or weights in the net stable
funding requirement could be relaxed for the funding of "green" investments, beyond what is estimated to be justified by empirical evidence on
default risk, etc., over the short run.[12] The supply of such funding would be
stimulated, while any cost would become apparent on the books of financial institutions only in the event that the investment fails. The cost would
be "socialized" if the financial institution fails outright.

Several governance-related considerations speak against the adoption by the
financial policy agencies of promotional policies related to climate change
mitigation.

First, the mandate of a typical financial policy agency seems to encompass
adaptation to climate change, not to expending resources on ineffectual efforts
to mitigate climate change. For all but the largest countries, national GHG
emissions are insignificant in the global total, so climate change will be unaffected by what a small county does or does not do; polices to reduce emissions
will not materially protect the environment or contribute the other objectives.
Less problematic is supporting the financing of adaptive projects, for example,
to improve water management, or the financing of projects to adjust to policies
imposed by other counties, such as border carbon adjustment. In the European
context, the texts quoted above suggest that the ECB has wider scope to pursue
the EU's objectives than do the supervisors.

Second, it will be very hard to hold a financial policy agency to account
for actions in these areas. While the staff resources devoted to these efforts
could be tracked, most of the costs and benefits would be non-measurable or
become apparent only after a very long lag. Parliament and the public would
have great difficulty in judging whether or not the use of public resources and
intervention in private business was worthwhile.

Third, the decision by a financial policy agency to institute non-financial
policy seems to face a "democratic deficit." In effect, the unelected board of
the financial policy agency would decide what is a non-financial priority, what
policy to take, and how many resources should be devoted to it. For the UK,
the Treasury periodically issues a pronouncement on (high-level) financial
sector policy priorities, which the Bank of England and regulatory agencies
must follow. For the ECB, there does not seem to be a mechanism to translate
"the general economic policies in the EU" into specific priorities. The legiti-

macy of a financial policy agency may be imperilled if it decides for itself what non-financial priorities are worth pursuing and how to do so.

Fourth, taking action in a non-financial area may set a dangerous precedent, one that ultimately jeopardizes independence. The danger is greatest where justification for the action relies on secondary objectives: if climate change is to be addressed for the sake of "a high level of protection and improvement of the quality of the environment," why not do something for the objectives of "balanced economic growth and a highly competitive social market economy, aiming at full employment and social progress" (or analogous objectives in non-euro area countries)? Central banks tend to be quite profitable. Hence, they could implement many other policies without endangering price or financial stability. For example, it could be established that better availability of childcare would promote balanced growth, etc. The central bank could use its refinancing facilities to promote childcare, thereby reducing its profits slightly. However, such "mission creep" would go against the spirit of current governance arrangements, and likely provoke a reaction by government and parliament aimed at reducing central bank autonomy.

4.   CONCLUSIONS

The climate crisis has already provoked substantial action by financial policy agencies, and so far the supervisory architecture and governance arrangements seem up to the task. Indeed, central banks and supervisors have become highly visible in promoting awareness of the need to try to limit climate change and to prepare for what cannot be avoided, without generating much opposition.

That opposition may start to emerge if policies are further intensified and the interests of powerful groups are affected. These powerful groups may include stakeholders in GHG-intensive industries and owners of other potentially stranded assets. The government itself may be made uncomfortable if the financial sector supervisors are fully open about policy risk and the limitations of the government's own policies.

Supervisors and central banks can defend themselves by demonstrating that they are fulfilling their well-established mandates to protect stability and consumers, using the best available information, taking costs into account, and implementing proportionality. That defence may be attacked on the basis of the large amount of uncertainty attached to all projections and models related to climate change, but the argument cuts both ways: the uncertainty and possibility of very adverse outcomes increases the value of precautionary measures.

The case for going further, for the financial policy agencies themselves actively promoting de-carbonization and the transition to a sustainable economy, must address governance concerns. A central bank or supervisor could use available instrument with the intention of accelerating structural change, without impinging on the attainment of its primary objective, in a manner consistent with legal requirements applicable to the European System of Central Banks. However, taking on such a program may run the risk that the concerned agency strays into quasi-fiscal activities, and is seen to do so. Good governance does not consist just of following the letter of the law; a commitment to good governance in practice, to accountability and restraint in the exercise of powers, is necessary for the system to work and for financial sector authorities' independence to be accepted. Hence, promotional action must offer the prospect of a large payoff, in terms of reduced climate change and related risks, if it is to be worth disrupting the European political economy equilibrium supporting the financial policies agencies' operational independence.

NOTES

1. The G20/OECD (2015) *Principles of Corporate Governance* states that "Corporate governance involves a set of relationships between a company's management, its board, its shareholders and other stakeholders. Corporate governance also provides the structure through which the objectives of the company are set, and the means of attaining those objectives and monitoring performance are determined" (p. 9).
2. It will be convenient to use the portmanteau term "financial policy agencies" for the monetary authority, the microprudential and macroprudential authorities, and the market conduct and consumer protection authority. (The bank resolution authority is of less relevance here.) They will be distinguished where necessary, but often enough they face comparable issues.
3. An extensive review of the literature is provided in Mitnick (1980) and Wilson (1980).
4. Similar objectives are found in national legislation.
5. https://www.europarl.europa.eu/factsheets/en/sheet/84/european-system-of-financial-supervision-esfs-
6. Dikau et al. (2019) provide a survey. NGFS (2020) offers more detail on supervisory approaches.
7. The jargon refers to a "Green Supporting Factor" and a "Brown Penalizing Factor," for example, in European Commission (2018), which in the first instance reflect verifiable differences in riskiness.
8. As discussed in ECB (op. cit.), section 7.3.2.
9. See https://www.ngfs.net/en
10. Durrani et al. (2020) note that, "A number of central banks and supervisory authorities [in the Asia Pacific Region] are already promoting sustainable financing options explicitly or implicitly."
11. Campiglio et al. (2018) propose that such an approach should be considered. Hines (2015) recommends the reconfiguration of the ECB asset purchase program to support infrastructure spending. See also Tooze (2019) and Monnin (2021).
12. Berenguer et al. (2020) refer to this as the "economic policy approach," as opposed to the traditional "risk approach." Robins et al. (2021) contains elements

of such as an approach. A French National Assembly report (2019) recommends that "Les banques doivent également mieux identifier l'impact climatique de leurs prêts et peuvent y être incitées par un bonus/malus prudentiel qui adapte les exigences de fonds propres en fonction de la part des prêts favorables ou défavorables à la transition bas-carbone dans les portefeuilles de prêts bancaires." This text can be interpreted as suggesting that risk weights should be adjusted to incentivize financing of investment supportive of the transition to a low-carbon economy.

REFERENCES

Assemblée Nationale (2019), "Mission d'évaluation et de contrôle (MEC) sur les outils publics encourageant l'investissement privé dans la transition écologique," Rapport d'Information en conclusion des travaux. https://www.assemblee-nationale.fr/dyn/15/rapports/mec/l15b1626_rapport-information

Bartholomew, Luke and Paul Diggle (2001), "Climate change and central banks: The case for violating neutrality," Voxeu blog. https://voxeu.org/article/climate-change-and-central-banks-case-violating-neutrality

Berenguer, M., M. Cardona and J. Evai (2020), "Integrating climate-related risks into banks' capital requirements," i4ce Working Paper. https://www.i4ce.org/wp-core/wp-content/uploads/2020/03/IntegratingClimate_EtudeVA.pdf

Campiglio, E., Y. Dafermos, P. Monnin, et al. (2018), "Climate change challenges for central banks and financial regulators," *Nature Climate Change* 8, 462–468.

Dikau, S. and U. Volz (2021), "Central bank mandates, sustainability objectives and the promotion of green finance," *Ecological Economics* 184. https://www.sciencedirect.com/science/article/pii/S092180092100080X

Dikau, S., N. Robins and M. Täger (2019), "Building a sustainable financial system: The state of practice and future priorities," Banca d'España, Revista de Establidad Financiera, Num. 37. https://www.bde.es/f/webbde/GAP/Secciones/Publicaciones/InformesBoletinesRevistas/RevistaEstabilidadFinanciera/19/noviembre/Building_sustainable_financial.pdf

Durrani, A., U. Volz and M. Rosmin (2020), "The role of central banks in scaling up sustainable finance: what do monetary authorities in Asia and the Pacific think?" ADBI Working Paper 1099, Tokyo: Asian Development Bank Institute. https://www.adb.org/publications/role-central-banks-scaling-sustainable-finance-asia-pacific

European Central Bank (2021), "Climate change and monetary policy in the euro area," ECB Occasional Paper No. 271. https://www.ecb.europa.eu/pub/pdf/scpops/ecb.op271~36775d43c8.en.pdf?c29941b5e2dbeb3168b6e48f362a2b87

European Commission (2018), "Sustainable finance: Commission's Action Plan for a greener and cleaner economy." https://ec.europa.eu/commission/presscorner/detail/en/IP_18_1404

G20/OECD (2015), *Principles of Corporate Governance.* https://www.oecd.org/daf/ca/Corporate-Governance-Principles-ENG.pdf

Hines, C. (2015), "The role of international financial institutions, central banks and monetary policies in the low-carbon transition," France Strategie article. https://www.strategie.gouv.fr/english-articles/role-international-financial-institutions-central-banks-and-monetary-policies-low

Mitnick, B. M. (1980), *The Political Economy of Regulation: Creating, Designing, and Removing Regulatory Forms*, New York: Columbia University Press.

Monnin, P. (2021), "ECB and climate change: The direction is clear – but ambition and speed are lacking," Council on Economic Policies blog. https://www.cepweb.org/ecb-and-climate-change-the-direction-is-clear-but-ambition-and-speed-are-lacking/

NGFS (2020), "Guide for supervisors integrating climate-related and environmental risks into prudential supervision," Network for Greening the Financial System Technical document. https://www.ngfs.net/sites/default/files/medias/documents/ngfs_guide_for_supervisors.pdf

Pointner, Wolfgang and Doris Ritzberger-Grünwald (2019), "Climate change as a risk to financial stability," *Financial Stability Report*, Oesterreichische Nationalbank (Austrian Central Bank), Issue 38, pp. 30–45.

Robins, N., S. Dikau and U. Volz (2021), "Net-zero central banking: A new phase in greening the financial system," Grantham Research Institute on Climate Change and the Environment Policy Report. https://www.lse.ac.uk/granthaminstitute/wp-content/uploads/2021/03/Net-zero-central-banking.pdf

Tooze, A. (2019), "Why central banks need to step up on global warming," *Foreign Policy* (July). https://foreignpolicy.com/2019/07/20/why-central-banks-need-to-step-up-on-global-warming/

UN Environment Inquiry (2017), "On the role of central banks in enhancing green finance," Inquiry Working Paper 17/1. https://wedocs.unep.org/bitstream/handle/20.500.11822/16803/Role_Central_Banks_Green_Finance.pdf?sequence=1&amp%3BisAllowed=

Wilson, J. Q. (1980), *The Politics of Regulation*, New York: Basic Books.

PART III

The role of central banks (II): microprudential supervision and financial stability

11. Entrusting central banks with microprudential supervision: implications for financial stability

Anca Maria Podpiera[1]

Should central banks be entrusted with microprudential supervision? I doubt the wisdom of raising this question in abstract terms.

Lamfalussy, 2011[2]

1. INTRODUCTION

Financial prudential supervision progressed alongside innovation, competition and pressure for profit that drove the financial systems. The evolution of formalized banking supervision has differed significantly among countries—dating back to the 1860s for banking supervision at the federal level in the U.S., the beginning of the 20th century for countries such as Colombia, Peru, Japan and Sweden, or the Great Depression for other developed countries.[3] In the U.K., the supervision of commercial banks started only in 1979 as a response to banks "failing to control themselves in a socially satisfactory fashion" that led to "fringe bank crisis" (Goodhart, 2018). As a result, the prudential supervision is often thought to be a recent phenomenon. In the same vein, its evolution is strongly associated with the need to circumvent negative externalities and political reactions to financial crises. Masciandaro and Romelli (2018) find that the occurrence of systemic banking crises as well as reforms in other countries are important drivers of reforms in supervisory structure. Nevertheless, for many countries it is documented as an "incremental institutional change" responding to the changes in the banking system, public and political leaders.[4]

Central bank involvement in supervision has been a long and slow process, in most cases (Grossman, 2010). Besides their traditional role in the conduct of monetary policy and, for some countries, in financial stability,[5] some central banks have also assumed banking supervision authority. Some countries with early formalization of supervision created institutions outside their central banks, as in Sweden, where the history of Riksbank as a commercial bank would have created a conflict of interest. Generally, younger central banks were more likely to be entrusted with banking supervision than their older counterparts (Grossman, 2010). Singapore and the U.K. gave the authority for regulation and supervision of banks to their central banks in 1970 and 1979, respectively. Despite their connection, monetary and prudential policies have been usually designed and analyzed in isolation from one another, with an increased interest in their optimal interaction in the aftermath of the global financial crisis (GFC) (Collard et al., 2017). As a source of liquidity though, central banks are naturally involved in preventing and managing systemic banking crisis.[6]

After the GFC, the considerations for the institutional design for macropru-dential policy and financial stability mandates for central banks added another layer of importance to their role in the architecture of microprudential super-vision. There has been a wide agreement that central banks should play an important role in the macroprudential policy (Edge and Liang, 2019). Yet, the conduct of macroprudential policy can interfere with that of microprudential policy, especially during bad times when a macroprudential standpoint may lean to facilitate the provision of credit while the microprudential perspec-tive may seek to preserve supervisory requirements (Claessens, 2014). This chapter reviews the recent changes in prudential structures, the pros and cons of entrusting central banks with prudential supervision in the light of changes in perspective after the GFC, and the recent empirical studies that underlie the implications of this for financial stability.

2.   MICROPRUDENTIAL SUPERVISION AFTER THE GLOBAL FINANCIAL CRISIS

2.1   Historical Perspective

The ravages of the GFC raised questions about many aspects of financial regulation and supervision—the lack of sufficient consideration for macropru-dential supervision and the effectiveness of microprudential supervision being major ones. In an attempt to tackle the effectiveness of prudential oversight some countries made significant, in some cases radical, changes in their institutional structures. Calvo et al. (2018) find that central banks got more supervisory powers in those jurisdictions more affected by the GFC. The 2016 survey of the World Bank (2019) finds that 93 countries out of 159 surveyed have their central bank as banking prudential supervisor and 12 countries have multiple bank supervisory agencies including the central bank.

The database of Melecky and Podpiera (2013), updated until 2021, which includes 98 countries ranging from upper-middle income to high-income countries across all continents reveals that one third of jurisdictions made changes in the supervisory architecture after the GFC.[7] While 19 changes were made shortly after the crisis, until 2012, others have been contemplated and occurred recently—with eight changes during 2017–2021.[8] Table 11.1 presents the evolution of supervisory structures starting from 2007. The majority of changes after the GFC have given more responsibility to central banks:

- Six countries (Belgium, Hungary, Ireland, New Zealand, the U.K. and more recently Iceland) in which central banks had no microprudential supervisory responsibilities during the GFC have entrusted them with prudential supervision of all financial sectors.
- Seventeen countries have now unified prudential supervision in central banks (five central banks hosting the prudential arm of a twin peaks supervisory structure) versus seven countries in 2007.
- Four countries added responsibilities for supervising insurance to central banks.
- Austria and Germany added microprudential supervisory responsibilities to their central banks while maintaining FSA[9] models.

Yet, were the changes in the role of central banks warranted by plausible improvements in the effectiveness of prudential oversight or were they mere political decisions? Brunnermeier et al. (2009) note that "there is a tendency, commonly observed amongst politicians, to review the structure of the regulatory system before considering the potential instruments to achieve better regulatory control." Similarly, Goodhart (2018) mentions that the establishment of the U.K.'s FSA in 1998 mandated with supervision of all subsectors of the financial sector happened "suddenly, and without any prior warning or justification." As for the 2012 return to the Bank of England of microprudential regulation, "there was little, or no, prior public discussion whether it was better to place the 'Resolution Authority' within, or outside the Bank."

However, transformations after the GFC appear more grounded in consultations—extensive in some cases. In Iceland, the merger of the central bank and the Financial Supervisory Authority—finalized in 2020—was preceded by "a wide-ranging examination and preparation."[10] Similarly, in Latvia, the approval in 2020 of the merger of the financial regulator with the central bank planned for 2022–2023 has been preceded by consultations, with expectations for increased effectiveness of both macro- and microprudential policies as well as of monetary policy and substantial decline in operating expenditures.[11] In Ireland, the Central Bank Reform Act of 2010 which established the central bank as a single fully integrated prudential structure also requires the conduct of an international peer review at least every four years to assess the performance of its regulatory functions in order to ensure and strengthen its accountability.[12] At the other end of the spectrum, the decisions to transfer responsibilities for financial regulation to the central bank in Azerbaijan in

Table 11.1   *Evolution of the organization of microprudential supervision*

Year	Banking microprudential supervision within the central bank (CB)					Banking microprudential supervision outside the central bank (CB)					Both[a]
	UCB	UCB TP	Insurance or securities supervision also in CB	Insurance and securities supervision unified outside of CB	Sectoral supervision	FSA	FSA TP	Insurance or securities supervision integrated with banking supervision	Insurance and securities supervision unified separately from banking supervision	Sectoral supervision outside the central bank	
2007	6	1	8	9	33	18	1	9	2	7	3
2012	9	3	8	11	30	19	1	6	1	7	3
2017	10	5	10	11	25	19	1	5	1	8	3
2021	12	5	10	11	24	19	1	6	0	7	3

Note: Number of countries: 98; UCB = unification in the central bank; TP = "twin peaks"; a = "Banking supervision both within and outside the central bank."

Source: Authors' calculations based on the updated database of Melecky and Podpiera (2013).

2019 from a FSA, and in Kazakhstan to a FSA from the central bank, were made by presidential decrees.

Adoptions of new "twin peaks" supervisory models also involved broad consultations. In New Zealand, the current model with the prudential mandate in the central bank, introduced in 2010, was based on the "Review of Financial Products and Providers" that took place during mid-2000s and had industry participants actively involved in the process (Reserve Bank of New Zealand, 2018). For South Africa's move to a twin peaks structure with prudential regulator under the administration of the central bank from a "sectoral" approach in 2017, the public comments received since 2013 on the draft bills resulted in significant amendments (Godwin et al., 2017). In Peru, the transition from an FSA to a twin peaks model with the prudential branch outside the central bank that started in 2020 "reflects the advice provided by the International Monetary Fund, as well as the comparative experience of globally integrated financial regulators."[13]

2.2   Pros and Cons of Entrusting Central Banks with Microprudential Supervision

Amid a surge in the attention to the conduct and institutional design for macroprudential policy, and recognized complementarities between micro- and macroprudential,[14] the role of central banks in the microprudential supervision is still pondered. We underline arguments in favor of as well as against the placement of prudential supervision in central banks, especially in the light of the experience during and after the GFC about its financial stability implications.

Bank supervision under one roof with the central bank could support the following efforts:

- **Coordination and synergies in systemic risk management, crisis preparedness, and crisis resolution.** The fundamental role of central banks in these areas was indubitable during the GFC (De Grauwe, 2007; Claessens et al., 2010). Two other factors stood out:
- – Combining the knowledge of prudential supervision with the central banks' expertise in evaluating macroeconomic and financial conditions and risks, especially in the case of financial systems containing systemically relevant financial institutions (Group of Thirty, 2008).
- – The proximity of the lender of last resort to the supervision of institutions that create credit. This is critical for the timely delivery of supervisory information about bank solvency and liquidity risk when key crisis management decisions are to be taken. The coordination for crisis management between the Bank of England and the U.K.'s Financial Services Authority

during the Northern Rock crisis in the U.K. in 2007 proved inadequate (Schoenmaker and Véron, 2017; Goodhart, 2018).

- **Prospects for supervisors in the central bank "to focus on the right questions in the accomplishment of their supervisory duties"** due to the central bank's direct access to market information stemming from its oversight responsibility of clearing, settlement and payment systems (Lamfalussy, 2011).
- **Enhanced effectiveness of central banks' main functions—indirectly benefitting the financial stability**. A precondition for an effective monetary policy is the soundness of banks as the "conduits" for monetary policy transmission, hence the need for accurate information from the supervision of the banking sector (Goodhart and Schoenmaker, 1995; Abrams and Taylor, 2000). This information is also necessary for the central bank's assessment of the participants in the payment system. The prospects for digital currencies add to the importance of this.
- **Improved capacity to coordinate cross-border supervision of regionally or globally systemic banks**. Central banks play a great role in the policy on international finance and the management of the balance of payments. The GFC havoc showed the need for more intense international cooperation in supervision, cooperation and coordination in crisis management (Financial Services Authority, 2009).
- **Central banks' capacity in attracting and retaining more skilled staff (Quintyn and Taylor, 2007).** Supervisory capacity is central to produce information useful for the risk assessment of banks. Abrams and Taylor (2000) emphasized that "this argument is particularly strong in countries where the absolute level of human capital with this skill is very small." The 2016 survey of the World Bank (2019) does not find significant differences in the average tenure of supervisors within versus those outside the central bank. Nevertheless, the same publication shows that the supervisory capacity has not kept pace with growing bank size and the complexity of regulations and of bank operations.

At the same time, there are substantial arguments for keeping the microprudential supervision outside the central bank:

- **More objectives, potential for less accountability.** An increase in the range of responsibilities for central banks could lead to a decline in accountability, if mechanisms to prevent this are not in place.
- **Threat on central bank independence.** The increased number of central bank responsibilities after the GFC, including on supervisory grounds, helped stir up the debate about the importance of maintaining central bank independence (De Haan et al., 2018). Recent empirical evidence though

reveals that central bank independence contributes, in fact, to financial stability (Doumpos et al., 2015; Andries et al., 2021).

• **Conflicts of interests between central banks' different mandates,** also apparent during the GFC, have been invoked as the most serious arguments for separating microprudential supervision from the central banks. The extent of these conflicts varies alongside the financial and economic cycle ("good times" versus "bad times").

− *Moral hazard related to the lender of last resort (LoLR) operations by the central bank.* Even before the GFC, many central banks limited the possibility of LoLR operations to systemic banks (Kremers et al., 2003). Nevertheless, during the financial panic in the U.S. during the fall 2008, some non-bank financial groups, such as Morgan Stanley and Goldman Sachs, converted to a status of bank holding company in order to access the federal banking safety net (Schoenmaker and Véron, 2017).

− *Microprudential supervision versus macroprudential supervision.* Serious concerns about the proximity of micro and macro supervision were expressed right after the GFC. Brunnermeier et al. (2009) highlight that the differences between the two types of regulatory measures "extend naturally to the ethos, discipline and cultures of the institutions involved," with the macro institution being the central bank, but they stress the need to maintain "direct links" with the systemic financial institutions. Danielsson et al. (2015) note that a source of this conflict, especially when both micro- and macroprudential policies are actively practiced and located within the same organization, is the fact that many micro-specific tools are useful and necessary for macroprudential supervision as well. The conflict becomes apparent when the two authorities "want to push the levers in opposite direction," depending on the state of economic cycle. Countries that relocate microprudential supervision within the central bank express the conviction that synergies rather than differences coming out of this proximity would prevail.

− *Business conduct supervision*[15] *versus macroprudential supervision.* Microprudential and business conduct supervisions are linked by institutional design in majority of cases, the twin peaks model being an exception. Concurrently, the majority of central banks have given a more formal mandate for macroprudential supervision after the GFC (Andries et al., 2021). Macroprudential and business conduct supervision could be in disagreement during times of crisis when there might be a temptation to neglect some problematic commercial practices because of enhanced focus on banks' capital and profitability, and even in non-crisis times when "business conduct mandate can be so all consuming that prudential considerations are neglected, as happened in the run-up to 2007 at U.K. FSA in its supervision of some British banks or at the U.S. SEC in its supervision of larger broker-dealers" (Schoenmaker and Véron, 2017).

Calvo et al. (2018) show that only about a quarter of jurisdictions appear to have structures in place to limit potential conflicts of interest stemming from additional supervisory functions, with the most common mechanism being assigning conflicting responsibilities to different departments or board members.

On practical grounds, in the 2018 New Zealand's Reserve Bank Act Review, some stakeholders favored institutional separation between microprudential supervision and the central bank—with the following main motivations: concerns about governance (potential conflicts of interest); perceived lack of resourcing of prudential policy and supervision; objectives being "vague and misspecified"; perceived lack of sufficient focus on prudential functions ("poor cousin" to monetary policy). Consequently, the Reserve Bank Amendment Act of 2018 introduced a number of enhancements to the Reserve Bank's governance and accountability arrangements (Reserve Bank of New Zealand, 2018).

3.   EMPIRICAL EVIDENCE

Earlier empirical studies analyzed preponderantly the determinants of quality of supervision owing to the idea that it is difficult to assess them due to an incomplete supervisor's contract. The supervisory architecture, including the role of the central bank, was a major factor considered. The findings were not conclusive, with some favoring placing banking supervision within the central bank for enhanced quality of supervision (compliance with Basel Core Principles) (Arnone and Gambini, 2006), while other studies (Cihak and Podpiera, 2008) do not find evidence of an improving role for the central bank. Eichengreen and Dincer (2011) conclude the superior efficiency of independent supervisors other than the central bank from a systemic risk point of view because of lower ratios of non-performing loans to GDP and lower capital ratios in these countries. Barth et al. (2003) found no bearing of bank supervisory structures on bank performance and suggested that the empirical studies look at the impact of the supervisory structure on bank safety and soundness, systemic stability, and the development of the banking system.

We highlight studies concentrating on the role of microprudential supervisors in supporting financial stability. Though very limited still, the empirical evidence shows that the central bank's involvement in microprudential supervision has a mitigating effect on systemic risk and the unfolding of financial crises.

Melecky and Podpiera (2015) show that having bank supervision in the central bank could generate financial stability benefits by, at a minimum, helping countries with significant financial depth or those undergoing extensive financial deepening to lessen their propensity for future systemic crises. They estimate a regression model explaining the probability of a banking crisis using their database described earlier and data from 124 countries, and confirm results from earlier studies that countries with greater financial deepening and countries taking greater aggregate liquidity risks are significantly more prone to banking crises. Placing bank supervision in the central bank can help reduce the positive effect of a greater financial deepening on the probability of crises by more than a half.

Doumpos et al. (2015) analyze primarily the effect that central bank independence exercises on bank soundness in a panel framework. Additionally, they include two indicators of the supervisory structures based on Melecky and Podpiera (2013)—central bank involvement in supervision as well as supervisory unification. They find that both factors improve bank soundness. Furthermore, the effect of a powerful unified supervisor on bank soundness is greater during banking crises than in normal times.

In a similar vein, Andries et al. (2021) find that greater central bank involvement in microprudential supervision helps reduce tail-event linkages between banks. The paper analyzes principally the relationship of central bank independence and banks' systemic risk measures in a panel framework[16] for the period 2001–2014, accounting for additional factors. It also confirms a significant decreasing effect of the degree of central bank involvement, measured by Masciandaro and Romelli's index (2018),[17] on the measures of banks' systemic risk relevance. The latest are also affected by bank characteristics, banking sector characteristics and macroeconomic variables.

4.   CONCLUSION

Central banks' role in financial prudential supervision has widened, naturally, owing to the relevance of financial sectors' performance for their operations. For many countries, the hard-won independence and better governance markers of central banks made them a better place to house financial microprudential supervision. The realization of fast-developing interconnectedness among financial subsectors during the late 1990s created a strong sense of urgency to unify prudential supervision across the main sectors and a trend to locate this unified supervisor outside the central bank. Unifications in the central bank also occurred during that time, but on a smaller scale.

The pace of change in the institutional structures of microprudential policy increased in the immediate aftermath of the GFC in many countries, especially among those most affected, as part of the effort to increase the effectiveness of prudential oversight. The GFC underscored important coordination benefits of having the bodies for preventing and managing systemic banking crises under the roof of the central bank. This is reflected in a significant increase in the number of countries that have assigned the prudential mandate, for banking as well as for other financial sectors, to the central bank, or that have merged a unified prudential supervisor with the central bank. In a sample of 98 countries, both developed and developing countries, the number with unification of prudential supervision in the central bank increased from seven in 2007 to 17 in 2021, whilst the number of countries having an FSA model increased only by one, from 19. Several additional countries included the supervision of insurance or securities to the banking supervision already in the central banks. Many of these changes appear to be not merely hastily taken political decisions but to have been based on extensive consultations with stakeholders.

The existing empirical evidence, though yet rather limited, finds that the proximity of prudential supervision to the central bank is beneficial for financial stability. There is some evidence that countries with deeper banking sectors could benefit from placing bank supervision in the central bank. Two other panel data analyses found that central bank involvement in supervision improves bank soundness and has mitigating effects on banks' systemic risk measures.

Hosting microprudential supervision in the central bank is not a panacea. Adrian and Narain (2019) report that compliance with Basel Core Principles[18] "failed to improve" since their 2012 revisions, especially on operational independence and appropriate resources, across the board—supervisory structure inside or outside the central bank. Central banks' experience with operational independence, accountability and transparency which rendered monetary policy effective has to be extended to prudential supervisors if they are under the same roof. Clear objectives, appropriate resources, a new robust governance framework to help reduce supervisory forbearance and foster credibility, as well as a proper legal framework to reflect these institutional underpinnings, are paramount to improve the effectiveness of microprudential supervision.

NOTES

1. The views expressed in this chapter are those of the author and do not reflect the views of the World Bank or its affiliated organizations.
2. Lamfalussy (2011, p. 11).
3. Hotori and Wendeschlang (2019). Formalization involves three dimensions: legal basis, a legitimate and empowered supervisory agency, and enforcement on a regular basis.
4. Hotori and Wendschlag (2019).

5. Historically, central banks' *de jure* mandates for financial stability have diverged widely despite their natural role in financial stability (Haltom and Weinberg, 2017).
6. See Masciandaro and Quintyn (2013, footnote 27) for a list of relevant papers.
7. The dataset distinguishes among the following types of institutional structures: sectoral, partial or unified, with banking supervision in or outside the central bank, and "twin peaks" supervisory models.
8. Calvo et al. (2018) also compared supervisory architecture before and after the GFC and found that 11 out of 79 jurisdictions made changes in the supervisory architecture.
9. FSA stands for Financial Supervision Authority, Financial Services Authority or Financial Services Agency.
10. https://www.cb.is/publications/news/news/2020/01/02/Financial-Supervisory-Authority-and-Central-Bank-of-Iceland-merge/
11. A new Bank Law was approved in April 2021 to accommodate this.
12. Baudino et al. (2020).
13. https://www.cmfchile.cl/portal/principal/613/w3-article-30109.html
14. Osiński et al. (2013).
15. Business conduct supervision includes financial consumer protection and market integrity supervision.
16. The sample in the regression analysis is composed of 323 publicly listed banks.
17. Masciandaro and Romelli (2018) provide an index that captures the roles of the central bank in supervising all, some or none of the different financial sectors.
18. This is based on assessments of compliance with the 2012 Basel Core Principles for Effective Banking Supervision under the World Bank-IMF Financial Sector Assessment Programs (FSAPs) during 2013–2017.

REFERENCES

Abrams, R.K. and Taylor, M.W., 2000. Issues in the Unification of Financial Sector Supervision, IMF Working Paper 00/213, Washington, DC.

Adrian, T. and Narain, A., 2019. Let Bank Supervisors Do Their Jobs, IMF Blog, February 13, 2019: https://blogs.imf.org/2019/02/13/let-bank-supervisors-do-their-jobs/

Andrieş, A.M., Podpiera, A.M. and Sprincean, N., 2021. Central Bank Independence and Systemic Risk, in *International Journal of Central Banking*, Volume 18, No 1, March 2022.

Arnone, M. and Gambini, A., 2006. Architectures of Supervisory Authorities and Banking Supervision. In Masciandaro, D. and Quintyn, M. (Eds.), *Designing Financial Supervision Institutions: Independence, Accountability and Governance*. Edward Elgar, Cheltenham.

Barth, J.R., Nolle, D.E., Phumiwasana, T. and Yago, G., 2003. A Cross-Country Analysis of the Bank Supervisory Framework and Bank Performance, in *Financial Markets, Institutions and Instruments*, Volume 12, Issue 2, May 2003.

Baudino, P., Murphy, D. and Svoronos, J.P., 2020. The Banking Crisis in Ireland, BIS Financial Stability Institute, FSI Crisis Management Series No 2, Basel.

Brunnermeier, M., Crocket, A., Goodhart, C., Persaud, A. and Shin, H., 2009. *The Fundamental Principles of Financial Regulation*. International Center for Monetary and Banking Studies Centre for Economic Policy Research, London and Geneva. Print.

Calvo, D., Crisanto, J.C., Hohl, S. and Gutiérrez, O.P., 2018. Financial Supervisory Architecture: What has Changed after the Crisis? FSI Insights on Policy Implementation No 8. Bank for International Settlements, April 2018.

Cihak, M. and Podpiera, R., 2008. Integrated Financial Supervision: Which Model?, in *The North American Journal of Economics and Finance*, Volume 19, Issue 2, August 2008: 135–152.

Claessens, S., 2014. An Overview of Macroprudential Policy Tools, IMF Working Paper 14/214, International Monetary Fund, Washington, DC.

Claessens, S., Del'Ariccia, G., Deniz, I. and Laeven, L., 2010. Lessons and Policy Implications from the Global Financial Crisis, IMF Working Paper 10/44, International Monetary Fund, Washington, DC.

Collard, F., Dellas, H., Diba, B. and Loisel, O., 2017. Optimal Monetary and Prudential Policies, in *American Economic Journal: Macroeconomics*, Volume 9, Issue 1: 40–87.

Danielsson, J., Fouché, M. and Macrae, R., 2015. The Macro-Micro Conflict. VoxEU CEPR Policy Portal: https://voxeu.org/article/macro-micro-conflict

De Grauwe, P., 2007. There is More to Central Banking than Inflation Targeting. VoxEU.org, November 14, 2007.

De Haan, J., Bodea, C., Hicks, R. and Eijffinger, S., 2018. Central Bank Independence Before and After the Crisis, in *Comparative Economic Studies*, Volume 60, Issue 2: 183–202.

Doumpos, M., Gaganis, C. and Pasiouras, F., 2015. Central Bank Independence, Financial Supervision Structure and Bank Soundness: An Empirical Analysis Around the Crisis, in *Journal of Banking & Finance*, Volume 61: S69–S83.

Edge, R.M. and Liang, N., 2019. New Financial Stability Governance Structures and Central Banks, Brookings Institution Hutchins Center Working Paper No. 50, Washington, DC.

Eichengreen, B. and Dincer, N., 2011. Who Should Supervise? The Structure of Bank Supervision and the Performance of the Financial System, NBER Working Paper 17401, National Bureau of Economic Research, Cambridge, MA.

Financial Services Authority, 2009. The Turner Review. A Regulatory Response to the Global Banking Crisis, FSA, London, UK (March).

Godwin, A., Howse, T. and Ramsey, A., 2017. Twin Peaks: South Africa's Financial Sector Regulatory Framework, in *South African Law Journal*, Volume 134, Issue 3: 665–702.

Goodhart, C., 2018. The Bank of England, 1694–2017. In Edvinsson, R., Jacobson, T. and Waldenström, D. (Eds.), *Sveriges Riksbank and the History of Central Banking. Studies in Macroeconomic History.* Cambridge University Press, Cambridge, 143–171.

Goodhart, C. and Schoenmaker, D., 1995. Should the Functions of Monetary Policy and Banking Supervision be Separated?, in *Oxford Economic Papers*, Volume 47: 539–560.

Grossman, R., 2010. The Emergence of Central Banks and Banking Supervision in Comparative Perspective. In Battilossi, S. and Reis, J. (Eds.), *State and Financial Systems in Europe and the USA: Historical Perspectives on Regulation and Supervision in the Nineteenth and Twentieth Centuries.* Ashgate, Aldershot, 123–137.

Group of Thirty, 2008. *The Structure of Financial Supervision. Approaches and Challenges in a Global Marketplace*. Washington, D.C.

Haltom, R. and Weinberg, A.J., 2017. Does the FED have a Financial Stability Mandate?, Economic Brief 17-06, Federal Reserve Bank of Richmond.

Hotori, E. and Wendschlag, M., 2019. The formalization of Banking Supervision in Japan and Sweden, in *Social Science Japan Journal*, Volume 22, Issue 2: 211–228. https://doi.org/10.1093/ssjj/jyz011

Kremers, J., Schoenmaker, D. and Wierts, P., 2003. Cross-Sector Supervision: Which Model? In Herring, R. and Litan, R. (Eds.), *Brookings-Wharton Papers on Financial Services: 2003*. Brookings Institution, Washington, DC.

Lamfalussy, A., 2011. Keynote speech in The Future of Central Banking under Post-crisis Mandates, BIS Papers, No. 55.

Masciandaro, D. and Quintyn, M., 2013. The Evolution of Financial Supervision: The Continuing Search for the Holy Grail, SUERF 50th Anniversary Volume Chapters. In Balling, Morten and Gnan, Ernest (Eds.), *50 Years of Money and Finance: Lessons and Challenges*, SUERF – The European Money and Finance Forum, 263–318.

Masciandaro, D. and Romelli, D., 2018. Central Bankers as Supervisors: Do Crises Matter?, in *European Journal of Political Economy*, Volume 52: 120–140.

Melecky, M. and Podpiera, A.M., 2013. Institutional Structures of Financial Sector Supervision, their Drivers and Historical Benchmarks, in *Journal of Financial Stability*, Volume 9: 428–444.

Melecky, M. and Podpiera, A.M., 2015. Placing Bank Supervision in the Central Bank. Implications for Financial Stability Based on Evidence from the Global Crisis, Policy Research Working Paper 7320, World Bank, Washington, DC.

Osiński, J., Seal, K. and Hoogduin, L., 2013. Macroprudential and Microprudential Policies: Toward Cohabitation, IMF Discussion Note 13/05, Washington, DC.

Reserve Bank of New Zealand, 2018. Safeguarding the Future of our Financial System. Background Paper 2: The Case for and against Separating Prudential Regulation and Supervision from the Reserve Bank of New Zealand, November 2018.

Schoenmaker, D. and Véron, N., 2017. A "Twin Peaks" Vision for Europe, Policy Contribution 30/2017, Bruegel.

World Bank, 2019. *Global Financial Development Report 2019/2020: Bank Regulation and Supervision a Decade after the Global Financial Crisis*. World Bank, Washington, DC. doi:10.1596/978-1-4648-1447-1. License: Creative Commons Attribution CC BY 3.0 IGO

12. Is this time different? Synergies between ECB's tasks

Karin Hobelsberger, Christoffer Kok and Francesco Paolo Mongelli[1]

1. INTRODUCTION

This chapter reviews the EU's and euro area's[2] financial history over the last 15 years, thus spanning three main crises: the Financial Turmoil (FT) in 2007 and subsequent Global Financial Crisis (GFC) in 2008–9, the euro area sovereign debt crisis (SDC) in 2010–12 and the ongoing coronavirus (COVID-19) crisis that started in early in 2020. Each crisis had distinct origins as well as economic, financial and social impacts. All three crises have been accompanied by important reforms of the EU's governance and financial architecture.

In hindsight, prior to the crises the EU had no common financial backstops for sovereigns or banks, and no crisis management and resolution framework for ailing banks. It was constituted of distinct national financial supervisory and regulatory frameworks, characterised by uneven exchange of information and weak coordination of un-harmonised national supervisory practices. Systemic risks to financial stability were not thoroughly taken into account in policy making. Such incomplete financial architecture exposed the EU, especially euro area countries, to adverse feedback loops between the financial system, sovereigns and the real economy that had severe negative implications for economic growth and welfare and repeatedly shook the foundations of the common currency.

In response to such existential challenges, today's financial policy framework is profoundly different than that prior to the crises. The reforms reviewed in this chapter also led to an enlargement of the ECB's tasks and responsibilities, beyond monetary policy, to encompass both micro- and macroprudential powers.[3] On the tail of the two preceding crises, the ongoing COVID-19 coronavirus crisis enables us to assess whether the set of financial reforms have had the intended impact in terms of improving the ability to confront major macro-financial shocks at the EU level.

The aim of this chapter is therefore to investigate whether and how the set of reforms has helped to reduce the sovereign-bank doom-loop, improve the overall resilience and resolvability of the EU banking sector and make it better able to withstand large, unexpected shocks while continuing to finance the real economy. In this chapter, we focus primarily on developments affecting the banking sector, while noting that during the same period major developments within the EU non-bank financial sector were observed.

The chapter is divided into three sections. In the first section, we briefly delineate the key EU financial reforms initiated in the aftermath of the Global Financial Crisis with a focus on the most important changes in the EU's/euro area's financial architecture and governance. In the second part, we compare various financial soundness and fragmentation indicators, analysing developments across the three crisis periods to gauge whether the last crisis was different in terms of the strength and persistence of financial distress. Finally, in the third section we focus specifically on the role of the new financial architecture in the coronavirus (COVID-19) crisis response.

2.   MAIN REGULATORY AND INSTITUTIONAL REFORMS SINCE THE FT AND THE GFC

In this section, we review the most important changes in the EU's/euro area's financial architecture and governance concerning banking supervision and the EU institutional framework.[4]

Main Reforms Connected to Banking Supervision Practices

At a global level, when the FT and the GFC crises struck, the dispersion of financial authorities and the fragmentation of tasks proved a stumbling block that slowed down policy responses. In Europe, the heterogeneity of banking supervisory practices and the regulatory framework helped to spread the financial crisis through a lack of information sharing and the erosion of trust, and it slowed its resolution. It accompanied an *adverse feedback loop* between weak banks, indebted sovereigns and fragile economies (Schoenmaker (2014) and Shambaugh et al. (2012)). Moreover, incentives to cooperate among supervisors remained weak until well into the GFC crisis, despite evident cross-border spillover effects (Cassola et al., 2019). In addition, there were no joint banking resolution procedures, despite some bank mergers and increasing interbank funding across borders (see Dorrucci et al. (2015), Enria (2019, 2021), and various ECB reports on Financial Integration).[5]

Furthermore, while there were already efforts by some central banks to identify and communicate threats to financial stability,[6] more systemic approaches to addressing financial stability concerns were scarce and there was a lack of systematic instruments to address and prevent identified financial stability risks from materialising (see the de Larosière Report, 2009). In retrospect, when the FT and GFC crises hit, it became clear that the Economic and Monetary Union's (EMU) architecture was incomplete. The euro area governance was unable to contain persistent real imbalances and spur national reforms, where needed, and financial market discipline was absent until well into the crisis (Brunnermeier, 2009).

The stress test conducted by the US Federal Reserve in Spring 2009 proved to be key in re-establishing confidence in US financial institutions during the crisis through increased transparency and the forced recapitalisations of banks. It set a precedent and set in motion the conduct of regular EU-wide stress tests coordinated by the Committee of European Banking Supervisors (CEBS) and later, by its successor, the European Banking Authority, and with the strong involvement of the ECB.

During the GFC, this window of opportunity was used to promote several financial reforms. At the global level, the FSB and later the G20 prepared the ground for the Basel Committee to issue, in December 2010, its so-called Basel III accord outlining new bank regulatory capital and liquidity standards. In accordance with the Basel package, the European Council of June 2009 also recommended establishing a 'European Single Rulebook' applicable to all financial institutions in the Single Market.[7] Plans for a new European System of Financial Supervision (EFSF) were launched in June 2009, becoming effective in January 2011. The first pillar of the EFSF is represented by the European Banking Authority (EBA), the European Insurance and Occupational Pensions Authority (EIOPA) and the European Securities and Markets Authority (ESMA). The second pillar of the EFSF is dedicated to macroprudential supervision and is centred on the European Systemic Risk Board (ESRB), which has a mandate to identify systemic risks.

On 29 June 2012, the European Council agreed to create a European banking supervision mechanism and to allow the ESM to recapitalise banks directly. This was the first step towards the banking union, which required a proposal by the European Commission. In September 2012, the latter issued a proposal for a Single Supervisory Mechanism (SSM) for banks in the euro area. The aim was to harmonise banking supervision practices and ensure that single market rules were applied consistently across banks. One year later, on 12 September 2013, the European Parliament voted in favour of creating the SSM at the ECB. In preparation, a Comprehensive Assessment of 130 significant banks' balance sheets was launched in October 2013. It was completed ahead of the SSM assuming its official supervisory role on 1 November 2014.

There were several reasons for conferring supervisory and macroprudential tasks to the ECB (Constâncio (2012) and Angeloni (2017a, 2017b)). As a central bank, the ECB due to its monetary policy function has an intrinsic and deep interest in a stable financial system and a well-developed, strong expertise in financial sector issues. In addition, there is a close relationship between microprudential supervision of individual institutions and the assessments of risks to the financial system, implying that there could be clear synergies in putting the two tasks under the same roof. Furthermore, an argument could be made for the importance of operational independence from political pressure for the effective conduct of supervisory tasks (see Nouy (2015), Beck and Gros (2012), Whelan (2012), and Melecky and Podpiera (2015)). Finally, there were also operational reasons for establishing the SSM at the ECB. The ECB had already built the infrastructure needed to operate the single monetary policy, gained the trust of financial markets, and successfully organised and run a network of Eurosystem technical committees. The ECB and the Eurosystem framework were thus expected and indeed proved to be able to support the rapid deployment of the SSM. There was also a political dimension, as any other option would have required a Treaty change.

On the flipside, by taking direct responsibility for banking supervision the central bank exposes itself to reputational risk that may arise when banks under its supervision run into problems. Also, a conflict of interest between the ECB's different mandates could potentially arise.[8] In order to minimise such conflicts of interest that could give rise to biased policy making, a strict 'separation principle' between the ECB's central bank tasks and its microprudential tasks has been implemented.[9] In other words, there is a clear separation between setting monetary policy, which pursues price stability for the euro area as a whole, and single banking supervision, which focuses on banks' stability.

Already the first few years of the SSM entailed significant microprudential actions including inter alia concerted efforts to reduce non-performing loans (NPLs) in former crisis countries, a gradual removal of existing options and national discretions, the targeted review of internal models (TRIM) from 2016 to 2021 and regular and reinforced stress testing of banks' resilience.

Likewise, euro area macroprudential authorities started introducing various policy measures including the phasing in of G-SIIs/O-SII buffers (Global/Other Systemically Important Institutions) and then in selected jurisdictions systemic risk buffers, countercyclical capital buffers (CCyBs) and various real estate-related borrower-based measures. Reflecting the ECB's new role, national and area-wide macroprudential measures are discussed and coordinated within the Eurosystem's Financial Stability Committee (see Constâncio et al., 2019).

As a reaction to the COVID-19 crisis, the ECB announced a range of mitigating supervisory measures. Specifically, the ECB allowed financial institutions to operate below Pillar 2 Guidance (P2G) levels until at least the end of 2022 and brought forward the use of Tier II and Tier III capital in meeting

Pillar 2 Requirements (P2R). The combined effects of these measures were equivalent to freeing up about €120 billion of CET1 capital that could be used to provide loans to the private sector. The ECB also compelled all euro area banks to suspend dividend payments and equity buybacks in order to avoid the regulatory forbearance to be distributed to shareholders and not be used to build up a capital buffer to provide for the expected significant increase in non-performing loans and other impaired assets. It also encouraged banks to fully implement the transitional IFRS 9 arrangements foreseen in Article 473(a) of the CRR.[10] In addition, macroprudential authorities across the euro area released or reduced more than €20 billion of capital buffer requirements, including the release of countercyclical capital buffers.

Reforms to the EU's Institutional Framework

In response to the GFC, numerous policy measures were deployed across Europe, such as a fiscal loosening via automatic stabilisers, as well as bank rescues in some countries. An important reform to the EU's institutional framework as a response to the GFC includes the easing of the EU's State Aid Rule in October 2008 by the European Commission, which ultimately allowed bank recapitalisations by sovereigns and thereby reassure markets. Moreover, the Stability and Growth Pact was revised and softened, and the Macroeconomic Imbalances Procedures (MIP) were launched.

As a response to the Sovereign Debt Crisis, two temporary sources of financial assistance to countries – subject to conditionality – were established in May 2010: the European Financial Stabilisation Mechanism (EFSM) and the European Financial Stability Facility (EFSF).[11] In December 2010, the European Council agreed to create a permanent mechanism for the provision of financial assistance to countries, whereby the European Stability Mechanism (ESM) took over the tasks of the EFSF.

Additional reforms to strengthen the EU's institutional framework included the 'six-pack' of December 2011, entailing a reform of the Stability and Growth Pact, minimum requirements for national fiscal frameworks and the launch of the macroeconomic imbalance procedure, a 'Fiscal Compact' of March 2012 promoting prudent fiscal behaviour and a 'two-pack' that strengthened coordination and monitoring of budgetary processes.

A few years later, as a response to the COVID-19 crisis, the Commission enabled greater flexibility on State Aid rules in March 2020. In April, the EU Council announced three novel safety nets worth a combined €540 billion which included:

- A Pandemic Crisis Support, to finance emergency healthcare costs related to the pandemic;[12]

- Temporary support to mitigate unemployment risks in an emergency (SURE), to face the incremental expenses of unemployment benefits stemming from the pandemic and lockdown policies; and
- A Guarantee Fund at the European Investment Bank, which would operate as a backup for loan guarantees extended by national development and promotional banks.

Once the full economic and labour market impact of the COVID-19 crisis became clear, the Commission discussed and finally agreed upon the scope of a Next Generation EU (NGEU) in July 2020. It includes the Recovery and Resilience Facility (RRF), funded by debt securities issued directly by the EU plus an increase in the EU's Own Resources.[13] In December 2020, the European Council amended ESM regulations to allow it to be used as backup for bank resolution. Thus, the resolution mechanism now has a financial backup, a further step forward for the Banking Union.[14]

3.   A COMPARISON OF FINANCIAL DEVELOPMENTS DURING THE CRISIS PERIODS

In this section, we focus on several key financial indicators comparing developments across the three crises. We start with market-based indicators of financial stress and financial fragmentation in the euro area, and then focus on bank credit developments in order to assess if and how crisis-induced distress impaired the smooth provision of credit to the real economy.

The CISS indicator[15] (Figure 12.1) and the CDS spreads of euro area banks (Figure 12.2) both signalled severe and persistent stress in the euro area financial sector during both the FT and GFC and the sovereign debt crises. At the same time, while these indicators of financial distress bounced back up in the early stages of the COVID-19 crisis – around March-April 2020 – not long thereafter they returned to more normal levels. This suggests that the concerted mitigating actions by fiscal, monetary and prudential authorities were highly effective.

Two Further Indicators Provide Additional Insights

In line with the above CISS indicator and bank CDS spreads, an indicator of Financial Crisis Probability over the next four quarters (Figure 12.3) rose to levels well below those observed during the GFC during the COVID-19 crisis period. The indicator is based on a standard early-warning logit regression[16] weighing the probability of a financial crisis occurring within the next 12 months. It captures developments in non-financial private sector debt sustain-

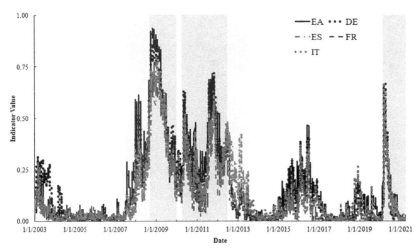

Source: ECB and ECB calculations.

Figure 12.1   The CISS indicator (daily)

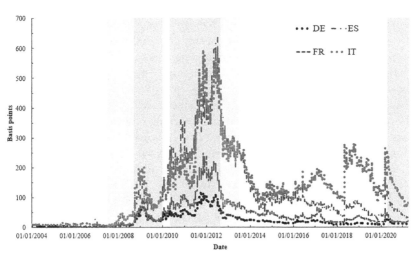

Source: ECB and ECB calculations.

Figure 12.2   Euro area bank CDS spreads (daily basis points)

ability, the real economy and financial markets.[17] However, in contrast with the more instantaneous CISS indicator and bank CDS spreads, the indicator of financial crisis probability remained elevated for the most part of 2020,

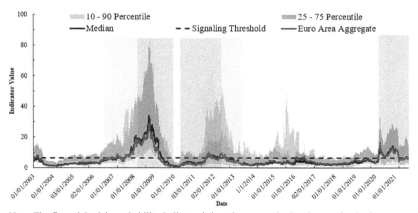

Note: The financial crisis probability indicator is based on a standard early-warning logit regression to assess the probability of a financial crisis occurring within the next 12 months.
Source: ECB and ECB calculations.

Figure 12.3   Financial crisis probability within four quarters (daily index)

returning to normal levels only at the beginning of 2021. The decrease since the beginning of 2021 could possibly be influenced by the brighter economic outlook given the announcement of COVID-19 vaccines at the end of 2020. It is also worth noting that the cross-country growth dispersion was much less pronounced during the COVID-19 crisis compared to the previous two crises.

The Systemic Risk Indicator (d-SRI in Figure 12.4) is a broad-based cyclical indicator, which captures risks stemming from domestic credit, real estate markets, asset prices and external imbalances (see Lang et al., 2019). The d-SRI has been found to have good early warning properties, reflected in the fact that the level of the d-SRI around the start of financial crises is highly correlated with measures of subsequent crisis severity, such as GDP declines. This is particularly evident from the peak levels of the d-SRI just prior to the GFC. By contrast, the d-SRI was relatively low in the period leading up to the COVID-19 crisis, underscoring the fact that this was a health-induced and not a financial crisis. It is notable though that the d-SRI indicator continued its upward trend even during the COVID-19 crisis, though still remaining at relatively moderate levels. Among other things, this may reflect the accommodative policy support measures and associated heightened debt sustainability concerns.

Concerning financial fragmentation, the Price-Based Indicator of Financial Integration (FINTEC, Figure 12.5) has tended to increase during boom times and to decline during periods of financial distress when cross-border financial intermediation is often reduced. This, again, was evident in the high levels

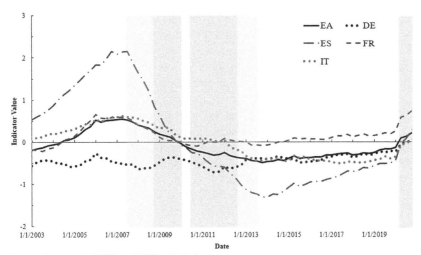

Source: Lang et al. (2019) and ECB calculations.

Figure 12.4   The d-SRI indicator (quarterly)

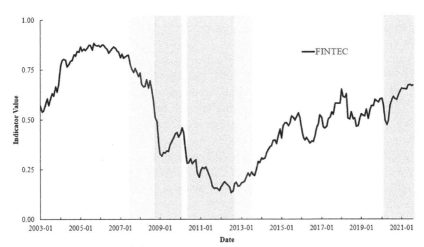

Source: ECB and ECB calculations.

Figure 12.5   The FINTEC indicator (monthly)

observed in the FINTEC indicator in the years leading up to the GFC and in the sharp falls during the subsequent crisis years with the indicator bottoming out in late 2012/early 2013. When the COVID-19 crisis broke out, financial markets in the euro area were immediately put under extraordinary stress, leading to an initial sharp fragmentation.[18] This was also reflected in an immediate sharp decline in the FINTEC indicator, which however was subsequently quick to recover and return to its pre-crisis level.

In terms of what concerns developments in the provision of credit to the real economy during each crisis, some distinct features are likewise notable. Bank credit conditions, as reflected by changes in credit standards (Figure 12.6) and (corporate[19]) loan growth (Figure 12.7), tend to be highly pro-cyclical. Hence, credit standards tend to be loose and loan growth to be strong during boom periods (such as in the run-up to the GFC) and when the crisis hits, and loan growth sharply declines amid tightening credit standards and reduced loan demand (for example during the GFC and the sovereign debt crisis). Notable cross-country heterogeneity was also observed among the major euro area countries with, for instance, pre-crisis loan growth and its subsequent correction during the crisis being particularly strong in Spain (and Ireland).

In recent years, loan growth has been robust, supported by the very accommodative monetary policy measures. Notably, corporate loan growth remained solid and positive (Figure 12.7) even as the COVID-19 crisis unfolded and despite a temporary tightening of credit standards (Figure 12.6). This resilience in lending activity, in spite of the unprecedented negative shock to economic activity in 2020 can be ascribed to the exceptional policy support measures, ranging from further monetary policy accommodation (e.g. PEPP and TLTRO III), various fiscal measures (e.g. state guaranteed loans, moratoria) as well as the relaxation of a number of prudential requirements.

Likewise, with respect to corporate lending rates in the decade since the GFC a gradual decline to historically low levels has been observed in line with the reduction of policy rates and other monetary measures aimed at easing financing conditions (Figure 12.8). At the same time, especially during the sovereign debt crisis, a notable cross-country dispersion was observed, reflecting the differences in sovereign yields spilling over to retail lending rates resulting in particularly high lending rates in the more vulnerable countries.

In the period since late 2012/early 2013 the lending rate dispersion has been gradually reduced in line with the fiscal consolidation in the euro area countries worst affected by the sovereign debt crisis, continued monetary accommodation and the general economic recovery. Notably, however, during the recent COVID-19 crisis the lending rate dispersion across euro area countries remained unchanged compared to pre-crisis levels. Again, this was likely reflecting the effectiveness of the various policy measures to support both banks and their corporate borrowers.

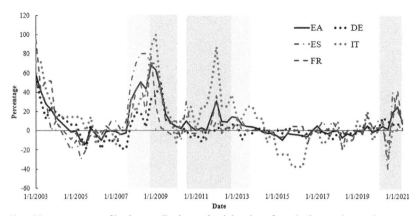

Note: Net percentages of banks contributing to the tightening of standards over the previous three months.
Source: ECB and ECB calculations.

Figure 12.6   Changes in credit standards

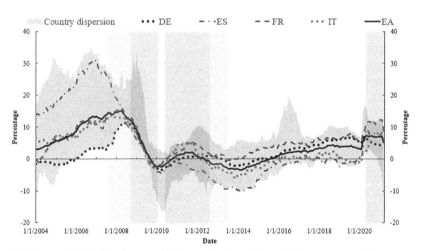

Note: Loans adjusted for sales, securitisation and cash pooling activities, non-seasonally adjusted. The country range is calculated as min/max over a fixed sample of 12 euro area countries.
Source: ECB and ECB calculations.

Figure 12.7   MFI loans to NFCs

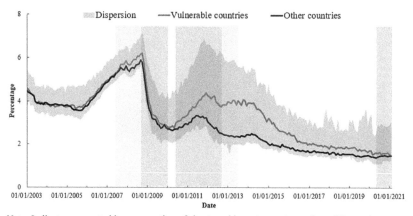

Note: Indicator computed by aggregation of short- and long-term rates, using a 24-month moving average of new business volumes. Vulnerable countries are IE, GR, ES, IT and PT. Other countries are BE, DE, FR, LU, NL, AT and FI. Within each country group, national rates are aggregated using 24-month moving averages of new business volumes as weights. At the beginning of the sample, weights are fixed at the first computable value. The cross-country dispersion displays the min-max range after trimming the two extreme values.
Source: ECB SDW and ECB calculations.

Figure 12.8   MFI lending rates to NFCs

One metric, where a somewhat similar pattern was observed both during the GFC and the COVID-19 crises, is the relative strength of cross-border versus domestic lending to non-financial companies (NFCs) (Figure 12.9). Indeed, cross-border lending is observed to have been increasing relatively strongly in boom periods, only to retract during periods of distress when banks have typically been deleveraging their non-core businesses while shielding domestic lending relationships. This was particularly notable pre-, during and post-GFC. Interestingly, to some extent a similar pattern can be observed during the more recent COVID-19 crisis – even if it may still be too early to draw firm conclusions. The fact that during the COVID-19 crisis domestic lending increased relative to cross-border lending could be related to policy support measures targeting the loan market. Measures, such as state guarantees or loan moratoria, were indeed primarily (if not exclusively) focused on supporting domestic borrowers.

Overall, the simplistic indicator-based analysis presented above seems to suggest that financial distress was significantly more contained and credit provision more resilient in the COVID-19 crisis compared to the two preceding major crisis episodes. At least part of this beneficial outcome can possibly be ascribed to the reformed institutional set-up of European prudential supervision, including the unification of banking supervision with ECB at the centre.

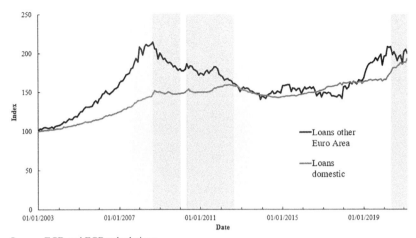

Source: ECB and ECB calculations.

Figure 12.9   MFI loans to NFCs – domestic vs. cross-border

4.   ROLE OF THE NEW FINANCIAL ARCHITECTURE IN THE CORONAVIRUS (COVID-19) CRISIS RESPONSE

This section describes how the combination of micro- and macroprudential measures taken during the COVID-19 crisis complemented simultaneous monetary and fiscal policy responses and herewith achieved a more effective policy mix in the COVID-19 crisis than in previous crisis episodes. Two of the main arguments for creating the Banking Union by setting up the SSM were to create a level playing field for banks and support delinking the nexus between banks and their sovereigns, which had proved to be pernicious during the sovereign debt crisis resulting in a 'doom loop', where distress in banks and/or sovereigns fed upon each other.

The COVID-19 crisis provided a litmus test of the SSM. The speed and concerted way with which these supervisory measures were taken early in the crisis stood in sharp contrast with the experiences from the previous crises (GFC and sovereign debt crisis), and significantly contributed to reducing the risks of financial fragmentation and avoiding the credit crunch experienced in those previous crises.

A clear indication that the EU's new financial architecture, underpinned by the Banking Union in particular but obviously also the extensive monetary policy accommodation, has helped break the link between bank funding costs and those of their sovereign is depicted in Figure 12.10. It is observed that the

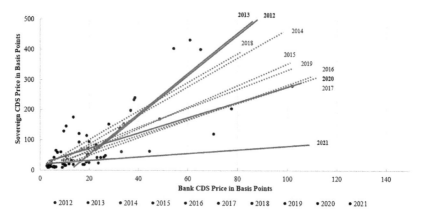

Note: X-axis: bank CDS spreads; y-axis: sovereign CDS spreads; in basis points. Banks' CDS prices are shown as value-weighted averages per country and year for the list of Significant Institutions, directly supervised by the Single Supervisory Mechanism, as published in May 2021). The dotted lines reflect the trend line for each year.
Source: ECB and ECB calculations.

Figure 12.10   CDS spreads of banks and sovereigns in the SSM area – by year (daily basis points)

relationship between bank and sovereign CDS spreads over time has become much less pronounced since 2015. This evidence speaks in favour of an effective conduct of the ECB's supervisory tasks and its operational independence from political pressure, as had been one of the goals and arguments for establishing microprudential supervision at the central bank.

While this does not allow us to draw firm conclusions regarding causality, it does seem to corroborate the empirical findings by Altavilla et al. (2020) suggesting that supranational banking supervision reduces excessive risk taking by banks. In the same vein, as argued by Ampudia et al. (2019), a large central supervisor can take advantage of economies of scale and scope in supervision and gain a broader perspective on the stability of the entire banking sector, which should result in improved financial stability (see also Maddaloni and Scopelliti, 2019).

Therefore, the novel centralised structure for banking supervision (SSM) entails significant benefits in terms of fewer opportunities for supervisory arbitrage by banks and less informational asymmetry, which may in turn have led to greater supervisory scrutiny and intrusiveness entailing a more differentiated pricing of bank CDS (see also Georgescu et al. (2017) and Kok et al. (2021)). Furthermore, both the ECB's 2020 Vulnerability Analysis and the EBA/SSM 2021 stress test confirmed that the large majority of euro area

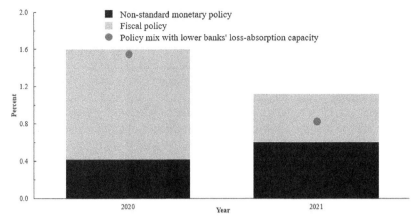

Note: The illustrative fiscal policy response abstracts from the effect of automatic stabilisers and off-budget items such as state guarantees on loans. The policy mix simulation with lower bank loss-absorption capacity evaluates the same fiscal and non-standard monetary policy measures but assumes tighter bank capital constraints so that banks would resist any temporary decline in net interest income through less accommodative lending policies.
Source: Darracq Pariès et al. (2020), box in the May 2020 ECB Financial Stability Review. Simulations based on Darracq Pariès et al. (2011, DKR model).

Figure 12.11   Model-projected real GDP growth (percentage point deviation from the baseline)

banks is resilient to even very severe adverse scenarios capturing uncertainties surrounding the COVID-19 pandemic (ECB, 2020, 2021).

A crucial feature of the response to the COVID-19 crisis was the rapid deployment of policy responses. The timely fiscal easing supported households' and firms' incomes, while central bank asset purchase and liquidity operations eased financing conditions for all economic agents. For example, the combined impact of a debt-financed fiscal impulse and central bank asset purchases could, according to model simulations by Darracq Pariès et al. (2020), support real GDP by 2.7 percentage points in 2020–1 (see Figure 12.11).[20]

However, the financial policy relief measures would help attenuate the economic impact of the pandemic by reducing pro-cyclicality. Altavilla et al. (2020) provide empirical evidence that the prudential measures stimulated lending and thus supported the monetary policy stimulus.[21] Combining the effects of the announced prudential capital relief measures, the measures to retain capital through dividend restrictions and the relaxation of IFRS 9 accounting rules, model-based simulations by Darracq Pariès et al. (2020) suggest that prudential policy in parallel reinforced the transmission of fiscal and monetary actions. Without the relief measures described above, banks' ability or willingness to absorb losses without constraining credit would be significantly lower.

With tighter bank capital constraints, the same fiscal and non-standard monetary measures might have yielded a smaller expansionary effect, notably in 2021 as banks would react to the downward pressures on their net interest income stemming from the central bank asset purchases and loan moratoria (see Figure 12.11). In the same vein, model simulations by Rancoita et al. (2020) indicate that the contributions of prudential policies are more evident in Spain and Italy where banks' management buffers[22] were relatively smaller and would have been eroded by more losses as the pandemic had a stronger economic impact, and smaller alternative mitigating measures such as direct support, tax deferrals and short-time working schemes were in place.

5.   CONCLUDING REMARKS AND DIRECTION FOR FURTHER RESEARCH

This chapter has tracked the main regulatory and supervisory reforms in the EU and the euro area vis-à-vis the unfolding of three crises: explicitly, the Financial Turmoil in mid-2007 and the 2008 GFC, the sovereign debt crisis of the euro area in 2010–12, and the ongoing COVID-19 crisis that started in early 2020. Briefly, some of the most important financial reforms include the Single Regulatory Framework (Single Rule Book), the implementation of Basel III in Europe, the establishment of the European System of Financial Supervision (ESFS), and ultimately the banking union with the Single Supervisory Mechanism (SSM) and the Single Resolution Board (SRB) and eventually a European Deposit Insurance Scheme (EDIS).

Against the backdrop of the changing financial landscape, we compared the three crises in terms of their severity and duration of financial distress, as well as bank credit developments. One overarching lesson is that it proved to be a good idea to establish microprudential supervision at the ECB by setting up the SSM. Yet, this would provide only part of the picture as the path towards the Banking Union was supported by institutional innovations as well as governance changes from mid-2007 onwards. These reforms also led to an enlargement of the ECB's tasks and responsibilities, beyond monetary policy, to encompass also shared macroprudential powers. Since early 2020, we also witnessed timely fiscal easing that supported households' and firms' incomes, while central bank asset purchase and liquidity operations eased financing conditions for all economic agents.

In the second part of the chapter, we have shown how these reforms and combined policies helped taper the sovereign-bank doom-loop, improve the overall resilience and resolvability of the EU banking sector and make it better able to withstand the ongoing large shocks while continuing to finance the real economy. The advancement in governance and financial architecture in the EU and the euro area enabled policy makers and regulators to counter the COVID-19 crisis with a swift and concerted crisis response. Information-related synergies between the ECB's mandates (in full respect of the strict 'separation principle') enabled it to counter the crisis with a coordinated, mutually-reinforcing, concerted and ultimately effective crisis response regarding both roles of the ECB.

NOTES

1. For their technical support and assistance we would like to thank Jan Hannes Lang, Marco Lo Duca, Marco Forletta, Richard James Sparkes, Marc Agustí I Torres and Laurent Abraham. For their comments and suggestions we would also like to thank: Teresa Messner, Marco Lo Duca and Luc Laeven. We accept full responsibility for any errors or omissions; the views expressed are our own and do not necessarily reflect those of the ECB.
2. For simplicity, we will be referring to the EU throughout most of the chapter, while noting that many of the developments we describe are related specifically to the euro area.
3. Financial reforms should also be seen against the backdrop of changes to the broader EU/euro area governance, including, but not limited to, the adoption of a financial backstop and a crisis management and resolution framework (European Stability Mechanism (ESM) backed by Outright Monetary Transactions (OMT) commitment), and a revised Stability and Growth Pact. Obviously, the implementation of various unconventional monetary policy measures by the ECB and other EU central banks also contributed in a major way to bolstering the crisis response capabilities at the aggregate EU/euro area level.
4. For an account of the ECB monetary policy actions during this period, see Hartmann and Smets (2018), Rostagno et al. (2019) and Rostagno et al. (2021).
5. Against this background, some – most prominently, Padoa-Schioppa (2003, 2006, 2007) – had argued that the EMU should be complemented by joint banking supervision.
6. For instance, the ECB has published a semi-annual Financial Stability Review since 2004.
7. Its three main pillars are: the Capital Requirements Directive IV (CRD IV) and Capital Requirements Regulation (CRR), implementing Basel III in the EU, and the Bank recovery and Resolution Directive (BRRD). The CRD IV and CRR address the problem of insufficient capitalisation of banks; the amended directive on Deposit Guarantee Schemes (DGS) endorsed the broadly agreed deposit guarantee of up to €100,000; the BRRD introduced a 'bail-in' mechanism.
8. For instance, a situation where the central bank would fear that an increase in microprudential capital requirements could hamper economic growth and the inflation outlook might induce it to take a more lenient supervisory stance. Vice versa there could be circumstances where if a number of banks would face solvency or liquidity problems this might induce the central bank to adopt a more accommodative monetary policy than would otherwise be the case.

9. Article 25(4) of the SSM Regulation requires the ECB to ensure that the operation of the Governing Council is completely differentiated with regard to monetary and supervisory functions. Such differentiation includes strict separation of meetings and agendas (see also Cassola et al., 2019).
10. On the regulatory side targeted revisions to the Capital Requirements Regulation (CRR) known as the 'quick fix' were published on 26 June. The revisions provide further flexibility to banks in responding to the challenging situation.
11. The EFSM was an intergovernmental agreement with a maximum lending capacity of €60 billion.
12. This is an ESM facility with no macro conditionality.
13. The NGEU is also to be linked with the Multiannual Financial Framework for 2021–7. The aim is to support EU countries' plans to recover, repair and emerge stronger from the pandemic while accelerating the Digital and Green Transitions.
14. For what concerns the third pillar – the common deposit insurance scheme – progress is still slow (Council of the European Union (2020, 2021) and Enria (2021)).
15. The CISS aims to measure the current state of instability in the financial system as a whole or, equivalently, the level of 'systemic stress' (see Kremer et al. (2012) and Hoffmann et al. (2019)).
16. The logit model is estimated on quarterly country-level data starting in 1990, covering the 19 euro area countries plus Denmark, Sweden and the UK. The logit model uses as the left-hand-side variable a vulnerability indicator that is equal to 1 during the four quarters ahead of past systemic financial crises. It is set to missing during actual crisis episodes and set to zero otherwise. The identification of systemic financial crises is based on the ECB/ESRB crisis database described in Lo Duca et al. (2017).
17. The variables used in the logit model are the annual change in the non-financial private sector debt service ratio, the European Commission consumer confidence indicator, the annual growth of equity prices, the realised equity price volatility over the last month, and the risk-free yield curve slope.
18. Between February and April 2020, the daily version of this indicator posted the second most severe drop during the 2007–21 period, see Borgioli et al. (2020).
19. Here we focus on corporate credit provision. However, developments with respect to credit to households displayed broadly similar patterns.
20. Note that this fiscal policy response neither includes the effects of automatic stabilisers nor off-budget measures, such as the various state guarantee schemes and equity injections.
21. Altavilla et al. (2020) find that the combined funding cost relief from the TLTROs and the capital relief from the prudential relaxation measures 'bears the potential to forestall an employment decline in the corporate sector over the next 2 years of 1:4%, equivalent to more than 1 million workers'.
22. The voluntary capital that banks hold on top of regulatory and prudential requirements.

REFERENCES

Altavilla, C., F. Barbiero, M. Boucinha and L. Burlon. 2020. The great lockdown: pandemic response policies and bank lending conditions, ECB Working Paper Series 2465.

Altavilla, C., M. Boucinha, J.L. Peydro and F. Smets. 2020. Banking supervision, monetary policy and risk-taking: big data evidence from 15 credit registers, ECB Working Paper 2349.

Ampudia, M., T. Beck, A. Beyer, J.-E. Colliard, A. Leonello, A. Maddaloni and D. Marques Ibanez. 2019. The architecture of supervision, ECB Working Paper 2287.

Angeloni, I. 2017a. 60 years on: promoting European integration in the banking union. Speech at the Università Bocconi, Milan, 24 March.

Angeloni, I. 2017b. Faraway or close? Supervisors and central bankers. Speech at the Halle Institute for Economic Research (IWH), Halle, 2 February.

Beck, G. and D. Gros. 2012. Monetary policy and banking supervision: coordination instead of separation, in *Monetary Policy and Banking Supervision, Monetary Dialogue*, December 2012, European Parliament.

Borgioli, S., C.W. Horn, U. Kochanska, P. Molitor and F.P. Mongelli. 2020. European financial integration during the COVID-19 crisis, ECB Economic Bulletin article, available at: https://www.ecb.europa.eu/pub/economic-bulletin/articles/2020/html/ecb.ebart202007_02~b27e8089c5.en.html

Brunnermeier, M.K. 2009. Deciphering the liquidity and credit crunch 2007–2008, *Journal of Economic Perspectives* 23(1), 77–100.

Cassola, N., C. Kok and F.P. Mongelli. 2019. The ECB after the crisis: existing synergies among monetary policy, macroprudential policies and banking supervision, ECB Occasional Paper 237.

Constâncio, V. 2012. Towards a European Banking Union. Lecture held at the Duisenberg School of Finance, Amsterdam, 7 September.

Constâncio, V., I. Cabral, C. Detken, J. Fell, J. Henry, P. Hiebert, S. Kapadia, S. Nicoletti Altimari, F. Pires and C. Salleo. 2019. Macroprudential policy at the ECB: institutional framework, strategy, analytical tools and policies, ECB Occasional Paper 227.

Council of the European Union. 2020. Statement of the Euro Summit in inclusive format, 11 December.

Council of the European Union. 2021. Remarks by Paschal Donohoe following the Eurogroup meeting of 17 June 2021.

Darracq Pariès, M., C. Kok and D. Rodriguez Palenzuela. 2011. Macroeconomic propagation under different regulatory regimes: evidence from a DSGE model for the euro area, *International Journal of Central Banking* 7.

Darracq Pariès, M., C. Kok and E. Rancoita. 2020. Macroeconomic impact of financial policy measures and synergies with other policies, box in the ECB Financial Stability Review, May.

Dorrucci E., D. Ioannou, F.P. Mongelli and A. Terzi. 2015. The four unions 'Pie' on the Monetary Union 'Cherry': a new index of European Institutional Integration, ECB Occasional Paper 160.

ECB. 2020. COVID-19 Vulnerability Analysis Results overview, ECB presentation of 28 July, available at: https://www.bankingsupervision.europa.eu/press/pr/date/2020/html/ssm.pr200728_annex~d36d893ca2.en.pdf?731039993a2a10392e3b7679d1669fb5

ECB. 2021. SSM-wide stress test 2021 – Final results, ECB presentation of 30 July, available at: https://www.bankingsupervision.europa.eu/press/pr/date/2021/html/ssm.pr210730_aggregate_results~5a1c5fb6bd.en.pdf?92e99add0bcf42344f5c4ec1e9913892

Enria, A. 2019. Foreword by A. Enria, in Bassani, G. 2019. *The Legal Framework Applicable to the Single Supervisory Mechanism: Tapestry or Patchwork?*, Alphen aan den Rjin: Wolters Kluwer.

Enria, A. 2021. How can we make the most of an incomplete banking union. Speech at the Eurifo Financial Forum, 9 September.

Georgescu, O., M. Gross, D. Kapp and C. Kok. 2017. Do stress tests matter? Evidence from the 2014 and 2016 stress tests, ECB Working Paper 2054.

Hartmann, P. and F. Smets. 2018. The first twenty years of the European Central Bank: monetary policy, ECB Working Paper 2219.

Hoffmann, P., M. Kremer and S. Zaharia. 2019. Financial integration in Europe through the lens of composite indicators, ECB Working Paper 2319.

Kok, C., C. Muller, S. Ongena and C. Pancaro. 2021. The disciplining effects of supervisory scrutiny in the EU-wide stress tests, ECB Working Paper 2551.

Kremer, M., Lo Duca, M. and Holló, D. 2012. CISS – a composite indicator of systemic stress in the financial system, ECB Working Paper 1426.

Lang, J.H., C. Izzo, S. Fahr and J. Ruzicka. 2019. Anticipating the bust: a new cyclical systemic risk indicator to assess the likelihood and severity of financial crises, ECB Occasional Paper 219.

Lo Duca, M., Koban, A., Basten, M., Bengtsson, E., Klaus, B., Kusmierczyk, P., Lang, J.H., Detken, C. and Peltonen, T.A. 2017. A new database for financial crises in European countries, ECB Occasional Paper 194.

Maddaloni, A. and A.D. Scopelliti. 2019. Rules and discretion(s) in prudential regulation and supervision: evidence from EU banks in the run-up to the crisis, ECB Working Paper 2284.

Melecky, M. and A.M. Podpiera. 2015. Placing bank supervision in the central bank; implications for financial stability based on evidence from the global crisis, World Bank Policy Research Working Paper 7320.

Nouy, D. 2015. Stable financial markets, stable Europe. Speech at the Economic Council, Berlin, 9 June.

Padoa-Schioppa, T. 2003. Central banks and financial stability: exploring a land in between, in V. Gaspar, P. Hartmann and O. Sleijpen (eds), *The Transformation of the European Financial System. Second ECB Central Banking Conference*, Frankfurt am Main: European Central Bank, 269–310.

Padoa-Schioppa, T. 2006. Intervento del Ministro dell'Economia e delle Finanze, Tommaso Padoa-Schioppa, alla celebrazione del ventesimo anniversario della scomparsa di Altiero Spinelli. Speech at an event to mark the 20th anniversary of Altiero Spinelli's death, Ventotene, 21 May.

Padoa-Schioppa, T. 2007. Europe needs a single financial rulebook, *Financial Times*, December.

Rancoita, E., M. Grodzicki, H.S. Hempell, C. Kok, J. Metzler and A. Prapiestis. 2020. Financial stability considerations arising from the interaction of coronavirus-related policy measures. Special feature in the November 2020 ECB Financial Stability Review.

Rostagno, M., C. Altavilla, G. Carboni, W. Lemke, R. Motto, A. Saint Guilhem and J. Yiangou. 2019. A tale of two decades: the ECB's monetary policy at 20, ECB Working Paper 2346.

Rostagno, M., C. Altavilla, G. Carboni, W. Lemke, R. Motto, R. and A. Saint Guilhem. 2021. Combining negative interest rates, forward guidance and asset purchases: identification and impacts of the ECB's unconventional policies, ECB Working Paper 2564.

Schoenmaker, D. (ed.). 2014. *Macroprudentialism*, London: CEPR Press.

Shambaugh, J.C., R. Reis and H. Rey. 2012. The Euro's three crises, *Brookings Papers on Economic Activity* 2, Spring, 157–231.

The de Larosière Group. 2009. de Larosière Report, High-level Group on financial Supervision in the EU, chaired by Jacques de Larosière, Brussels, 25 February.

Whelan, K. 2012. Should monetary policy be separated from banking supervision?, in *Monetary Policy and Banking Supervision, Monetary Dialogue*, December 2012, European Parliament.

13. Money, supervision, and financial stability: a money-credit constitution entrusted to independent but constrained central banks

Paul Tucker

> I insist that neither monetary policy nor the financial system will be well served if
> a central bank loses interest in, or influence over, the financial system.
> Paul Volcker, 1990

Paul Volcker's words, delivered just a few years after retiring from the Federal Reserve, combined wisdom with prophecy. In the years leading up to the 2007–9 Great Financial Crisis, there were two dominant international financial centres. In one, the Federal Reserve had lost interest in the financial system. In the other, the Bank of England had been stripped of its regulatory powers. Chaos ensued.

This chapter is about why Volcker was right, and what that means for central banks in constitutional democracies.[1]

1. INTEREST: MONETARY STABILITY AND FINANCIAL STABILITY ARE INTRINSICALLY CONNECTED

Volcker's two concerns are obviously distinct. It does not follow that a public authority should have a formal role (meaning powers of direction or constraint) merely because it has an interest in a particular field. Monetary policy makers have a clear interest in the structure of labour markets and, more generally, the supply side of the economy, but no one argues central banks should be responsible for such policies. Volcker's normative stipulation must, then, rest on something special about the nature of central banks' interest in the financial system. That stems, essentially, from the place of banking in the monetary system, and that of central banks in the banking system.

1.1   Fractional-reserve Banking: Private Liquidity Insurance and Money Creation

We live in a world with both state money creation and private money creation. This takes the state out of credit allocation but lands it with the problem of preserving financial stability.[2]

A banking system provides liquidity insurance to the rest of the economy. Banks do this by allowing customers to withdraw deposits on demand, and to draw down committed lines of credit on demand. Their capacity to provide this liquidity insurance stems from their deposit liabilities being treated by people and businesses as money: meaning instruments regarded by holders as so safe, there is no need to monitor information about banks' creditworthiness (known to economists as information insensitivity: Holmstrom, 2015).

When a bank makes a loan, it simply credits its customer's deposit account, expanding the supply of money. Even if the deposit is immediately transferred to another bank, the monetary liabilities of the system as a whole expand. *Banks are monetary institutions.* In fact, most of the money in today's economies is the deposit money issued by private banks, known as 'broad money'.

This is not a riskless business. It is known to economists as *fractional-reserve banking* and, for once, the jargon conveys something important. While commercial banks undertake to repay deposits on demand, they employ *only a small fraction* of those deposits in truly low-risk, liquid assets (of which the lowest risk and most liquid are balances with the central bank, known as *reserves*). Most of their assets comprise illiquid loans to risky borrowers. In other words, banks transform portfolios of risky assets into (apparently) safe deposit liabilities.

The resulting balance-sheet structure is inherently fragile. If a bank is faced with a surge of withdrawals, it may have to sell assets at discounted prices – either because it is straining the liquidity of the markets for those instruments or because it is treated as a forced seller. Suffering a loss on the sale will impair the bank's net worth (solvency), reducing the security of its remaining liabilities. There is, in consequence, a first-come-first-served incentive for customers to draw on their liquidity insurance before it is too late. Such runs will tend to afflict not only unsound banks, but also any sound bank that is liable to be rendered insolvent *ex post* by the fire sales necessary to meet withdrawals, in what amounts to a self-fulfilling panic (broadly captured in Diamond and Dybvig, 1983).

As well as hurting those depositors who get stuck when the doors close, liquidity crises have much wider social costs. The afflicted part of the banking system loses its capacity to make loans to businesses and households once its deposits are no longer accepted as money. If the crisis is widespread, other parts of the banking system might not be able to substitute seamlessly or might themselves be pulled into the vortex through direct losses and contagion. As credit supply tightens, economic activity contracts, causing more people to default on loans, and so fuelling the incentive to run on banks.

All of which is to say that we live in a world in which payments and loans – and, therefore, the *monetary system* and the *credit system* – are inextricably intertwined, surviving or falling together. So, there can be no doubting central banks have an interest in banking stability.

This highlights the significance of their apparently humdrum but core operational role, as banker to the banks. Banks settle claims amongst themselves across the central bank's books, in its money, the economy's final settlement asset, essentially to remove the involuntarily counterparty credit exposures they would otherwise incur, and so reduce one source of systemic fragility. Echoing the words of Francis Baring over two centuries ago, this makes central banks the pivot of the money-credit system: the liquidity *re*-insurer for the banking system, and thus for the economy as a whole (Baring, 1797).

1.2   The Two Components of Monetary System Stability: From Interest to Influence

Monetary policy and financial stability are not separate fields. Better to think of the goal as being *monetary system stability*, with two components:

- stability in the value of central bank money in terms of goods and services; and also
- stability of private-banking system deposit money (and any other 'safe assets') in terms of central bank money.[3]

Articulating that broad account of monetary system stability is, however, insufficient to carry us as far as Volcker's institutional prescription. A monetary policy organization (and its political principals) might think it can rely on an arms-length regulator to ensure banking-system stability, money-market efficiency, and so on. In fact, as the system's pivot central banks can hardly avoid a functional role of the kind Volcker entertained.

A central bank must accommodate sudden shifts in the demand for its money if it is to avoid inadvertent restraint on economic activity. Runs on the banking system – people demanding their deposits be redeemed in cash, now – are one of the more dramatic manifestations of increased demand for central bank money. If a bank does not hold sufficient central bank money (or assets that can be converted into central bank money via the market) to meet its customers' demand for cash, it will fail unless it can go to the central bank and exchange illiquid assets for cash. In agreeing to lend, the central bank is doing two things at the same time. It is stabilizing banking by acting as a lender of last resort, and it is ensuring that the liquidity crunch does not interfere with the course of monetary policy. In other words, the missions of preserving banking stability and price stability are intimately intertwined not only for society but for the central banks themselves in their most elemental function: creating money on demand.

That being so, central banks, as lenders of last resort, have more than a mere interest in stability. They need to be able to influence those elements of the financial system's regulation and supervision that materially affect its resilience. At the most basic level, when they lend, they want to get their money back! They need to be able to judge which banks (and possibly near-banks) should get access to liquidity, and on what terms. Even proponents of narrow conceptions of central banking generally accept that, as the lender of last resort, the central bank cannot avoid inspecting banks that want to borrow. Events in the UK in 2007 demonstrated that doing so from a standing-start is hazardous for society. A central bank must be in a position to track the health of individual banks during peacetime if it is to be equipped to act as the liquidity cavalry, and to judge how its monetary decisions will be transmitted through the economy.

1.3   Not Merely Influence but Formalized Powers and Responsibilities: Accountability under Constitutional Democracy

In some jurisdictions, this practical need to know about banking and banks is reflected in a set-up where the central bank conducts inspections of banks but does not take *formal* regulatory decisions. I once asked former Bundesbank President Helmut Schlesinger why he publicly maintained that central banks should not be the bank supervisor when, as a matter of brute fact, many Buba staff were engaged on bank supervision. The response was that as the central bank was not formally responsible or accountable, banking problems would not infect the Bundesbank's reputation and standing as a monetary authority (viz. Dombret, 2014).

It is an odd perspective. In many constitutional democracies, the central bank could not escape censure over a banking crisis by saying that it was only one of a number of *de facto* supervisors, not the *de jure* regulator. Some of our deepest political values demand that *if* central banks are to be involved materially in supervision, their role should be formalized so that it is clear what they are expected to deliver and can be held accountable for. Otherwise, we are ruled by the unaccountable.

Much the same follows even if the central bank plays no role – *de facto* as well as *de jure* – in supervision. Given the lender of last resort is pretty well certain to find itself at the scene of any financial disaster, societies typically expect their central bank to give an account of how things could have come to such a pretty pass. After the collapse of Northern Rock in 2007, the front cover of the British edition of the *Economist* magazine was a photograph of the then Governor of the Bank of England under the headline 'The bank that failed' (*Economist*, 20 September 2007). Not, note, a tryptic of central banker, separate regulator, and finance minister – the members of the UK's then non-statutory Tripartite Committee for stability – but the first only. Even in a set-up where supervision and regulation were formally and practically at arm's length, the central bank could not, when it mattered most, insulate its reputation as a monetary authority from prudential problems, as some in the UK and elsewhere had (fancifully) argued would be possible. Responsibility without power is as unattractive – and can be almost as bad for society as the converse.

So, we arrive at constitutional republics needing formally to give their central banks a formal role in supervision and regulation. Something like that used to be orthodoxy at central banking's summit. After becoming sidelined during central banking's cultural revolution of the 1990s, it is now restored – for the time being.[4]

2.   FROM INFLUENCE TO INSULATION: TRUSTEES FOR MONETARY-SYSTEM STABILITY

This leaves an awkward question. Arguing that central banks warrant some kind of formal role in stability policy is not the same as establishing that they should be insulated from day-to-day politics – independent – in pursuing those responsibilities.

It is sometimes argued, including occasionally by central bankers, that a multiple-mission central bank could properly be granted different degrees of independence in different fields.[5] While technically feasible, that would put monetary independence at risk. If politicians held formal levers over some of a central bank's policy instruments and powers, they would be sorely tempted to use them as informal bargaining chips over monetary policy. That's just how the world works, and it is a mistake to pretend otherwise.

If that is broadly right, it matters whether independence in the supervisory role can be grounded. I believe it can be, but on condition that the role is constrained in various ways.

2.1 One Argument for an Independent Stability Supervisor: Credible Commitment

It is surely uncontentious that booms in the supply of credit and asset prices can be deeply alluring once underway. A political decision-maker would be tempted to substitute their own interests (re-election, popularity) for the country's interests. That might involve allowing a potentially destabilizing credit boom to persist in order to harness the 'feel-good factor' or, more subtly, shading policy to serve political backers and constituents.

That is a classic problem of credible commitment: society would like to tie itself to the mast of stability but finds it difficult to do so. This is the standard argument for handing the reins to an independent *trustee-type* agency.

This, it must be stressed, demonstrates only that independent central banks cannot sensibly be excluded (or exclude themselves) from responsibility for banking stability, not that they have a unique claim to regulatory/supervisory powers. If, however, the central bank and the lead stability authority are separate, they need to co-operate to an unusually high degree. Information flows would need to be frictionless. That is more easily stipulated and promised than secured. For individual bureaucrats, clashes that can be painted as 'turf wars' can be highly damaging, leaving underlap as an institutional equilibrium that suits the private interests of those concerned. For society, meanwhile, underlap can be a lot more damaging than overlap. The world discovered exactly that in London, Washington DC and elsewhere when the 2007/8 crisis broke.[6]

3. CONDITIONS AND CONSTRAINTS

What, then, of constraints? They are needed to ensure that unelected power does not escape the people's control or undermine our deepest political values. Just a few will be sketched here.

3.1 Insulation From Politics: Fiscal Risks Must be Bracketed Away

A precondition for formal independence being credible is that elected politicians do not have to get involved in day-to-day matters. But given the fiscal and other costs of crises, that is exactly what happens when preventative measures fail and all that remains is a choice between the abyss and taxpayer rescue. A necessary condition for insulating stability policy is, therefore, that there exists a credible regime and credible plans for resolving fundamentally broken firms in a tolerably orderly way without taxpayer solvency support.[7]

Interestingly, that also addresses one of the most frequently advanced arguments against central banks acting as supervisors. As summarized by Steve Cecchetti, who favours the dual role (Cecchetti, 2007):

> The most compelling argument for separation is the potential for conflict of interest … The central bank will protect banks rather than the public interest. Making banks look bad makes supervisors look bad. So, allowing banks to fail would affect the central banker-supervisor's reputation.

Effective resolution regimes are, then, vital to liberating supervisors from fear of failing banks, and monetary policy makers from any temptation to soften policy in order to bail out their supervisory colleagues. Given the reforms to resolution regimes over recent years, I am going to assume here that they are sufficiently credible for independent central banks not to be ruled out as supervisors.[8]

3.2   Mandates that Should NOT be Given to Independent Central Banks

Secondly, in order to ensure focus and avoid unnecessary powers in one unelected agency, central banks should *not* be responsible for:

- competition policy, which would make them more powerful than they need to be;
- the structure of the financial-services industry, as it involves high-level trade-offs between efficiency and resilience;
- its external competiveness, as that invites political pressure to relax resilience standards and adopt 'light touch regulation';
- sponsoring the industry's interests in government or in society, which would be liable to lead to capture by sectoral interests and so to lower resilience than desired;
- consumer protection, which would confuse the public about the nature of a broader stability mandate, as well as taking most central bankers beyond their comfort zone and vocational drive;
- market regulation, as it unavoidably incorporates consumer protection and, separately, would make central banks too powerful.

3.3   Objective: A Standard for System Resilience

An unelected but independent policy body needs to be set an objective that can be understood, and which is monitorable. An objective that is complex, vague, or otherwise not monitorable leaves the trustee for stability in a position to mark its own work, a set-up where it is liable to maintain that everything is going well until it is too late.

Given the public policy purpose of stability policy, this objective should be framed as a *standard for resilience*: just how much stress should the system, and key intermediaries within it, be able to withstand. In democracies, that standard needs to be set by elected politicians – the legislature – as a political society's tolerance for crisis is not at root technocratic; financial crises could be eliminated by suppressing financial intermediation, but if taken too far that might constrain economic dynamism and allocative efficiency. Stress testing could be used to help legislators articulate such a standard, but that would require them to move away from using scenarios the banks 'pass', enabling central banks to declare victory when no such thing is achieved.

A central bank with a system-resilience objective should be constrained from getting into regional or sectoral policy, or from intervening in order to reallocate resources or change the distribution of income and wealth; we elect governments to do that precisely because there is no deep consensus on distributional questions. Plainly there are sometimes particular hot spots in property and other markets, but they should not concern an independent central bank unless the resilience of the system as a whole is threatened.

These constraints matter because politicians will want to shift lots of things to unelected technocrats in order to avoid responsibility themselves, free up their time, and so on. Central bankers need to exercise self-restraint.

4. MICRO- AND MACROPRUDENTIAL SUPERVISION

Up to this point, a distinction has not been drawn between regulation and supervision, nor between micro- and macroprudential endeavours. Here we confront another intrinsic feature of finance: its capacity to avoid or evade any set of static rules.

4.1 Supervision as Well as Regulation: System Resilience as a Common Good Plagued by Hidden-action Problems

The financial system's resilience can be thought of as a *common good*: the benefits accrue to everyone but can be eroded by individual members of the system. Each intermediary has incentives to take more risks than they would willingly incur if the system were not believed to be resilient. So long as they are not spotted, they will be undercharged for risk by their customers and market counterparties. In other words, it is hard for individual firms to remain prudent. If, however, many firms succumb, in aggregate some of the resilience of the system as a whole is eroded, invalidating the assumption upon which their private risk appetites were predicated. This is an example of the *problem of the commons*, where historically individuals would overuse the common grazing land, leaving everybody worse off (Ostrom, 1990).

But unlike a local, physical commons, the erosion of the financial system's resilience creeps up on us, because firms are able to disguise their true state via what economists call *hidden actions*. When the authorities write rules to constrain intermediaries' balance-sheet choices, regulated firms find ways of taking more risk than contemplated in the calibration of those rules; and unregulated intermediaries structure themselves so as to stay outside the scope of the rules, even though the economic substance of their business is essentially the same. In other words, finance is a shape-shifter. Regulatory arbitrage is endemic, and the rule-writers can end up chasing their tails.

Microprudential supervision, focused on hidden actions, is called into existence to break this problem. It occupies a distinct space between financial-stability policy making and the enforcement of the rule books in which headline capital, liquidity, and other requirements are enshrined.

4.2   Judgement-based Supervision

A micro-supervisor has to make judgements of the following kind: 'Firm X is managed so imprudently that there is no reasonable prospect of its meeting the required *standard of resilience* in the states of the world it might plausibly confront.' In such circumstances, the micro-supervisor needs to be ready (and so legally empowered) to revoke the firm's license, or place (monitorable and enforceable) constraints on its risk-taking.

The basic criteria underpinning the supervisor's findings – e.g., prudence, competent management, a separation of powers within the intermediary – have to be established in law and interpreted in the light of the regime's purpose. When applying them to individual firms, the micro-supervisor is called upon to comply with the canons of procedural fairness and reason.

4.3   Micro- and Macroprudential Supervision Don't Really Exist
(On Their Own)

That distinction between supervision and regulation operates at the macro level too. Threats to stability cannot always be identified by looking at intermediaries one by one because the financial system is just that, a *system*, with component parts connected within sectors; across sectors and markets; via interactions with the real economy; and across countries. As the first chairman of the Basel Supervisors Committee, George Blunden said back in the mid-1980s (Blunden, 1987):[9]

> [i]t is part of the [supervisor's] job to take [a] wider systemic view and sometimes to curb practices which even prudent banks might, if left to themselves, regard as safe.

Similarly, any set of regulatory requirements calibrated to deliver the desired standard for resilience in more or less normal conditions might prove insufficient in the face of extraordinarily strong booms or changes in the structures through which losses are transmitted around the financial system. This is what has become known as *macroprudential* policy, involving dynamic adjustments to regulatory requirements.[10]

5. OPERATING A SYSTEM OF SPECIALIST COMMITTEES, AND SO FRAGMENTED POWER

The kind of limited central bank described here is very powerful. It is important, given our republican values, to avoid concentrating such power in one or a few individuals, and to ensure there are proper forms of accountability without undermining independence.

This points to legislators establishing separate policy committees for each regime delegated to a central bank. That, more or less, is the post-crisis set up in the UK.[11] It is approximated in the euro area, with the ECB having separate monetary and micro-supervisory committees, albeit with the former having a right to override the latter (and both being too big to be properly deliberative bodies). It is also approximated in the Fed's long-standing structure, with monetary and regulatory responsibilities split between the Federal Reserve Board and the FOMC.

Members of multiple committees (monetary policy, and stability) might sustain their public standing by, say, delivering price stability even if they mess up financial stability. By contrast, those members who are on only the stability/ regulatory committee are unambiguously impaled on their track record in maintaining the stability of the financial system as a whole. That helps ensure they accept personal responsibility for the resilience of the system. So far, parliamentary oversight has not recognized their vital role.

5.1 Transparency as a Means to Accountability: Resolution Plans and Stress Testing

While *regulatory* outputs – rules and regulations – are obviously observable, historically the activities of prudential *supervisors* have been largely invisible, except to the individual regulated firms themselves. Neither *outputs* nor *outcomes* have been monitorable.

This is not an accident. Within the community of prudential supervisors, there has long been a culture-cum-doctrine of secrecy. While understandable given the risks, this is at odds with prudential supervisors being insulated from day-to-day politics. If prudential supervision *must* be opaque, then it should be open to day-to-day political control.

Fortunately, potential solutions to this dilemma have emerged in recent years. One is transparency in resolution plans, the other is stress testing. Supervision need no longer be a mystery – accessible to the public and their elected representatives only after something goes badly wrong.

In particular, the regularity and transparency of stress testing could transform public debate and accountability, taking prudential supervision towards the kind of oversight exercised over monetary policy. Year by year, everyone sees the severity of the chosen stress scenarios as well as the firm-by-firm results. This ought to help legislators think about the degree of resilience they want to require in the financial system, about how well the statutory regime is working, where it needs reform, where responsibilities should be rejigged, and so on.

That rosy prospect depends, however, on the integrity of the tests, which should not be taken for granted. Some assurance might be provided by each major jurisdiction's supervisors allowing in observers or participants from foreign authorities; and by independent reports on the integrity of each centre's process (Cecchetti and Tucker, 2015).

6.   SUMMING UP: CENTRAL BANKS IN THE REGULATORY STATE

In concluding, we need a way of joining up the central banking regimes necessary for monetary-system stability. I call that a *Money-Credit Constitution*. It would cover the constraints on the business and risks in banking, what central banks must do (their mandate), may do, and may not do – all grounded in shared principles so as to generate a coherent whole.

At a schematic level, a modern Money-Credit Constitution might have five components: a target for inflation (or some other nominal magnitude); a requirement to hold reserves (or assets readily exchanged for reserves) that increases with a bank's leverage/riskiness and social significance; a liquidity-reinsurance regime for fundamentally solvent banks and shadow banks; a resolution regime for bankrupt banks and shadow banks; and constraints on how far the central bank is free to pursue its mandate and structure its balance sheet.

How strict those constraints need to be is a vital question. For the banking (and shadow banking) sector, it matters that the availability of liquidity reinsurance gives banks (and others) incentives to take more risk than otherwise since it shields them from some of the costs of their own actions and choices. This 'moral hazard' problem makes crises more likely through the very efforts of the state to contain their social costs. Partly for that reason, I have come to favour a regime where 100% of a banking business' short-term liabilities must be covered by assets eligible at the central bank's lending facility. It is a regime where the monetary authority's collateral-haircut policy becomes the financial stability analogue of its monetary policy rate of interest. Industry lobbying (and associated political pressure) would be directed at the definition of 'short-term liabilities', the population of eligible instruments, and the level of central bank haircuts. Not fool proof, but a lot better (King (2016) and, with elaboration, Tucker (2019)).

NOTES

1. This chapter draws heavily on chapters 20 and 21 of Paul Tucker's *Unelected Power* (Tucker 2018).
2. This, by the way, is the best way of framing the debate about central bank digital currencies.
3. To be clear, the second leg absolutely does not entail that no banking institutions can be allowed to fail; only that the monetary liabilities of distressed firms must be transferable into claims on other, healthy deposit-taking firms or otherwise mutualized so that payments services are not interrupted.
4. At the Bank of England's 1994 tercentenary conference, banking supervision was stressed only by leading figures from the 1980s: former Governors Larosière, Richardson and Volcker and BIS head Lamfalussy: 'The Philosophy of Central Banking' and 'Central Banking in Transition' in Capie et al. (1994).
5. Bernanke (2010) has argued that, in its regulatory/supervisory functions, the Fed has and should have no more independence than other regulators, and thus less than in its monetary policy functions, including the discount window and LOLR. Based on my argument, that might be the wrong way round. In fact, the Fed has pretty much the same political insulation in supervision and regulation as it does in monetary policy, and a lot closer to that than to, say, the position of other regulatory agencies: job security, instrument autonomy, and, unusually in the US, budgetary autonomy.
6. In the UK, confidence that information would flow smoothly was strongly, but naively and damagingly, asserted by various commentators when Bank of England independence was debated during the early 1990s: notably, Roll (1993, pp. 44, 68).
7. An independent central bank cannot decently lend to fundamentally broken firms as it entails fiscal and distributional effects (Tucker, 2020).
8. In fact, serious work is still needed in this area, and it is striking how little central bank leaders talk about resolution policy (Tucker, 2014).
9. Blunden had by then retired as chair of the Basel Committee but was Deputy Governor of the Bank of England.

10.   Too often described as 'macroprudential instruments', they are standard pru-
        dential regulatory measures used in pursuit of macroprudential (or system-wide)
        goals.
11.   The Bank of England has separate statutory committees responsible for micro-
        and macroprudential policy, essentially so that a majority on the latter is not
        infected by any lapses in micro-oversight and to draw on different types of
        technocratic skill. Reflecting proposals that George Blunden and I had each aired
        in the late 1970s, mid-1980s, early 1990s and mid-2000s, the micro body was ini-
        tially established, on the French model, as a formal subsidiary in order, amongst
        other things, to give the external members a statutory role in internal organization
        and resources given that some supervisory outputs are effected at desk level and
        that the central bank's leaders might favour resourcing the monetary side.

REFERENCES

Baring, Francis (1797). 'Observations on the Establishment of the Bank of England.
     And on the Paper Circulation of the Country'.
Bernanke, Benjamin (2010). 'Central Bank Independence, Transparency, and
     Accountability'. Institute for Monetary and Economic Studies International
     Conference, Bank of Japan, 26 May.
Blunden, George (1987). 'Supervision and Central Banking'. *Bank of England
     Quarterly Bulletin*, August.
Capie, Forrest et. al., (eds) (1994). *The Future of Central Banking: The Tercentenary
     Symposium of the Bank of England*. Cambridge: Cambridge University Press.
Cecchetti, Stephen G. (2007). 'Why Central Banks Should Be Financial Supervisors'.
     Vox Subprime Series, part 3. *CEPR Policy Portal*, 30 November.
Cecchetti, Stephen G. and Paul Tucker (2015). 'Is there Macro-Prudential Policy
     without International Cooperation?' In *Policy Challenges in a Diverging Global
     Economy: Proceedings of the Asia Pacific Policy Conference*, edited by R. Glick and
     M. Speigel, Federal Reserve Bank of San Francisco, November.
Diamond, Douglas W. and P. H. Dybvig (1983). Bank Runs, Deposit Insurance, and
     Liquidity'. *Journal of Political Economy* 91, no. 3: 401–19.
Dombret, Andreas (2014). 'What is "Good Regulation"?' Speech at the Bundesbank
     Symposium 'Banking Supervision in Dialogue?', Frankfurt, 9 July.
Holmstrom, Bengt (2015). 'Understanding the Role of Debt in the Financial System'.
     BIS Working Paper No. 479.
King, Mervyn (2016). *The End of Alchemy: Money, Banking and the Future of the
     Global Economy*. London: Little Brown.
Ostrom, Elinor (1990). *Governing the Commons: The Evolution of Institutions for
     Collective Action*. New York: Cambridge University Press.
Roll, Eric et al. (1993). *Independent and Accountable: A New Mandate for the Bank of
     England*. Report of an Independent Panel, CEPR.
The Economist (2007). The Bank that failed. Published 20 September 2007. Accessed
     25 July 2022, https://www.economist.com/leaders/2007/09/20/the-bank-that-failed.
Tucker, P. (2014). 'The Resolution of Financial Institutions without taxpayer solvency
     support: Seven retrospective clarifications and elaborations'. Comments at the
     European Summer Symposium in Economic Theory, Gerzensee.
Tucker, P. (2018). *Unelected Power: The Quest for Legitimacy in Central Banking and
     the Regulatory State*. Princeton, NJ: Princeton University Press.

Tucker, P. (2019). 'Is the Financial System Sufficiently Resilient? A Research Programme and Policy Agenda'. BIS Working Paper No 792.

Tucker, P. (2020). 'Solvency as a Fundamental Constraint on LOLR Policy for Independent Central Banks: Principles, History, Law'. *Journal of Financial Crises* 2, no. 2.

Volcker, Paul (1990). 'The Triumph of Central Banking?' The 1990 Per Jacobsson Lecture, Per Jacobsson Foundation.

14. Politicians, central banks and macroprudential supervision

Donato Masciandaro

1. INTRODUCTION

By the early 2000s, an increasing number of countries had adopted a well-defined central bank framework in which the central bank was independent and accountable for achieving monetary policy goals, while its traditional responsibilities for pursuing financial stability had become less important. Essentially, central banks were designed as monetary policy actors. The economic rationale was well-known and the theoretical bottom line can be summarized as follows: for various reasons, policymakers tend to adopt a short-term perspective when using monetary tools. They use these tools to smooth out macroeconomic shocks and to exploit the trade-offs between real gains and nominal costs.

However, the more markets are efficient and rational, the greater the risk that short-sighted monetary policy will generate negative macroeconomic distortions. Therefore, banning the use of monetary policy for myopic purposes became a social goal and the institutional setting gained momentum, with the aim of separating the central bank from the government and from all fiscal and banking responsibilities.

The fundamental effect was that the supervisory role of central banks generally decreased. However, following the 2008–2009 Great Crisis, central banks again became involved in supervision in many countries, suggesting a sort of 'Great Reversal' towards prudential supervision in the hands of central banks.

The 2008–2009 economic crisis highlighted the need for financial stability. In numerous countries, reforms of financial regulations were motivated by the fact that a focus solely on monetary stability and micro-supervision (i.e., the stability of individual institutions and markets) could not guarantee the safety and soundness of the financial industry. The key response has been the formation of macroprudential committees.[1]

How can the role played by central banks in financial stability be explained? From the perspective of traditional economics, the extension of central bank influence into this field has both pros and cons. In other words, this perspective does not provide a clear answer as to whether assigning a supervisory role to central banks or other independent institutions is socially optimal.[2] Two conflicting views can be found regarding the merging of monetary and supervisory functions within the central bank: the integration view and the separation view.[3] The integration view underscores the informational advantages and economies of scale derived from bringing all functions under the authority of the central bank. In contrast, the separation argument suggests a higher risk of policy failure if central banks have supervisory responsibilities, as financial-stability concerns might reduce the effectiveness of monetary policy action. The extant empirical research into the relative merits of putting banking-sector supervision in the hands of central banks provides mixed results.[4]

Therefore, policymakers must address a series of possible trade-offs between the expected benefits and costs of allowing the monetary authority to have more or less influence on macroprudential strategies. Consequently, the political economy perspective becomes relevant,[5] as arguments supporting either the integration view or the separation view can be more or less important in the minds of those who design and implement the supervisory regime. In other words, we have to focus on the agent responsible for the institutional setting – the policymaker. Consequently, the question that naturally arises is genuinely empirical: Is it possible to identify common drivers that explain political choices concerning central bank involvement in supervision?

The aim of this chapter is to illustrate how empirical analyses can shed light on the political drivers that might explain the central bank's involvement as a supervisor. Section 2 highlights the empirical drivers that may explain central bank involvement in the macroprudential perimeter using a cross-country analysis. Section 3 adds a temporal dimension and discusses the possible role of financial crises. Section 4 concludes.

2.   POLITICIANS, CENTRAL BANKS AND MACROPRUDENTIAL GOVERNANCE

Is it possible to identify common drivers that explain political decisions regarding central bank involvement in macroprudential governance? In a recent econometric cross-sectional analysis of the determinants of central bank involvement in this area, Masciandaro and Volpicella (2016) test different assumptions made in the theoretical and institutional literature. In general, the empirical results indicate that: (a) central banks acting as micro-supervisors of the banking industry are more likely to be given more macroprudential powers, (b) higher central bank political independence is associated with lower involvement in macro-supervision, and (c) central banks pursuing specific price-stability objectives are more likely to be endowed with macro-supervisory responsibilities. These results can be interpreted using a political economy perspective.

The political economy perspective differs from the extant literature in two main respects. First, while interactions between macroprudential policies and monetary policies have been studied, few analyses have examined the drivers of governance arrangements (Masciandaro 2006, 2007, 2009, Masciandaro and Volpicella 2016, Masciandaro and Romelli 2015, 2018a, 2018b, Gaganis et al. 2021, Moschella and Pinto 2021). Second, this perspective enriches research focusing on the effects of statutory central bank independence (CBI). Since it emerged in the 1990s, CBI has been viewed as a major determinant of macroeconomic performance. In the empirical analysis (Masciandaro and Volpicella 2016) the broader picture is enriched by exploring the relationship between CBI and an important institutional feature – macro-supervision. The results suggest that CBI is relevant not only owing to its beneficial effects on macroeconomic variables but also because it influences policymakers' decisions.

The empirical analysis is based on data available in 2013 covering 31 countries that were heterogeneous in terms of their institutional frameworks and stages of economic development. In order to shed light on the drivers that influence the development of macroprudential settings, qualitative information must first be transformed into quantitative variables. Two main indicators can be used to measure the key features of the central bank's role in financial supervision. The central bank's involvement in macro-supervision is our dependent variable in the econometric tests, while the central bank's role as a micro-supervisor serves as a proxy for its role as the leading authority in micro-supervision, as discussed above.

The macroprudential index[6] (MAPP) was used to measure central bank involvement in macro-supervision and the CBBA index[7] was applied to measure central bank involvement in micro-supervision of the banking industry. The latter index is a dummy variable that takes a value of one if the central bank is the main banking supervisory authority, and zero otherwise. In addition, I use an index of involvement for central banks' micro-supervision of the financial system as a whole (i.e., banking, securities and insurance). To do so, I adopt a two-step procedure that starts from the Financial Supervision Herfindahl Hirschman (FSHH) Index. The FSHH measures the extent to which supervisory powers are consolidated using the classical index proposed by Herfindahl and Hirschman.[8] In the second stage, the methodology can be used to build an index of central bank involvement in micro-supervision: the Central Bank Supervisor Share (CBSS) index.[9] As a result, we have two alternative indexes that measure the impact of the central bank's role as micro-supervisor. The expected sign of both variables is undetermined: higher levels of either the CBBA or the CBSS are likely to be associated with higher MAPP levels if the information-gain effect prevails. The opposite is true if the capture-risk effect dominates.

In addition, it is necessary to measure two potential shortcomings that politicians may associate with deep central bank involvement in macro-supervision: too much bureaucratic independence in the institutional setting and excessive discretion in defining monetary policy. A proxy for CBI with respect to the monetary policy function can be found in the extant literature. Acknowledging that *de facto* independence can sometimes lead to a different framework than *de jure* independence – especially in emerging and developing countries[10] – our analysis focuses on the legal features of independence. This choice is justified by the fact that CBI cannot be ensured without proper legal provisions.

In terms of determining the most relevant index for capturing either the political or operational dimensions of CBI among those proposed in the literature,[11] this study uses the GMT index[12] mainly owing to its robustness. In fact, the literature on CBI generally uses two different strategies to capture the degree of CBI: (a) indices based on central bank legislation (*de jure*) or (b) indices on the turnover rate of the central bank governor (*de facto*).[13]

Given this overall setting, we can frame the results regarding the drivers of central bank involvement in macro-supervision. The empirical results show that: (a) central banks acting as micro-supervisors of the banking industry are more likely to be given more extensive macroprudential powers, (b) higher central bank political independence is associated with lower involvement in macro-supervision, and (c) central banks pursuing specific price-stability objectives are more likely to be endowed with macro-supervisory responsibilities.

What is the political economy interpretation of these results? First, the empirical analysis suggests that a central bank's role as a micro-supervisor of the banking industry can be a key driver of its macroprudential involvement. In other words, micro-supervisory powers serve as a proxy for the information advantages available to the central bank and politicians seem to appreciate this feature, with the argument that goes as follows: the central banker can effectively perform her role as macro supervisor if she is also responsible for the supervision of the institutions that make up the banking system. Second, from the politicians' perspective, greater central bank political independence, which increases the risk of an overly powerful monetary authority, seems to imply fewer macro-supervisory powers. However, it is worth noting that the potential risks in having too much power in the hands of an unelected central banker when independence is combined with supervisory involvement could be addressed – at least theoretically – with a proper accountability design.

Finally, rule-based monetary policy focused on inflation targeting, which reduces the central bank's discretion, weakly increases the odds of a central bank being involved in macro-supervision. Politicians seem to dislike situations in which central bankers have too much discretion. At the same time, regarding the potential conflicts of goals – inflation targeting versus banking stability – that may arise, it is worth recalling that such conflicts can arise in any institutional structure and – if we assume that the probability of conflict is exogenous – the issue becomes whether it is more efficient to resolve these conflicts internally within the central bank or between agencies if a different agency is responsible for bank supervision.

All in all, politicians appear to be wary of placing too much power in the hands of independent and/or discretionary central banks, although it is worth noting that independence seems to be the more relevant characteristic.

3.   POLITICIANS AND SUPERVISORY CENTRAL BANKS: DO CRISES MATTER?

The stability and generalizability of the above-mentioned results regarding politicians' incentives must be checked in future research. At the same time, other assumptions regarding what drives politicians to modify supervisory architectures over time should be tested in the field of macro-supervision. Recently, Masciandaro and Romelli (2018a) undertook an empirical analysis of 105 countries over the period 1996 to 2013. Their results suggest the existence of two main drivers of reforms. First, systemic banking crises significantly increase the probability that a country will change its supervisory structure. Second, an equally important 'bandwagon' effect seems to matter – countries are more likely to change their supervisory architectures when the share of countries undertaking reforms around the world or on the same continent is high.

Masciandaro and Romelli's (2018a) results show that the number of financial crises previously experienced by a country positively influences the incentives to increase central bank involvement in supervision. Moreover, they show a negative effect of independence on the degree of central bank involvement in financial supervision. These findings further support the idea that the greater the independence of the supervisor, the greater the fear of powerful institutions or bureaucratic misconduct.

It is also possible to analyse the extent of central bank involvement in macroprudential policy. In fact, it has been suggested[14] that supervision reforms are more important in countries undertaking macroprudential policies. Hence, we might expect countries in which central banks are more involved in macroprudential policies to also have central banks with greater overall supervisory powers. The positive and statistically significant coefficient in Masciandaro and Romelli (2018a) provides strong support for this argument. Among the other explanatory variables, the negative sign for the civil law dummy and the country's latitude signal that countries with a civil legal system and countries characterized by higher latitudes tend to have financial services supervision responsibilities outside the central bank.

All in all, we find evidence that the extent to which supervision is concentrated in the hands of the central bank is influenced by a cumulative index of past financial crises, the degree of CBI, real GDP per capita, openness and financial sector development. The positive relationships between the number of previous financial crises and the CBIS index suggest that countries that experienced more financial turmoil in the past two decades are more likely to put their supervisory architecture in the hands of the central bank.

4.   CONCLUSION

Since the 2008–2009 financial crisis, financial stability has been a general priority. When thinking about ways to prevent financial disasters in the future, it has been natural to reconsider the relationship between central banks and financial stability. Some researchers claim[15] that central bank independence, inflation targeting and financial stability represent the major changes in the monetary policy landscape in recent decades.

The crucial point is that traditional economics offers two main and contradictory results that can be summarized as opposing answers to the following question: Given two policies – monetary policy and macro-supervision policy – with their own macro goals, what is the optimal degree of involvement for the monetary agent (i.e., the central bank) in supervisory responsibilities? Thus far, two answers have been offered: the integration view and the separation view.

This chapter highlighted the potential usefulness of adding another perspective: the political economy view. The political economy view is based on the fact that the player who decides to maintain or reform a supervisory regime is the politician in charge. This politician follows his or her own preferences when weighing the arguments of the integration and separation views. In this perspective, the central bank's involvement in supervision is an endogenous variable. In other words, the optimal institutional setting *does not* exist per se.

Moreover, the central bank's involvement is likely to change over time based on political preferences favouring the delegation of more (or less) supervisory power to the monetary authority. Today, this consideration deserves even more attention given the role of a 'special' kind of politicians – the populists. Populist policies revolve around presenting solutions that are welfare enhancing in the short run for a majority of the population but costly in the long run for the overall population. Given this definition, the narratives of central bankers seem to highlight them as a natural target for populist policies. Some researchers have argued that the rise of populism may negatively affect the consensus in favour of CBI evident from the late 1980s until the 2008–2009 economic crisis.[16] The same arguments could be tested when exploring the role of central banks as supervisors.

In addition, politicians are generally viewed as 'Econs' – rational players in the sense of the traditional economic mainstream. Future research could explore the behavioural perspective and investigate the consequences of the fact that politicians are 'Humans', as behavioural biases might distort their decisions. In general, politicians are subject to the same sources of behavioural bias that all individuals face. In the presence of behavioural biases, the outcomes of different information sets and/or governance rules can differ. At the same time, governance rules are based on the assumptions that central bankers are bureaucrats and that bureaucrats are rational players. Recent research[17] has shown how the perspectives associated with modern economics, political economy and behavioural economics can serve as fruitful and complementary tools when analysing the design and implementation of monetary policy.

NOTES

1. Edge and Liang (2017), Aikman et al. (2019). On the relationship between the governance structure of new macroprudential regimes and the use of new bank capital tools see Edge and Liang (2020).
2. For analyses on the interaction between the institutional architecture and the policy mandates concerning monetary and supervisory policies see Dalla Pellegrina and Masciandaro (2008), Gros et al. (2014), Lazopoulos and Gabriel (2018), Matsumoto (2020), Mertzanis (2020). For a case study – i.e. South Africa – see Liu and Molise (2020). Regarding the interactions between monetary policy and banking stability see Albertazzi et al. (2020), Cozzi et al. (2020), Adrian et al. (2020), Wall (2021), Schularick et al. (2021).
3. The taxonomy was introduced in Masciandaro and Quintyn (2016).
4. Recently the literature is discussing the 'paradox of credibility': inflation targeting central banks are blamed for the build-up of financial instability (Blanchard et al. 2010, Borio 2006). Fazio et al. (2015) provided evidence against the credibility paradox, Frappa and Mesonnier (2010) provided mixed results, while Musa and Jun (2020) found that when the supervisory role is situated within central banks focusing on price stability financial imbalances are more likely to occur.
5. Baker (2015) and Bengtsson (2018).
6. Lim et al. (2013).
7. Masciandaro and Volpicella (2016). See also Masciandaro (2019).
8. Masciandaro and Quintyn (2016).
9. Masciandaro and Quintyn (2016).
10. Cukierman (2008).
11. For surveys, see Alesina and Stella (2010), Reis (2013), Masciandaro and Romelli (2015), and de Haan and Eijffinger (2016).
12. Grilli et al. (1991) developed the index, which was updated by Arnone et al. (2009).
13. *De jure* indices are more likely to capture the extent of CBI for several reasons. First, turnover rates relate the independence of central banks to the autonomy of their governors. While extensively used, this approach has been shown to be

less robust in empirical estimations than the GMT index of legal independence. Second, the legal measures associated with CBI are more likely to reflect the true relationships among the central bank, the policymakers and the bankers, especially in countries where the rule of law is strongly embedded in the political culture, as in many developed economies. Third, it is currently most relevant to capture changes in the extent of CBI after 2008. Given that many post-crisis reforms revolved around central bank involvement in supervision, it is more efficient to restrict our attention to *de jure* indices that can capture such changes; see de Haan et al. (2008) and Masciandaro and Romelli (2018b).
14. Blanchard et al. (2010).
15. Reis (2018).
16. Buiter (2014), de Haan and Eijffinger (2017), Goodhart and Lastra (2017), Rajan (2017), Rodrik (2018), Masciandaro and Passarelli (2020).
17. Favaretto and Masciandaro (2016).

REFERENCES

Adrian, T., Duarte, F., Liang, N. and Zabczyk, P., (2020), Monetary and Macroprudential Policy with Endogenous Risk, CEPR Discussion Paper Series, n. 14435.

Aikman, D., Bridges, J., Kashyap A. and Siergert, C., (2019), Would Macroprudential Regulation Have Prevented the Last Crisis?, *Journal of Economic Perspectives*, 33(1), 107–130.

Albertazzi, U., Barbiero F., Marques-Ibanez D., Popov A., Rodriguez D'Acri C. and Vlassopoulos, T., (2020), Monetary Policy and Bank Stability: The Analytical Toolbox Reviewed, ECB Technical Paper Series, n. 2377.

Alesina, A. and Stella, A., (2010), The Politics of Monetary Policy, in *Handbook of Monetary Economics,* pp. 1001–1054.

Arnone, M., Sommer, M., Laurens, B. and Segalotto, J.F., (2009), Central Bank Autonomy: Lessons From Global Trends, IMF Staff Papers, 56, 263–296, 10.1057/imfsp.2008.25.

Baker, A., (2015), The Bankers' Paradox: The Political Economy of Macroprudential Regulation, SRC Discussion Paper Series, n. 37.

Bengtsson, E., (2018), The Political Economy of Macroprudential Policy, mimeo.

Blanchard, O., Dell'Ariccia, G. and Mauro, P. (2010), Rethinking Macroeconomic Policy, *Journal of Money, Credit and Banking*, 42(s1), 199–215.

Borio, C., (2006), Monetary and Financial Stability: Here to Stay?, *Journal of Banking and Finance*, 30, 3407–3414.

Buiter W.H., (2014), *Central Banks: Powerful, Political and Unaccountable*, CEPR Discussion Paper Series, n. 10223.

Cozzi, G., Darracq-Paries, M., Karadi, P., Koerner, J., Kok, C., Mazelis, F., Nikolov, K., Rancoita, E., Van der Ghote, A. and Weber, J., (2020), Macroprudential Measures: Macroeconomic Impact and Interaction with Monetary Policy, ECB Technical Paper Series, n. 2376.

Cukierman, A., (2008), Central Bank Independence and Monetary Policymaking Institutions: Past, Present and Future, *European Journal of Political Economy*, 24(4), 722–736.

Dalla Pellegrina, L. and Masciandaro, D., (2008), Politicians, Central Banks, and the Shape of Financial Supervision Architectures, *Journal of Financial Regulation and Compliance*, 16(4), 290–317.

de Haan, J. and Eijffinger, S., (2016), The Politics of Central Bank Independence, DNP Working Papers, n. 539, 399–410.

de Haan, J. and Eijiffinger S., (2017), Central Bank Independence under Threat?, CEPR Policy Insight, n. 87.

de Haan, J., Masciandaro, D. and Quintyn, M., (2008), Does Central Bank Independence Still Matter? *European Journal of Political Economy*, 24(4), 717–721.

Edge, R. and Liang, N., (2017), New Financial Stability Governance and Central Banks, in J. Hambur and J. Simon (Eds), *Monetary Policy and Financial Stability in a World of Low Interest Rates*. Conference proceedings Reserve Bank of Australia's conference in 2017: https://www.rba.gov.au/publications/confs/2017/.

Edge, R.M. and Liang, J.N., (2020), Financial Stability Committees and the Countercyclical Capital Buffer, Deutshe Bundesbank, Discussion Paper Series, n. 4.

Favaretto, F. and Masciandaro, D., (2016), Doves, Hawks and Pigeons: Behavioral Monetary Policy and Interest Rate Inertia, *Journal of Financial Stability*, 27, 50–58.

Fazio, D.M., Tabak B.M. and Cajueiro D.O., (2015), Inflation Targeting: Is It to Blame for Banking System Instability?, *Journal of Banking and Finance*: https://doi.org/10.1016/j.jbankfin.2015.05.016

Frappa, S. and Mesonnier, J.S., (2010), The Housing Price Boom of the Late 1990s: Did Inflation Targeting Matter? *Journal of Financial Stability*: https://doi.org/10.1016/j.jfs.2010.06.001

Gaganis, C., Pasiouras F. and Wohlschlegel A., (2021), Allocating Supervisory Responsibility to Central Bankers: Does National Culture Matter?, *International Review of Law and Economics*: https://doi.org/10.1016/j.ijle.2021.105991

Goodhart, C.A. and Lastra, R., (2017), Populism and Central Bank Independence, CEPR Discussion Paper Series, n. 2017.

Grilli, Vittorio, Donato Masciandaro and Guido Tabellini, (1991), Political and Monetary Institutions and Public Financial Policies in the Industrial Countries, *Economic Policy*, 6(13), 341–392. https://doi.org/10.2307/1344630

Gros, D., Langfield, S., Pagano, M. and Schoenmaker, D., (2014), Allocating Macro Prudential Powers, European Systemic Risk Board, Advisory Scientific Committee, Reports, n. 5.

Lazopoulos, I. and Gabriel, V.J., (2018), Policy Mandate and Institutional Architecture, mimeo.

Lim, C.H., Columba, A., Costa, P., Kongsaamut, P., Otani, A., Saiyid, M., Wezel, T. and Wu, X., (2013), Macroprudential Policy: What Instruments and How to Use Them?, IMF Working Paper Series, International Monetary Fund, n. 238.

Liu, G. and Molise, T., (2020), The Optimal Monetary and Macroprudential Policies for the South African Economy, ERSA Working Paper Series, n. 811.

Masciandaro, D., (2006), E Pluribus Unum? Authorities' Design in Financial Supervision: Trends and Determinants?, *Open Economies Review,* 17, 73–102.

Masciandaro, D., (2007), Divide et Impera: Financial Supervision Unification and Central Bank Fragmentation Effect, *European Journal of Political Economy,* 23, 285–315.

Masciandaro, D., (2009), Politicians and Financial Supervision outside the Central Bank: Why Do They Do it?, *Journal of Financial Stability*, 5(2), 124–147.

Masciandaro, D., (2019), Central Banks as Macroprudential Authorities: Economics and Politics, in D.W. Arner, E. Avgouleas, D. Busch and S.L. Schwarcz (Eds), *Systemic Risk in the Financial Sector: Ten Years after the Global Financial Crisis*, McGill-Queen's University Press, 151–164.

Masciandaro, D. and Passarelli, F., (2020), Populism, Political Pressure and Central Bank (In)dependence, *Open Economies Review*, forthcoming.

Masciandaro, D. and Quintyn M., (2016), The Governance of Financial Supervision: Recent Developments, *Journal of Economic Surveys*, 30, 982–1006. https://doi.org/10.1111/joes.12130

Masciandaro, D. and Romelli, D., (2015), Ups and Downs of Central Bank Independence from the Great Inflation to the Great Recession: Theory, Institutions and Empirics, *Financial History Review*, 22(3), 259–289.

Masciandaro, D. and Romelli, D., (2018a), Central Bankers as Supervisors: Do Crises Matter?, *European Journal of Political Economy*, 52, 120–140.

Masciandaro, D. and Romelli, D., (2018b), Peaks and Troughs: Economics and Political Economy of Central Bank Independence Cycles, in D. Mayes, P.L. Siklos and J.E. Sturm (Eds), *Oxford Handbook of the Economics of Central Banking*, Oxford University Press.

Masciandaro, D. and Volpicella, A. (2016), Macro Prudential Governance and Central Banks: Facts and Drivers, *Journal of International Money and Finance*, 61, 101–119.

Matsumoto, H., (2020), Monetary and Macroprudential Policies against Currency Crises, Bank of Japan, mimeo.

Mertzanis, C., (2020), Financial Supervision Structure, Decentralized Decision-Making and Financing Constraints, *Journal of Economic Behavior and Organization*, 174, 13–37.

Moschella, M. and Pinto, L., (2021), The Multi-Agencies Dilemma of Delegation: Why Do Policymakers Choose One or Multiple Agencies for Financial Regulation?, *Regulation and Governance*: doi:10.1111/rego.12435

Musa, U. and Jun, W., (2020), Does Inflation Targeting Cause Financial Instability?, *North American Journal of Economics and Finance*, 52: https://doi.org/10.1016/j.najef.2020.101164

Rajan, R., (2017), Central Banks' Year of Reckoning, Project Syndicate, 21 December, mimeo.

Reis, R., (2013), Central Bank Design, *Journal of Economic Perspectives*, 27(4), 17–44.

Reis, R., (2018), Is Something Really Wrong with Macroeconomics?, *Oxford Review of Economic Policy*, 34(1–2), 132–155.

Rodrik, D., (2018), *In Defence of Economic Populism*, Project Syndicate, 8 January.

Schularick, M., Steege, L. and Ward, F., (2021), Leaning against the Wind and Crisis Risk, *American Economic Review: Insights*, 3(2), 199–214.

Wall, L.D., (2021), Bank Supervisory Goals versus Monetary Policy Implementation, Federal Reserve Bank of Atlanta, Policy Hub, n. 3, March.

PART IV

The FinTech revolution: implications for optimal supervisory architecture

15. Regulating and supervising BigTech in finance

José Manuel González-Páramo

1. NEW TECHNOLOGIES IN BANKING

Banks have always managed to make the most of technology to improve their efficiency and the service provided to their customers, but now they are facing a new wave of innovation with much wider and disruptive implications. "Digital" – meaning the combination of immense masses of data generated via interconnectivity thanks to mobility and the internet of things, together with the utilization of big data techniques, artificial intelligence and machine learning to generate new value propositions – is the name of the game.

In a static environment, digital technologies offer the potential to help banks to survive the pressures of low growth, lackluster profitability and strict regulation, and to solidly re-establish customers' trust and reputation with society. If banks could offer a better user experience and improve variety and affordability, they would again come closer to what customers demand and need to satisfy their aspirations. But the world is not static anymore. The disruption in finance is reflected in profound and irreversible changes in both the demand for and the supply of financial services. On the demand side, we are already witnessing a radical refashioning in the patterns of consumption and savings behavior, with interactions defined by online standards: convenience, transparency, affordability, simplicity and advice.

As for the supply side, digital technologies have lowered the barriers to entry in the financial sector in a way, and at a speed never seen before. Over the past few years, we have seen an increase in the number of new players coming from the digital world, the FinTech startups and the BigTechs. The former are born in the financial sector, and concentrate on specific segments of the value chain (foreign exchange, payments, loans, trade, asset management or insurance, for example), unbundling or disaggregating the services previously originated and sold by the banking sector. These companies start without the burden of having to maintain a physical distribution network, the rigidities of corporate culture, the upkeep of obsolescent technological systems or tough banking regulations. As to the latter, the BigTechs are major digital companies arriving to finance from other areas, and differ from FinTechs in brand recognition, large membership, and outstanding financial and technological strengths. This chapter will focus on the risks raised by BigTech's business model and the inconsistencies in the regulation and supervision of their activities.

2.   FROM FINTECH TO BIGTECH

In the aftermath of the Great Financial Crisis, the banking sector was confronted with several challenges. First, the need to boost profitability from modest levels. Second, the requirement to adapt to a demanding set of multiple new regulations coordinated internationally, in many domains (capital, liquidity, governance, interconnectedness, systemic relevance, etc.). And, third, the imperative necessity to recover from the enormous reputational loss suffered by the financial sector.

Cost-cutting, revenue diversification and mergers were the most salient initiatives of the banking industry, often overtly supported by supervisors. But as much as these reactions contributed to financial stability, arguably they did so at the expense of more concentration and a less competitive cost of financial intermediation. This is the context in which the advent of FinTech was greeted by regulators like Mark Carney, then Chair of the Financial Stability Board (FSB): "FinTech may make conventional banking more contestable, improving efficiency and customer choice (…)" (Carney, 2017).

The potential contribution of FinTech to contestability springs from two fronts: the massive and adept use of enabling digital technologies, and regulatory and supervisory advantages – warranted or not – vis-à-vis banks. Albeit available to incumbents as well, digital native FinTechs could fully exploit digital technologies thanks to the leaner organization and the absence of legacy technologies and systems. The threat of unbundling banking would thus work for the benefit of clients and society at large.

The first wave of FinTech innovation failed to deliver on this promise. The reasons why FinTech are prone to fail are manifold (FinTech News Singapore, 2018; Sevlin, 2019): overestimation of the clients' willingness to change their behavior and pay for new services in addition to what they already pay for; lack of brand recognition; underfunding; and overlooking of legal and compliance aspects, among others. Just a very small share of startups has matured to viable models. However, FinTech startups must be credited for an acceleration of the digital transformation of incumbent institutions through a wide array of partnerships and collaborative models: incubators, open innovation, licensing, white label solutions or full integration (European Banking Authority, EBA, 2018; Van der Kroft, 2021).

A second wave of digital innovation has come from the entry of BigTechs into financial activities, with potentially disruptive effects. Companies like Google, Apple, Facebook, Amazon and Microsoft come to finance with huge customer bases, unmatched information about clients' preferences and experiences thanks to data superiority, brand recognition and full access to finance. If the promise of FinTech was unbundling banking, BigTechs come to re-bundle financial products and services (payments, credit, asset management, advice, and many others) with the rest of the services in their ecosystem. In so doing, BigTechs do not primarily seek large profits (currently just 11% of BigTechs' revenues; see Carstens, 2021) or positioning thanks to regulatory arbitrage (Oliver Wyman, 2020). Their desire is to complement and reinforce their core commercial activities by increasing convenience (re-bundling), as well as to diversify their revenue streams and to access new sources of data (FSB, 2019).

As is the case of FinTech startups, BigTech platforms in finance bring with them potentially many benefits: cost reductions, financial inclusion, tailoring of products to clients and convenience. However, this is just one part of the story. Unlike FinTech, BigTech activities may end up impairing competition in the medium to long term, as well as harming consumer protection, market integrity and financial stability. If these risks materialize, BigTech may end up reducing welfare. The two main drivers behind this potential outcome are BigTech's business model, and regulatory asymmetries.

3.   BIGTECH BUSINESS MODEL

BigTechs were not born large. They originated as startups that established multi-sided platforms (see Rochet and Tirole, 2003; Sánchez-Cartas and León, 2021) enabling online interactions between buyers and sellers in areas like e-commerce, search, and social networks. After a platform has attracted a critical mass of users on both sides, network externalities kick in, whereby a larger number of sellers increases the value of the platform to buyers and vice versa, thus embarking on a phase of accelerated growth. In this period platforms feature enhancements of user experience and start to benefit massively from economies of scale. As they mature, BigTechs may also profit from economies of scope (i.e., expanding to other activities in a cost-effective way), and from a more stable membership thanks to high switching costs in the ecosystem.

At this point, the platforms exploit to the fullest what the Bank for International Settlements has coined as BigTechs's DNA: **D**ata analytics, **N**etwork externalities and interwoven **A**ctivities (BIS, 2019). More users generate more data. Data analytics allows to enhance existing services and to provide others, thus attracting more users as complementary activities are added to the offering.

The relevance of BigTechs in finance comes not just from their scale and their growth potential, but also from the interactions within and across platforms, and with incumbent financial actors. The comparatively low cost of provision of financial services and the potential to grow fast could put at risk the most profitable segments of banks' business, particularly in the distribution of retail products. In addition, BigTechs usually operate in various platforms, which allows for cross-subsidization that could be used to "envelop" other platforms to capture their business and their data (De la Mano and Padilla, 2018).

In sum, it appears that the BigTechs' DNA features an in-built leaning towards monopolization. It is not just that BigTech business model may "envelop" banks' most profitable lines of business and interfaces with clients. They could also make today's disruptors the new firmly established incumbents, unassailable to contestability from future would-be disruptors. Current incumbents and prospective disruptors would face three main barriers from BigTech's DNA (see Curzon Price et al., 2020). First, lack of access to data on consumer preferences and behavior, and misuse of such data, could be utilized to block potential competitors. Second, network effects enable BigTechs to become gatekeepers, thus influencing access to the market and to specific services and data. Gatekeeping and high switching costs may end up harming clients in the long term. And, third, clients' inertia and gatekeeping could also be exploited to create a competitive imbalance with products from competitors (via bundling of services and "self-preferencing"). In this environment, "killer" mergers and buyouts, algorithmic pricing and product selection might exacerbate competition issues, putting at risk the prospective benefits to customers of platformization and the contestability of the markets.

4. REGULATORY AND SUPERVISORY ASYMMETRIES

In the domain of financial regulation, however, favoring competition is only secondary to social objectives like consumer protection, market integrity and financial stability (Restoy, 2021). As much as the DNA business model may create or aggravate financial risks, financial authorities generally lack the mandate and the instruments to promote a level playing field.

Yet the financial industry and relevant regulatory bodies (BIS, 2019, p. 68) have for some time demanded from authorities to apply the principle "same activity, same regulation" (SASR). Admittedly, both the policy line of regulators (see Carstens, 2021; Carstens et al., 2021) and the position of the banking industry (see, for instance, Pacheco, 2021; European Banking Federation, EBF, 2021) have evolved in recent years. The initial demands from the banking industry to apply SASR to BigTechs could be interpreted as a call for urging action from the authorities to prevent the regulatory playing field from becoming increasingly lopsided. Today's established common ground is that the same activities could lead to different risks, and thus may warrant a differentiated regulatory and supervisory treatment.

But BigTechs are indeed regulated by SASR rules when entering finance, as are FinTechs and other actors. Such rules depend on the specific financial activity performed. This is the so-called "activities-based regulation," or ABR, which is aimed at implementing the SASR principle.

BigTechs are subject to two distinct levels of regulation. First, they must comply with the general laws and regulations that apply to all sector or activities. These horizontal, or cross-industry regulations are, fundamentally: (1) competition general law and rules on specific aspects of relevance (for example, mergers, cartels, market abuse, etc.), and case law; (2) data use and data protection; (3) consumer protection and business conduct; and (4) other regulations (for example, cybersecurity rules and standards).

Second, BigTechs or specific entities within their group must also submit to finance-specific regulations when providing financial services. In principle, they face the same requirements as other actors when conducting regulated activities, either directly or through partnerships with other financial institutions. Thus, when performing activities like payment services, e-money operations, credit, or wealth management, BigTechs or entities within their groups need to hold appropriate licenses. And as licensed institutions they become subject to standard and specific requirements on consumer protection and business conduct, anti-money laundering and countering the financing of terrorism (AML/CTF), on competition, on data management, and so on.

Yet, despite being subject to general cross-sector regulations and standard financial industry requirements, there is a host of reasons to argue that current regulatory requirements and supervisory practices create asymmetries which hamper competition, while overlooking the risks that size, growth potential and interconnectedness may pose to the overarching goals of financial regulation: financial stability, consumer protection and market integrity. The first source of imbalance is the regulatory and supervisory approach towards credit institutions. Banks perform a variety of regulated activities that involve risk transformation. Deposit-taking for long-term lending is an essential activity for financial stability and economic growth. The need to protect the system from the consequences of bank failure is what justifies, and rightly so, that prudential rules and the supervision of banks follow an "entity-based regulation," or EBR. Banks are regulated and supervised as consolidated entities, by a dedicated supervisor, on all their activities, regulated or not, as non-core operations might impinge upon their soundness. They bear a heavy regulatory burden, and frequently a very intrusive supervision, which affects both core and ancillary activities, or matters largely unfamiliar to BigTechs concerns, such as: capital, liquidity, leverage, financial governance, risk management culture, remuneration caps or payout guidelines. In addition, globally systemic banks – which are much smaller in size than the main BigTechs – must submit to additional prudential requirements on loss absorbency, recovery and resolution.

Relating in part to the above, a second asymmetry springs from the different intensities of supervision and enforcement of financial regulations (see Oliver Wyman, 2020; Restoy, 2021). Admittedly, lighter standards may be justified in the case of most FinTechs, but certainly not when it comes to issues of consumer protection, or AML/CTF prevention associated to BigTechs' activities. Differences in the intensity of supervision and enforcement of oversight may result in undesirable outcomes. A third origin of competitive disadvantage for incumbents is the existence of an asymmetry of overarching importance in the context of the DNA business model: data sharing arrangements tend to benefit BigTechs precisely where their skills are unmatched. For instance, in the European Union (EU) the revised Payments Services Directive, PSD2 (EU, 2015), allows third-party providers, including BigTechs, to access banks' customers' account information and to initiate payments services from those accounts. But third-party providers are obliged to facilitate data portability under the General Data Protection Regulation (EU, 2016) only when "technically possible," which is seldom the case. This absence of reciprocity unavoidably hinders innovation and competition.

The combination of these asymmetries in regulatory standards and in the intensity of oversight and supervision could unintentionally drive or contribute to relatively fast changes in markets structures and sources of risk. This remark is pertinent to a fourth, arguably more relevant, source of asymmetry between incumbents and BigTechs, namely the limited extent to which financial stability risks created or heightened by the latter are effectively mitigated by current rules and practices. Those risks have come under increased scrutiny by regulatory bodies (see FSB, 2019). A first concern relates to scale and potential to grow fast: failure of a large BigTech – or of a significant entity within the group – could cause severe disruptions to the financial system. Second, the expansion of BigTechs into store-of-value services (i.e., mobile wallets) might significantly shrink the pool of funds controlled inside the banking sector, thus increasing the cost of banks' funding, and diminishing its stability and the profitability of incumbents. Third, when massively entering the credit market, a few additional new risks could emerge. For instance, we know little about the functioning of their credit assessment and performance monitoring models, only data-based as opposed to the traditional hybrid data/relationship-based approach. Lending standards might also suffer in credit models where the platform retains only a small portion of the risk involved in the loans they originate. And, fourth, a significant volume of credit flowing outside the regulated banking system may hinder the effectiveness of macroprudential policies, particularly when BigTechs act as mere intermediaries between clients and credit institutions, as the platforms are not subject to measures aimed at containing systemic risk and may not be even constrained by strict rules protecting market integrity. This observation echoes the concerns about "shadow banking."

Interconnectedness between BigTechs and incumbents stands out among the most relevant potential sources of financial stability risks. New operational and financial links may provide extra channels of propagation of risks. One such linkage is the significant dependency of banks from cloud services providers, like Google or Amazon. Severe operational or cyber-security incidents affecting cloud services providers could have systemic effects. Financial regulation subjects outsourcing by credit institutions, but no standards exist for the providers themselves. Additional interdependencies emerge when BigTechs interact with banks as customer-facing layers, or partner with them in many other ways. Operational or financial shocks might further amplify financial stability risks.

5.   WHAT CAN BE DONE?

The answer to this question is far from obvious, given the ramifications and complexities of the subject at all levels, including the financial, economic, regulatory, geographic and geopolitical dimensions. We may start by referring to two alternatives which do not represent constructive options: letting things stay as they are and forbidding BigTechs' presence in the most risky financial activities, including lending services. None of these avenues is consistent with the principles of good regulation (see, for instance, Financial Conduct Authority, FCA, 2020). Doing nothing would imply that identified risks to efficiency, financial stability, consumer protection and market integrity are left unaddressed. Furthermore, regulatory and supervisory inertia would possibly lead to increasing financial stability and consumer protection risks, along with a bumpy transition to a new steady state with a limited role of competition from incumbent credit institutions. The alternative choice of banning BigTechs from business would deprive society from the benefits accruing from competition – wider variety, convenience, inclusion, innovation, etc. – as effective contestability from FinTechs or new entrants faces many limitations (Vives, 2016).

In the face of the rapid changes taking place in technology and finance, there is a need to find a compromise balance between the promotion of the new digital solutions provided by FinTechs, BigTechs and incumbents, and the necessary changes and reforms to the regulatory and the oversight framework. To make it fit for purpose, such a framework would need to mitigate the emerging risks with proportionality and transparency, while recognizing the differences in business models. Openness to financial innovation demands, first and foremost, that financial authorities understand it in all its most relevant implications. Setting up innovation hubs, sandboxes and, most importantly, investing in technological knowledge and engaging with all stakeholders are key initiatives in this respect. Authorities ought to embark in consultations and fact-finding exercises (see, for instance, EBA, 2021), establish a transparent and collaborative environment with market participants, and make all efforts to upgrade the skills of their staff in relation to digital finance innovations (González-Páramo, 2017).

For the immediate future, arguably the most realistic way forward would be to endeavor to close regulatory gaps in the ABR framework, while maintaining the EBR regulation and supervision for banks. As incumbents increasingly depend on and compete with platforms and digital enablers, closing existing loopholes calls for a systematic exercise to identify those with a view to modifying current regulations and/or extending the regulatory perimeter, as well as enhancing supervisory practices. A good example is provided by the EU's call for advice from the European Supervisory Authorities on digital finance, issued in February 2021 (EU, 2021), an exercise the result for which are expected to be published in early 2022. A taste of the kind of issues that can be expected to come out of this cross-examination is provided by EBA's report on the use of digital platforms (EBA, 2021): an overwhelming majority of national competent authorities in the EU report challenges in monitoring compliance with consumer protection and business conduct in the case of digital enablers and platforms.

The list of issues which merit discussion in this ABR gap-closing exercise is long. As a matter of proportionality, it could be argued that large-scale provision is likely to increase risks, which would call for some tightening of licensing and supervisory intensity in all dimensions: prudential rules, operational resilience, resolution, risk governance, reporting, disclosures, and so on (see Pacheco and Urbiola, 2020). Specific themes regularly mentioned in industry surveys (for instance, EBA, 2021) include the following: the convenience to examine new business models in the light of AML/CTF and consumer protection risks and reporting obligations, with a view to bring them into regulation; risk attribution and compliance rules, particularly in the case of third-party providers and marketplace models; limits and thresholds in the imposition of regulation (i.e., solicitation of clients, pooling of assets, etc.) (see De la Mano and Padilla, 2018); group consolidation and remuneration rules hindering the ability of incumbents to attract talent; crypto-currency transactions and exposures, specifically in connection with decentralized platforms, with potential AML/CTF implications; etc. A list of concrete proposals is expected from the EU authorities in 2022 following the above-mentioned call for advice to financial supervisors on potential changes to be made to better reflect BigTech activities and associated risks to consumer protection, market integrity and financial stability (EU, 2021).

Granting the fact that these initiatives could help to mitigate some important asymmetries and somewhat rebalance the playing field, they would do little to tackle two of the most relevant sources of risk to the economy: the effects of BigTechs on competition, and the operational resilience of platforms. To be sure, in the medium term the changes to be implemented need to be deeper and more consistent if regulation is to rise to the challenge. A promising avenue to tackle operational resilience risks is to reinforce ABR requirements to all agents in the financial industry, including BigTechs. For instance, the European Union has proposed a Digital Operational Risk Act which would introduce strict requirements for all financial institutions and ICT services providers (EU, 2020a).

Certainly, however, the argument that it is precisely the bundle of tasks and activities performed by banks, and the impact of this combination on risks to the goals of good regulation that justifies that bank are subject to EBR, is applicable to BigTechs, particularly in the light of the competition concerns coming from their business model. These platforms usually offer a wide array of financial and non-financial services. It is this amalgamation, together with the size and the interconnectedness of platforms, and the risks linked to the DNA business model, that could justify a recalibration of regulation in the direction of a more EBR-based framework complemented with strengthened ABR standards (see Restoy, 2021; Crisanto et al., 2021).

The change of approach to BigTech regulation is arguably necessary, but it is difficult as well since those platforms perform most of their activities in the non-financial sphere, and competition policy is not under the direct authority of financial regulators. On the other hand, a brand-new EBR would need to define what the key features of a "big" platform need to be to become subject to the new regime. And in any case, the principal supervisor of BigTechs would not be the financial authority. The competition authority is the natural candidate if adequately resourced for the task. The creation of a brand-new specialized authority should be explored as an option. An example is the Furman proposal to create a Digital Markets Unit in the UK's Competition and Markets Authority (UK Digital Competition Expert Panel, 2019). This unit would be responsible for setting up a code of conduct for BigTechs, securing data mobility and open standards, as well as requiring access to non-personal and anonymized data. The unit would complement the existing Competition and Markets Authority, which would retain (upgraded) powers on mergers (UK HM Government, 2021). The US is also working on new legislation. A variety of proposals is being discussed, from the creation of a new authority dedicated in full to digital markets (Wheeler, 2021), to beefing up the Federal and Trade Commission, FTC, and the Department of Justice, to declaring

BigTechs as Systemically Important Financial Markets Utilities (see Carstens, 2021). While the US Congress is debating a number of measures to tackle competition concerns, one of the star leaders behind the new thinking calling for ex ante codes of conduct for BigTechs and using regulatory powers in a preventive and timely fashion, Professor Khan (Khan, 2017; Chopra and Khan, 2020), has been at the helm of the FTC since June 2021.

For its part, the EU took a decisive step in tacking the competition concerns raised by BigTechs when proposing the Digital Markets Act to upgrade and refine the competition rules applying to "gatekeeper platforms" (EU, 2020b). The regulation includes obligations of access by third parties to BigTechs' own services and to data generated by users, while banning "self-preferencing," limiting lock-in effects and forbidding other non-competitive practices. The EU Commission will designate "gatekeepers," update their obligations, propose remedies – including divestures of (parts of) a business – and eventually impose financial penalties and fines (up to 10% of global annual turnover). "Gatekeepers" will be subject to an annual independent audit, on-site inspections and, ultimately, to interim measures in the case of potentially irreparable consequences for users.

These moves towards limiting abuses of dominant position and other anti-competitive practices are clearly signaling a way forward, with competition authorities taking care of big platforms' cross-sector competition matters, in close coordination with regulators at the industry level. In such a context, it would be all too natural that the financial services provided by BigTechs, as well as non-financial services relevant for financial activities provided by them, including cloud services, would be regulated, and supervised under an EBR approach complemented by strengthened ABR requirements. Under this new regime, financial authorities would need to work in very close coordination with competition, data-protection, cyber-security and other cross-sector regulators and supervisors, both at the national and the international levels. In the medium to long term, complex home-host issues would need to be discussed and settled if regulatory fragmentation is to be avoided (Adrian, 2021).

6.   CONCLUSION

The presence of BigTech platforms in finance brings potentially many benefits: cost reductions, higher productivity, financial inclusion, tailoring of products to clients, and convenience. However, this is just one part of the story. Unlike FinTech, BigTech activities may end up impairing competition in the medium to long term, as well as harming consumer protection, market integrity and financial stability. If these risks materialize, BigTech may end up reducing welfare. The two main drivers behind this potential outcome are BigTech's business model, and regulatory and supervisory asymmetries.

Competition is a fundamental cornerstone of a vibrant digital economy. However, BigTechs' business model is visibly leading to a significant concentration of economic dominance. This has triggered doctrinal and policy debates that are coalescing around a new approach to competition policy, with entity-based proposals of various types. These initiatives pave the way for significant changes in the approach through which large digital platforms are regulated and supervised in finance. Albeit currently financial services represent only a small fraction of their revenues, BigTechs' influence goes much beyond that, as they also offer non-financial services that are essential for all financial competitors. And they could very quickly become too big to fail. Removing the most critical regulatory asymmetries which hinder the attainment of authorities' objectives calls for strengthening fundamental horizontal regulations – in particular, operational resilience – as well as for treating BigTechs as entities performing financial and non-financial roles of crucial importance for financial and economic stability.

REFERENCES

Adrian, T. (2021), BigTech in financial services, International Monetary Fund, June 16 (https://www.imf.org/en/News/Articles/2021/06/16/sp061721-bigtech-in-financial -services).

BIS (2019), Big tech in finance: opportunities and risks, in BIS Annual Economic Reports 2019, chapter III (https://www.bis.org/publ/arpdf/ar2019e3.pdf).

Carney, M. (2017), The promise of FinTech – Something new under the sun?, Deutsche Bundesbank G20 Conference on "Digitising finance, financial inclusion and financial literacy," Wiesbaden, 25 January (https://www.bankofengland.co.uk/speech/ 2017/the-promise-of-fintech-something-new-under-the-sun).

Carstens, A. (2021), Public policy for big techs in finance, Asia School of Business Conversations on Central Banking webinar, "Finance as information," Basel, January 21 (https://www.bis.org/speeches/sp210121.pdf).

Carstens, A., Claessens, S., Restoy, F. and Shin, H.S. (2021), Regulating big techs in finance, BIS Bulletin No. 45, August 2 (https://www.bis.org/publ/bisbull45.htm).

Chopra, R. and Khan, L.M. (2020), The case for "unfair methods of competition" rulemaking, *The University of Chicago Law Review*, 87, pp. 357–379.

Crisanto, J.C., Ehrentraud, J. and Fabian, M. (2021), Big techs in finance: Regulatory approaches and policy options, Financial Stability Institute, FSI Briefs, 12, March (https://www.bis.org/fsi/fsibriefs12.pdf).

Curzon Price, T., Gee, C., Reynolds, G. and Morrison, E. (2020), BigTech and data disruption, Insight, Financial Conduct Authority (United Kingdom), October (https:// www.fca.org.uk/insight/future-market-dynamics-part-2).

De la Mano, M. and Padilla, J. (2018), BigTech banking, *Journal of Competition Law & Economics*, 14, pp. 494–526 (https://academic.oup.com/jcle/article-abstract/14/4/ 494/5429927).

EBA (2018), EBA report on the impact of FinTech on incumbent credit institutions business models, July (https://www.eba.europa.eu/sites/default/documents/ files/documents/10180/2270909/1f27bb57-387e-4978-82f6-ece725b51941/Report

%20on%20the%20impact%20of%20Fintech%20on%20incumbent%20credit
%20institutions%27%20business%20models.pdf?retry=1).

EBA (2021), EBA report on the use of digital platforms in the EU banking and payments sector, EBA/REP/2021/26, September 21 (https://www.eba.europa.eu/sites/
default/documents/files/document_library/Publications/Reports/2021/1019865/
EBA%20Digital%20platforms%20report%20-%20210921.pdf).

EBF (2021), EBF Position Paper on the European Commission's proposal for a regulation on digital operational resilience for the financial sector (DORA), April 28
(https://www.ebf.eu/wp-content/uploads/2021/05/EBF-Position-Paper_DORA.pdf).

EU (2015), Directive 2015/2366/EU of the European Parliament and of the Council of
25 November 2015 on payment services in the internal market, amending Directives
2002/65/EC, 2009/110/EC and 2013/36/EU and Regulation (EU) No 1093/2010,
and repealing Directive 2007/64/EC, December (https://eur-lex.europa.eu/legal
-content/EN/TXT/PDF/?uri=CELEX:32015L2366&from=EN).

EU (2016), Regulation 2016/679 of the European Parliament and of the Council of
27 April 2016 on the protection of natural persons with regard to the processing of
personal data and on the free movement of such data, and repealing Directive 95/46/
EC (General Data Protection Regulation) (https://eur-lex.europa.eu/legal-content/
EN/TXT/PDF/?uri=CELEX:02016R0679-20160504&from=EN).

EU (2020a), Proposal for a regulation of the European Parliament and of the Council
on Digital Operational Resilience for the financial sector and amending Regulations
(EC) No 1060/2009, (EU) No 648/2012, (EU) No 600/2014 and (EU) No 909/2014
(https://eur-lex.europa.eu/legal-content/EN/TXT/PDF/?uri=CELEX:52020PC0595
&from=EN).

EU (2020b), Proposal for a regulation of the European Parliament and of the Council on
contestable and fair markets in the digital sector (Digital Markets Act), SEC(2020)
437 final, December 15 (https://eur-lex.europa.eu/legal-content/EN/TXT/PDF/?uri=
CELEX:52020PC0842&from=en).

EU (2021), Request to EBA, EIOPA and ESMA for technical advice on digital finance
and related issues (https://ec.europa.eu/info/sites/default/files/business_economy
_euro/banking_and_finance/documents/210202-call-advice-esas-digital-finance_en
.pdf).

FCA (2020), What is the Financial Conduct Authority (FCA) UK? (https://psplab.com/
kb/what-is-the-financial-conduct-authority-fca-uk/).

FinTech News Singapore (2018), 8 reasons why FinTech startups fail, June 20 (https://
fintechnews.sg/20296/fintech/reasons-why-fintech-startups-fail/).

FSB (2019), BigTech in finance. Market developments and potential financial stability implications, December 9 (https://www.fsb.org/wp-content/uploads/P091219-1
.pdf).

González-Páramo, J.M. (2017), Financial innovation in the digital age, *Financial
Stability Review*, 32, Bank of Spain, May, pp. 9–38 (https://www.bde.es/f/webbde/
GAP/Secciones/Publicaciones/InformesBoletinesRevistas/RevistaEstabilidadF
inanciera/17/MAYO%202017/Articulo_GonzalezParamo.pdf).

Khan, L.M. (2017), Amazon's antitrust paradox, *The Yale Law Journal*, 126,
pp. 712–815 (https://www.yalelawjournal.org/pdf/e.710.Khan.805_zuvfyyeh.pdf).

Oliver Wyman (2020), Big banks, bigger techs? Joint report with the International
Banking Federation (https://www.oliverwyman.com/content/dam/oliver-wyman/
v2/publications/2020/jul/Big%20Banks%20Bigger%20Techs%20Final%20Version
.pdf).

Pacheco, L. (2021), Implementing the principle of "same activity, same risk, same regulation of supervision": activity vs. entity-based frameworks, BBVA, *Economic Watch*, October 14 (https://www.bbvaresearch.com/en/publicaciones/global -implementing-the-principle-of-same-activity-same-risk-same-regulation/).

Pacheco, L. and Urbiola, P. (2020), From FinTech to BigTech: An evolving regulatory response, Working Paper 20/09, BBVA Research (https://www.bbvaresearch .com/wp-content/uploads/2020/06/WP_From_FinTech_to_BigTech_an_evolving _regulatory_response_WB_.pdf).

Restoy, F. (2021), FinTech regulation: How to achieve a level playing field, Financial Stability Institute, Occasional Paper, 17, February (https://www.bis.org/fsi/ fsipapers17.pdf).

Rochet, J.-C. and Tirole, J. (2003), Platform competition in two-sided markets, *Journal of the European Economic Association*, 1(4), pp. 990–1029 (https://doi.org/10.1162/ 154247603322493212).

Sánchez-Cartas and León (2021), Multi-sided platforms and markets: A survey of the theoretical Literature, *Journal of Economic Surveys*, 35(2), pp. 452–487 (https://doi .org/10.1111/joes.12409).

Sevlin, R. (2019), Why FinTech startups fail?, *Forbes*, July 29 (https://www.forbes .com/sites/ronshevlin/2019/07/29/why-fintech-startups-fail/?sh=66c747c86440).

UK Digital Competition Expert Panel (2019), Unlocking digital competition, March (https://assets.publishing.service.gov.uk/government/uploads/system/uploads/ attachment_data/file/785547/unlocking_digital_competition_furman_review_web .pdf).

UK HM Government (2021), A new pro-competition regime for digital markets (Consultation), July (https://assets.publishing.service.gov.uk/government/uploads/ system/uploads/attachment_data/file/1003913/Digital_Competition_Consultation _v2.pdf).

Van der Kroft, J. (2021), Collaboration at the core: Evolving partnerships between banks and FinTechs, EY, March 23 (https://www.ey.com/en_nl/banking-capital -markets-transformation-growth/collaboration-at-the-core-evolving-partnerships -between-banks-and-fintechs).

Vives, X. (2016), *Competition and Stability in Banking: The Role of Regulation and Competition Policy*, Princeton University Press.

Wheeler, T. (2021), A focused federal agency is necessary to oversee Big Tech, Brookings brief, February 10, (https://www.brookings.edu/research/a-focused -federal-agency-is-necessary-to-oversee-big-tech/).

16. The emerging autonomy–stability choice for stablecoins[1]

Maarten R. C. van Oordt

1. INTRODUCTION

The emergence of cryptocurrencies has enabled the storage and transfer of digital assets in a decentralized manner using distributed ledgers ("blockchains"). The exchange rates of cryptocurrencies such as Bitcoin have witnessed high levels of volatility (Yermack, 2015; Dwyer, 2015).[2] Many initiatives have explored different arrangements to create digital tokens or "coins" that maintain a stable value and that could be used as a form of money in transactions on distributed ledgers. Coins initiated with this goal in mind have been labeled *stable*coins after their objective of a stable value.

Most stablecoins target a fixed exchange rate against a fiat currency such as the dollar or the euro.[3] Two types of stablecoin arrangements that target a fixed exchange rate against a fiat currency tend to be most popular. The first type can be characterized as stablecoins that are backed with assets denominated in a fiat currency that are held in the traditional financial system, or *fiat*-backed stablecoins. The supply of the two largest stablecoins of this type (Tether and USD Coin) represented a total value of 121 billion U.S. dollars at the end of 2021. The second type can be characterized as stablecoins that are backed with digital assets such as cryptocurrencies that are held in distributed ledgers, or *crypto*-backed stablecoins. The market capitalization of the largest stablecoin of this type (DAI) was 9 billion U.S. dollars at the end of 2021. The precise meaning of *backing* I leave intentionally vague, but one can think broadly about backing as assets that are meant to be available to the stablecoin arrangement to redeem tokens or to intervene whenever a stablecoin deviates from the targeted exchange rate.

Stablecoin arrangements have not remained unnoticed by regulators worldwide (Financial Stability Board, 2020, 2021). Many policy makers have raised the importance of the solvency, liquidity and transparency of stablecoin arrangements as well as the importance of their compliance with regulations aimed at financial consumer protection, investor protection, operational resilience and the prevention of money-laundering and terrorist financing

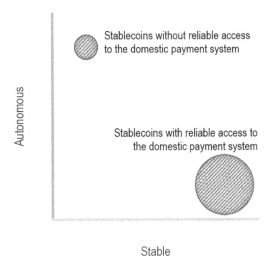

Figure 16.1   The autonomy–stability choice of stablecoins

(European Central Bank, 2020; U.S. President's Working Group et al., 2021; Garcia et al., 2021; Bolt et al., 2022).[4] Less attention has been paid to the fact that stablecoin transactions are processed by decentralized networks that may largely operate outside the sphere of control of the relevant authorities.

The topic of this chapter is the need for the issuer of a fiat-backed stablecoin to maintain reliable access to the domestic payment system of the jurisdiction that issues the fiat currency in order to maintain a stable peg. In particular, I show how substantial deviations of the one-to-one peg occurred for the largest fiat-backed stablecoin when its access to the domestic payment system was interrupted. This is an important observation for regulators, because the need for reliable access to the domestic payment system in order to maintain a stable value provides an important foothold for regulators to exercise control over fiat-backed stablecoins.

The chapter then discusses the potential implications of regulation for the universe of stablecoins. As regulators pay more and more attention to stablecoins, I expect stablecoins to increasingly face the choice between either *less autonomy* in the sense of subjecting themselves to regulatory control or *less stability* due to a lack of reliable payment system access. Conditional upon domestic regulators having little control over the operators of some distributed ledgers, this is likely to lead to a situation where the users of stablecoins ultimately face a choice between stablecoins with a stable value but little autonomy (the lower-right corner of Figure 16.1) and alternatives with more autonomy but a less stable value (the upper-left corner of Figure 16.1).

2.   PAYMENT SYSTEM ACCESS

The issuers of the most popular form of stablecoins, fiat-backed stablecoins, effectively manage their exchange rates by providing a possibility for their users to redeem or convert their stablecoin tokens into fiat currency and vice versa at a rate that is close to the target rate. The redemption or conversion of fiat-backed stablecoin tokens may either be directly with the issuer or indirectly, for example, through a third-party such as a cryptocurrency exchange or a market maker who acts as a middleman.

The redemption of stablecoin tokens requires two flows of transactions to take place that are each processed in different systems. First, it must be possible for the issuer to either directly or indirectly receive the stablecoin tokens that were sent by the stablecoin users. The flow of stablecoin tokens takes place in the realm of distributed ledgers and is processed by a decentralized network. Second, it must be possible for the stablecoin issuer to send either directly or indirectly fiat currency to the bank accounts of the stablecoin users. The flow of fiat currency is processed by the domestic payment system of which the direct participants (e.g., banks) and indirect participants (e.g., respondents of correspondent banks) provide bank accounts to their customers.

Enabling the redemption or conversion of a fiat-backed stablecoin ultimately requires the issuer to have the ability to receive, store and send funds using the traditional financial system. After all, if the demand for a stablecoin drops substantially and users wish to convert their stablecoin into fiat money – that is, balances in their bank accounts – then the funds held by the issuer of the stablecoin will need a channel to flow to the users' bank accounts. The issuer could obtain access to the domestic payment system to facilitate this flow of fiat currency, for example, through a banking relationship of either the stablecoin issuer or its payment processor with a direct or indirect participant.

When the flow of fiat currency between the stablecoin issuer and the users becomes disrupted, then the issuer can no longer remit fiat currency to users who redeem or convert their stablecoin tokens. Although users would still be able to sell tokens to each other, there is no mechanism that guarantees that the price of the tokens traded among users would be close to the targeted exchange rate. Hence, the prevailing exchange rate may deviate from the target rate if the access of the issuer to the domestic payment system becomes disrupted.

The crucial role of reliable access to the domestic payment system for the issuer of a fiat-backed stablecoin in order to maintain a stable peg can be well illustrated by some episodes in the early history of Tether which currently is the largest stablecoin in terms of market capitalization.[5]

2.1   Losing Payment System Access

For a long time, the stability of Tether's exchange rate was supported by the closely related cryptocurrency exchange Bitfinex. Bitfinex customers could adjust their dollar balances held with the exchange either through wire transfers from their bank accounts, or through deposits and withdrawals of Tether where Bitfinex would apply a one-to-one exchange rate when adjusting the customers' dollar balances at the exchange (Bitfinex, 2018). This provided users of Tether with the indirect ability to convert their Tether tokens into U.S. dollars held in their bank accounts at a one-to-one exchange rate. At least, this possibility existed as long as Bitfinex continued to be able to send and receive payments in U.S. dollars through the traditional financial system. Bitfinex and Tether relied on Taiwan-based banks to send and receive U.S. dollar wire transfers with Wells Fargo providing access to the domestic payment system as the corresponding bank. At the end of March 2017, Wells Fargo elected to no longer process the wire transfers for Bitfinex and Tether (New York AG, 2021).

As a consequence, Bitfinex and Tether were essentially cut off from the domestic payment system, which disrupted the ability of users to convert their Tether tokens at a one-to-one exchange rate through U.S. dollar withdrawals at Bitfinex (Bitfinex, 2017; Tether, 2017).

Without reliable access to the traditional payment system, the exchange rate peg of Tether to the U.S. dollar started to fickle. At the end of March 2017, another cryptocurrency exchange called Kraken – arguably a platform with better access to the traditional payment system at the time – had started to support the trading of Tether without guaranteeing its exchange rate (Kraken, 2017). When both Bitfinex and Tether were cut off from the traditional payment system, users could in principle continue to convert their Tether tokens into dollar balances in their bank accounts by selling Tether tokens to other users at Kraken. In return, they would receive U.S. dollar balances at Kraken which could be withdrawn by relying on Kraken's access to the payment system.[6] The price received for Tether tokens at Kraken would depend on the prevailing exchange rate rather than the fixed one-to-one exchange rate applied to Tether deposits at Bitfinex. Tether's exchange rate at the Kraken exchange is shown by the black line in Figure 16.2. Initially, the price dropped substantially below the peg to around 90 cents on the dollar, before recovering and even overshooting the peg.[7]

Although Bitfinex continued its practice to credit balances for Tether deposits at a one-to-one exchange rate throughout this episode, this did not prevent the occurrence of deviations from the one-to-one peg that customers experienced in practice when converting Tether into U.S. dollar balances in their bank accounts. With Bitfinex being cut off from the domestic payment system,

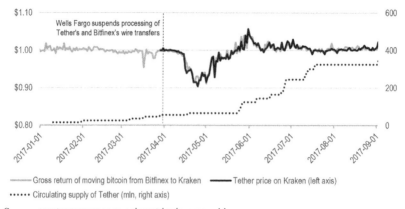

Source: cryptocompare.com, coinmetrics.io, messari.io.

Figure 16.2   Tether's exchange rate when losing payment system access in 2017

an alternative route for users to convert Tether tokens into dollars in their bank accounts was to purchase bitcoins or other cryptocurrencies at Bitfinex – which could be withdrawn using blockchain transactions – and to subsequently sell those bitcoins at Kraken. However, this was costly too. Differences in the exchange rates of cryptocurrencies at Bitfinex and Kraken started to emerge as customers started to discount the dollar balances held with Bitfinex that couldn't be withdrawn to their bank accounts. The gray line in Figure 16.2 reports how much customers could receive at Kraken per U.S. dollar of balances at Bitfinex that they would convert into bitcoin after accounting for the differential in the bitcoin exchange rates at both exchanges.[8] The discount (and later, premium) closely follows the deviation in the peg of the exchange rate of Tether. In other words, the support of Bitfinex for the one-to-one peg could not prevent the peg that users experienced in practice from becoming unstable when Bitfinex was cut off from the domestic payment system.

2.2   Bitfinex Dropping the Peg

A second episode illustrating the importance of access to the domestic payment system for maintaining the peg of a fiat-backed stablecoin happened during the fall of 2018. After the earlier banking troubles, Bitfinex had started increasingly to rely on third parties to handle customer deposits and withdrawals, and the stability of the exchange rate of Tether improved during the first half of 2018. However, customers started to experience substantial delays in withdrawals of balances from the Bitfinex trading platform to their bank

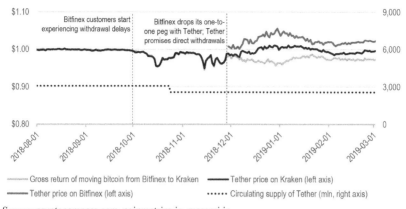

Source: cryptocompare.com, coinmetrics.io, messari.io.

Figure 16.3   Tether's exchange rate after Bitfinex drops the peg

accounts in the fall of 2018 (Coindesk, 2018b) after Bitfinex started experiencing trouble with their major payment processor, Crypto Capital, and lost control over a significant amount of funds (New York AG, 2021). As in the earlier episode, this resulted in both a deviation in the peg of Tether as well as a discount on the amount of fiat currency customers would get when moving bitcoin from Bitfinex to Kraken (Figure 16.3).

What makes this episode particularly interesting is that, by the end of November, Bitfinex (2018) announced it would no longer apply a one-to-one exchange rate for Tether deposits and withdrawals. Instead, it would start offering customers the ability to buy and sell Tether through a Tether-U.S. dollar trading pair like the one on Kraken. When the pair started trading the day after, Tether traded at a *premium* at Bitfinex – consistent with customers discounting dollar balances held in Bitfinex relative to holding Tether tokens – even though Tether itself continued trade for a while at a *discount* at Kraken.[9] Hence, for a while, there were two unstable "pegs" rather than one. Tether tokens were discounted compared to U.S. dollar balances at Kraken which could be withdrawn, and dollar balances held with Bitfinex were discounted even more.

3.   REGULATORY IMPLICATIONS

The need for reliable access to the domestic payment system in order to maintain a stable peg has substantial implications for the regulation of stablecoins. Regulators may have relatively little effective control over the operators of distributed ledgers (e.g., miners), but the participants in their domestic payment systems (e.g., banks) tend to be within their sphere of control.[10] The control of regulators over the participants in the domestic payment system provides them with substantial leverage to directly or indirectly enforce regulatory compliance for any entity that requires reliable access to the domestic payment system, including fiat-backed stablecoin issuers that wish to maintain a stable peg.

The empirical evidence in this chapter suggests that – if regulators exercise this control – the issuers of fiat-backed stablecoins will face the choice between *less autonomy* in the sense of subjecting themselves to regulatory control or a *less stable peg* as operating their stablecoins without regulatory approval would leave them without reliable access to the domestic payment system. Regulators are likely to subject stablecoin issuers to a wide variety of standards and rules given the concerns they have raised. For example, the U.S. President's Working Group et al. (2021, p. 16) suggest that legislation should require stablecoin issuers to be insured depository institutions which would subject them to intensive regulatory oversight. Moreover, stablecoin issuers would likely need to comply with regular requests from law enforcement agencies and financial supervisors to freeze balances (e.g. Cointelegraph, 2020a, 2020b).[11] Conditional upon domestic regulators having little control over the operators of distributed ledgers, users of stablecoins are then likely to face a choice between stablecoins with a stable value but little autonomy (the lower-right corner of Figure 16.1) and stablecoins with more autonomy but a less stable value (the upper-left corner of Figure 16.1).

Three types of candidates for the less stable stablecoins in the upper-left corner of Figure 16.1 emerge.

First, an obvious candidate is the issuer of a fiat-backed stablecoin that is willing to accept the risk of being cut off from the payment system in a cat-and-mouse game with regulators. Such an issuer would expose its users to an unstable peg but could potentially experience a higher level of autonomy for as long as it lasts.

Second, there may be hurdles for domestic regulators to force the issuer of a fiat-backed stablecoin that is pegged to a foreign fiat currency to comply with regulations in their jurisdiction. Even though domestic users of a "foreign" fiat-backed stablecoin would face some foreign exchange rate risk, they could still benefit from such a stablecoin when the exchange rate risk of the foreign fiat currency is less than that of cryptocurrencies like Bitcoin and Ethereum. The operator of such a foreign stablecoin could maintain a peg with a fiat currency of a jurisdiction that allows them to operate with a higher degree of autonomy. Initiatives for international cooperation and harmonization in the area of stablecoin regulation (e.g., Financial Stability Board, 2020) could help to reduce some of the hurdles domestic regulators would face with respect to foreign stablecoins.

Third, crypto-backed stablecoins may experience a high degree of autonomy because these type of stablecoins require no access to the traditional payment systems. The management of the supply of crypto-backed stablecoins involves transactions with tokens and assets on a distributed ledger only, so these stablecoins may experience a high degree of autonomy as long as regulators continue to have little control over the operators of distributed ledgers.[12] However, crypto-backed stablecoins are unlikely to maintain a stable one-to-one peg with a stable supply in the event where a deep crash in the prices of the underlying crypto-assets occurs.[13]

4.   CONCLUDING REMARKS

The continued existence of "more autonomous – less stable" stablecoins as the regulatory pressure rises would rely on the continued existence of some decentralized networks that can operate outside the sphere of control of the relevant authorities. There are some reasons to believe that some decentralized cryptocurrency networks do not operate completely independently of the local regulatory stance. For example, China's crackdown on mining activities in May 2021 (*Economist*, 2021) was followed by an approximately 40 percent drop in the computational power of the Bitcoin network. This does not imply that the operators of all decentralized networks will be within the sphere of control of the relevant authorities. First, decentralized networks may operate from jurisdictions that take a more lenient stance. Second, the operators of the Bitcoin network rely on specialized hardware to maintain the integrity of the ledger (Garrat and Van Oordt, 2020; Prat and Walter, 2021) which requires ties to a physical location. Some other decentralized cryptocurrency networks rely on protocols that do not use specialized hardware (e.g., "proof-of-stake"), which allows their operators to move virtually anywhere at a low cost. This suggests that some of the autonomous stablecoins are here to stay, although they may turn out to become limited in scale and importance compared to their stable regulated counterparts.

NOTES

1.   I am grateful to Jonathan Chiu, Robert Holzmann and Anneke Kosse for helpful comments and suggestions.
2.   Reasons mentioned for the high volatility of cryptocurrency exchange rates include the unresponsiveness of their supply to transactional demand, their limited use for real payments – which causes their exchange rate to be highly sensitive to the actions of speculators (Bolt and Van Oordt, 2020) – and the fundamental uncertainty regarding the popularity of a cryptocurrency while many other cryptocurrencies exist that could act as potential substitutes (Garratt and Wallace, 2018).

3. A complete taxonomy is not my purpose at present but would include among others stablecoins pegged to commodities and so-called algorithmic stablecoins (e.g., Bullmann et al., 2019).
4. See also Lyons and Viswanath-Natraj (2020), Gorton and Zhang (2021) and Lipton et al. (forthcoming).
5. Some of the largest and most persistent deviations in Tether's exchange rate were during periods where the issuer's access to the traditional payment system was disrupted. That said, solvency concerns may play a role too. Whether Tether always held enough high-quality liquid assets (e.g., cash and cash equivalents) to redeem each token has been the subject of considerable controversy (Faux, 2021; Griffin and Shams, 2020). The issuer of Tether provided a loan of 625 million U.S. dollars to the close-related cryptocurrency exchange Bitfinex that experienced financial headwinds at the time without informing the public (New York AG, 2021). These type of concerns are not without historical precedent (Frost et al., 2020).
6. It seems this remained a popular route in subsequent episodes (Coindesk, 2018a).
7. When the exchange rate started to overshoot the peg in the second half of May 2017, Tether issued a substantial number of additional tokens to increase the supply. From the 2021 settlement agreement, it seems that these additional tokens may have been accounted for through an account receivable from Bitfinex; see New York AG (2021).
8. The figure abstracts from transaction costs.
9. Tether's exchange rate at Kraken recovered relatively quickly towards the target rate while the discount on dollar balances held in Bitfinex remained more persistent. The simultaneous announcement of Tether (2018) promising the reopening of the possibility for direct redemptions of Tether tokens for large customers through their new banking relationship may have contributed to this recovery. However, it is not entirely clear to what extent customers were truly able to redeem their Tether tokens at that time.
10. The sphere of control extends to payments from and to indirect participants (e.g., foreign respondent banks) as regulators have the ability to set standards that correspondent banks need to adhere to when providing services to respondent banks (Coelho et al., 2020). For example, the allegations of Australia's regulator against Westpac that resulted in an AUD 1.3 billion settlement agreement included deficiencies in Westpac's oversight of its correspondent banking relationships (AUSTRAC, 2019).
11. Such requests could be used by regulators to not only freeze balances that are suspected to be linked to crime, but also to potentially target balances held by unregulated centralized exchanges and balances held in smart contracts and decentralized exchanges that facilitate the trade between regulated and unregulated digital assets.
12. A potential exception could be a crypto-backed stablecoin that is backed with digital assets of which the issuers are within the sphere of control of the regulator (e.g., a fiat-backed stablecoin that is within the control of the regulator). For example, the multi-collateral version of the crypto-backed stablecoin DAI (MakerDAO, 2020) is partially backed by the fiat-backed stablecoin USD Coin; see https://daistats.com/. The regulator could request the issuer of USD Coin to freeze the relevant balances.
13. Some early empirical evidence on the stability of crypto-backed stablecoins is provided by Bellia and Schich (2020), who report their exchange rates to be more

volatile than those of fiat-backed stablecoins, and Kozhan and Viswanath-Natraj (2021), who find that their stability depends on the stability of the collateral. See, e.g., Li and Mayer (2021) for a theoretical analysis.

REFERENCES

AUSTRAC. AUSTRAC Applies for Civil Penalty Orders Against Westpac. Press Release (November 20), 2019. https://www.austrac.gov.au/about-us/media-release/civil-penalty-orders-against-westpac

Bellia, M. and S. Schich. What Makes Private Stablecoins Stable? Working Paper, 2020.

Bitfinex. Pausing Wire Deposits to Bitfinex. Online Announcement (April 17), 2017. https://www.bitfinex.com/posts/200

Bitfinex. Bitfinex Announces Tether Neutrality and Launches New Stablecoin Pairs. Online Announcement (November 27), 2018. https://www.bitfinex.com/posts/319

Bolt, W. and M.R.C. Van Oordt. On the Value of Virtual Currencies. *Journal of Money, Credit and Banking*, 52(2): 835–862, 2020.

Bolt, W., V. Lubbersen and P. Wierts. Getting the Balance Right: Crypto, Stablecoin and CBDC. *Journal of Payments Strategy & Systems*, (forthcoming), 2022.

Bullmann, D., J. Klemm and A. Pinna. In Search for Stability in Crypto-assets: Are Stablecoins the Solution? ECB Occasional Paper, 230, 2019.

Coelho, R., J. Fishman, A. Hassan and R. Vrbaski. Closing the Loop: AML/CFT Supervision of Correspondent Banking. *Financial Stability Institute Insights*, 28, 2020.

Coindesk. Tether Floods into Kraken Exchange, Where Crypto Traders Can Get Dollars. News Report (October 19), 2018a. https://www.coindesk.com/markets/2018/10/19/tether-floods-into-kraken-exchange-where-crypto-traders-can-get-dollars/

Coindesk. For Bitfinex Users, Dollar Withdrawals Are Now a Weeks-Long Struggle. News Report (November 9), 2018b. https://www.coindesk.com/markets/2018/11/09/for-bitfinex-users-dollar-withdrawals-are-now-a-weeks-long-struggle/

Cointelegraph. Centre Freezes Ethereum Address Holding $100K USDC. News Report (July 9), 2020a. https://cointelegraph.com/news/centre-freezes-ethereum-address-holding-100k-usdc

Cointelegraph. Tether Blacklists 39 Ethereum Addresses Worth Over $46 Million. News Report (July 10), 2020b. https://cointelegraph.com/news/tether-blacklists-39-ethereum-addresses-worth-over-46-million

Dwyer, G.P. The Economics of Bitcoin and Similar Private Digital Currencies. *Journal of Financial Stability*, 17: 81–91, 2015.

Economist. America is the Big Winner of China's Crypto Crackdown. News Report (October 22), 2021. https://www.economist.com/graphic-detail/2021/10/22/america-is-the-big-winner-of-chinas-crypto-crackdown

European Central Bank. Stablecoins: Implications for Monetary Policy, Financial Stability, Market Infrastructure and Payments, and Banking Supervision in the Euro Area. Occasional Paper, 247, 2020.

Faux, Z. Anyone Seen Tether's Billions? *Bloomberg Businessweek* (October 7), 2021. https://www.bloomberg.com/news/features/2021-10-07/crypto-mystery-where-s-the-69-billion-backing-the-stablecoin-tether

Financial Stability Board. Regulation, Supervision and Oversight of "Global Stablecoin" Arrangements. Institutional Report, 2020.

Financial Stability Board. Regulation, Supervision and Oversight of "Global Stablecoin" Arrangements: Progress Report on the Implementation of the FSB High-Level Recommendations. Institutional Report, 2021.

Frost, J., H.S. Shin and P. Wierts. An Early Stablecoin? The Bank of Amsterdam and the Governance of Money, BIS Working Paper, 902, 2020.

Garcia, A., B. Lands and D. Yanchus. Stablecoin Assessment Framework. *Bank of Canada Staff Analytical Note*, 2021-6, 2021.

Garrat, R.J. and M.R.C. Van Oordt. Why Fixed Costs Matter for Proof-of-Work Based Cryptocurrencies. Bank of Canada Staff Working Paper, 2020-19, 2020.

Garratt, R. and N. Wallace. Bitcoin 1, Bitcoin 2 ...: An Experiment on Privately Issued Outside Monies. *Economic Inquiry*, 56(3): 1887–1897, 2018.

Gorton, G.B. and J. Zhang. Taming Wildcat Stablecoins. Working Paper, 2021.

Griffin, J.M. and A. Shams. Is Bitcoin Really Untethered? *Journal of Finance*, 75(4): 1913–1964, 2020.

Kozhan, R. and G. Viswanath-Natraj. Decentralized Stablecoins and Collateral Risk. Working Paper, 2021.

Kraken. Kraken Announces Support for "Crypto dollar" Tether (USDT). Online Announcement (March 29), 2017. https://blog.kraken.com/post/206/kraken -announces-support-for-crypto-dollar/

Li, Y. and S. Mayer. Money Creation in Decentralized Finance: A Dynamic Model of Stablecoin and Crypto Shadow Banking. CESifo Working Paper, 9, 260, 2021.

Lipton, A., A. Sardon, F. Schär and C. Schüpbach. Stablecoins, Digital Currency, and the Future of Money. In A. Pentland, A. Lipton and T. Hardjono (eds.), *Building the New Economy*. MIT Press, forthcoming.

Lyons, R.K. and G. Viswanath-Natraj. What Keeps Stablecoins Stable? NBER Working Paper, 27, 136, 2020.

MakerDAO. The Maker Protocol: MakerDAO's Multi-Collateral Dai System. White Paper, 2020.

New York AG. Settlement Agreement between the OAG, Bitfinex, and Tether. 2021. https://ag.ny.gov/sites/default/files/2021.02.17_-_settlement_agreement_- _execution_version.b-t_signed-c2_oag_signed.pdf

Prat, J. and B. Walter. An Equilibrium Model of the Market for Bitcoin Mining. *Journal of Political Economy*, 129(8): 2415–2452, 2021.

Tether. Announcement. Online Announcement (April 22), 2017. https://tether.to/ 2017/04/

Tether. Announcement. Online Announcement (November 27), 2018. https://tether .to/tether-reopens-account-verification-and-direct-redemption-of-fiat-from-its -platform/

U.S. President's Working Group, FDIC, and OCC. Interagency Report on Stablecoins. Institutional Report, 2021. https://home.treasury.gov/system/files/136/ StableCoinReport Nov1 508.pdf

Yermack, D. Is Bitcoin a Real Currency? An Economic Appraisal. In D.L.K. Chuen (ed.), *Handbook of Digital Currency*, pp. 31–43. Elsevier, 2015.

PART V

Lessons from the COVID-19 crisis for the optimal supervisory architecture

17. Some lessons from COVID-19 for the EU financial framework

Ignazio Angeloni

Remember the Millennium Bug? Late in the 1990s, as the world relished the tailwinds of the technology revolution and the end of the Cold War and people prepared for a special New Year's celebration, all humans seemed to worry about was that computers may ignore that the first digit of the year was changing and that this may bring us back – digitally – to the Middle Ages. In the end, nothing happened. As we soon discovered, the real threats of the New Era were elsewhere.

We have since experienced four of those threats – terrorism, financial meltdown, pandemic and, more recently, war in Europe – and we had an unpleasant foretaste of a fifth one: climate disaster. Another risk, the potential impact of an asteroid on Earth, is increasingly discussed by scientists but is expected to become real only from the 22nd century onward. These threats are all foreseeable in nature but unpredictable in their actual occurrence, timing and modalities. Then there are the unforeseeable ones: the "unknown unknowns" that we cannot even imagine.

Therefore, farsighted policymakers must be concerned not only about the present crisis or how to deal with similar ones in the future. They should focus on building "systems" (social, political, infrastructural, financial) which can withstand unforeseen shocks without fatal or unbearable adverse consequences. This task requires developing plausible scenarios but also safeguards which are effective against a variety of imponderable circumstances.

As we struggle to contain the (hopefully) last of COVID-19 tail whisks, it may be a good time to reflect on what aspects of the European financial architecture need rethinking in light of our recent experiences. In the following pages I offer some reflections on this, focused on two areas, monetary policy and financial stability policies. For this purpose, I find it useful to first recall some recent discussions, also inspired by the COVID-19 experience but more general, on how disruptive societal risks should be managed.

1.   TOWARDS SYSTEM RESILIENCE

The Princeton economist Markus Brunnermeier (2021) discusses in a recent book some conceptual issues and practical ways to make our societies more "resilient." He distinguishes between "robustness," the ability to stand firm under an adverse shock, and "resilience," the aptitude to endure the shock by adapting to it and restoring balance once the shock subsides. The first characteristic emphasizes strength and ability to resist; the second highlights adaptation, flexibility and ability to recover. One example relates to flood protection. Dams effectively control floods, but only up to a point – until the dam breaks or is overwhelmed. Once that "tipping point" is reached, the adverse consequences can be dramatic. An alternative approach (or perhaps a complementary one) is to move water-sensitive infrastructures higher and reinforce rescue systems. This approach does not prevent floods, but mitigates their impact and facilitates the resumption of the status quo ante.

Another concept discussed in that book is that of "sustainability." Sustainability can be defined as an extended form of resilience: a system is sustainable if its resilience is maintained over time. Here things become more subtle, because one has to worry about the possibility that the very actions that make a system resilient at one point in time may compromise its sustainability at a later time. Going back to the flood example, the existence of mitigation measures may make people feel more protected and hence less alert and prompt when a flood actually occurs. This concept is relevant for the design of financial architectures, such as fiscal rules, banking and insurance regulation, monetary and supervisory charters, etc. These are all cases in which moral hazard may arise. Certain features intended to make the financial architecture more resilient may affect individual behavior in a way that jeopardizes later resilience.

An implication of considering dynamics and endogenous behavior is that risk minimization is not necessarily appropriate. A certain amount of risk can be necessary, indeed optimal for society to develop inner defences that make those or other risks more survivable.[1] Vaccination is a relevant example here; small amounts of pathogen help develop antibodies which protect against grave illnesses.

These ideas are relevant in other contexts as well.[2] For example, consider the comparison between "autocratic" and "democratic" political systems in their relative aptness in delivering societal resilience. Autocratic systems (more centralized, less depended on public opinion, less transparent) may have an advantage in making the society more robust, by building stronger defences to change. However, compared to democratic systems, they may be less effective in delivering resilience, which implies or requires adaptability, diversity of views and multiple inputs into the decision-making processes, freedom of information, ability to change course and correct mistakes. This distinction is relevant also with regard to financial architectures. The latter can differ, for example, in the extent to which policy decisions rely on fixed rules, rigid in their application and hard to change, as opposed to discretionary decisions, entrusted to independent and accountable agencies. Even if constrained by charters and accountability frameworks, discretionary decision-makers are in a better position to react to unforeseen circumstances and take into account broader and changing information sets.

Recent analyses bordering with psychology and behavioral science, applied to decision-making approaches in both corporate and public policy environments, have also emphasized the distinction between "tunnel vision" (exclusive focus on limited information sets) and "peripheral" or "lateral vision" (preparedness to take into consideration also apparently unrelated evidence and intelligence).[3] In a world characterized by rapid change and imponderables (little-known or unknown unknowns), tunnel vision may result in delayed awareness of and reaction to risk. Again, the concept is relevant for the design of financial architectures. For example, legal and regulatory constraints forcing decision-makers to consider only certain parameters, or respond only in predefined ways, or to entertain only certain forms of cooperation with other policy actors[4] can lead to sub-optimal decisions in presence of unforeseen developments or crises.

According to Brunnermeier (2021), central banks are particularly well-suited to provide resilience to the financial and the broader economy, because of their ability to provide last-resort lending to financial institutions and broad-based monetary support, with a certain degree of discretion, when the economy is hit by adverse demand shocks. His book discusses instances in which central banks have performed such role in the COVID-19 crisis, mitigating its impact. It is worth noting that in most of these cases, central banks have typically had to make decisions rapidly, with limited information sets, in many cases reaching the limits of their mandates to introduce new intervention criteria and modalities.

The next two sections discuss two areas of the existing European financial architecture where the above considerations may apply, starting with monetary policy and then moving on to financial stability, in particular to banking regulation and supervision.

2.   MONETARY POLICY

The euro area's monetary policy framework, agreed upon in the late 1980s and enshrined in the EU Treaty (of which the ECB statute is part), rests on four main conceptual pillars.

The first is the notion that price stability is the overriding objective of the ECB monetary policy (art. 127 of the Treaty and art. 2 of the ECB statute). The exclusive focus on a single objective is mitigated by the provision, in the same article, that without prejudice to the objective of price stability, the ECB should contribute to the general economic policies of the European Union; yet, price stability remains the overriding goal without escape clauses and regardless of circumstances. The second pillar is given by the detailed enumeration of the instruments that the central bank can use to attain is goal. The list contained in chapter 4 of the ECB statute mirrors the practices followed by most central banks in advanced economies for most of the 20th century, in most (though not all) circumstances.[5] The use of "other instruments" is admitted but only by qualified majority in the Governing Council. The third element underpinning the ECB charter is its independence (art. 130 of the Treaty and art. 7 of the ECB statute): the members of the ECB Governing Council cannot seek or take instructions by any public or private body. The last one is the explicit prohibition of monetary financing of public entities (art. 123 of the Treaty and art. 21 of the ECB statute), in the form of overdrafts or any other type of credit facilities.

The fact that all these elements feature in a legal text that has constitutional status such as the European Treaty is remarkable. It constitutes a unique case in the international comparison. In the United States, for example, the monetary powers are entrusted by the Constitution to Congress; the Federal Reserve, created at a later time, is accountable to Congress. The most peculiar aspect, is, perhaps, the enumeration of the central bank intervention techniques, an eminently technical matter. The prohibition to grant credits or overdrafts to public entities can be seen as another limitation in the use of monetary instruments. There are, as well-known, important historical reasons for such provisions. The ECB charter reflects the experiences and political sensitivities of the time when that text was written: primarily the great inflation of the 1970s (which, however, most analyses show not having been caused primarily by monetization of excessive public deficits).

More important, perhaps, is the fact that the ECB is a supra-national institution whose inner rules reflect different experiences, views and "red lines" of the constituent countries. One of them is the concern that the lax attitude towards the financing of state deficits built in the historical record of some constituent national central banks may affect the common monetary policy. These views and arguments are well known and understandable. Still, once the ECB has established its own record and it moves deeper into the 21st century, with its new prospects and challenges, one may ask whether those extraordinary statutory constraints may not hamper its action – more specifically, its crucial role in contributing to the "resilience" of the European financial system in crisis situations.

One may think that, in practice, the problem is less serious than it appears; that some of those limitations may be more apparent than real. Legal provisions, even constitutional ones, are subject to interpretation. To translate into practice, they need to be qualified and made "operational." The brief history of the ECB contains examples that go in this direction. Among the most interesting ones is, perhaps, the argument according to which the pursuit of price stability encompasses and requires the safeguard of the "monetary policy transmission mechanism" – the causal linkages through which monetary policy affect the economy via the financial sector. The single monetary policy – so the argument goes – requires a well-functioning transmission mechanism. Therefore, the pursuit of price stability allows, in fact requires, actions by the central bank that preserves the well-functioning of monetary transmission to the *whole* euro area, including all jurisdictions. From 2011 onwards, this argument has been used to support "unconventional" monetary interventions, from the Securities Market Program (SMP, in place between 2010 and 2013), to the Asset Purchase Program (APP, from 2014) and finally to the Pandemic Emergency Purchase Program (PEPP, 2020), all of which made use of considerable and increasing flexibility in the amounts and composition of the assets purchased.

Another consideration is that, when securities markets are large and liquid, the effects of central bank purchases of public securities at issue, formally prohibited under the Treaty, are essentially the same as those of purchases in the open market, which are instead allowed and encouraged. On this basis, one may doubt that the prohibition of monetary financing, as presently formulated, is of much practical significance.

Of the four cornerstones of the ECB monetary framework mentioned earlier, those concerning price stability and central bank independence are the most significant, and those for which a constitutional basis is more clearly justified. The existence of independent delegated agencies is a cornerstone of the way modern democratic societies are governed. In particular, the benefits of an independent central bank are quite firmly established (for a recent discussion supportive of the concept, see Haldane, 2020). The price stability mandate counterbalances such independence, by providing a measure on the basis of which performance can be assessed and accountability can be exercised.

Yet, qualifications must be made regarding the way these principles are applied. International experiences differ. In the euro area, the definition and the measurement of price stability is left to the central bank itself, which could, in extreme cases, act in a way to elude its constitutional goal. In practice, the ECB has used this leeway sparingly, with small changes both in the numerical reference (the 2% level, previously an upper bound, now a central target) and in the price index used as reference (headline consumer price inflation according to a harmonized definition, though lately more weight is accorded to measures of core inflation and, in future, the index will be broadened to include imputed home rentals). The possibility of changing the inflation target, and the possibility to make amendment without recourse to complex and lengthy legislative procedures, provides flexibility to the monetary policy process. This underpins resilience.

The broader implications of central bank independence are potentially more complex. Two issues have been debated recently. The first is whether independence is compatible with the broader spectrum of monetary policy instruments now prevailing (large-scale asset purchases of private and public securities), which have arguably blurred the distinction between monetary and fiscal policy.[6] Non-conventional instruments of monetary policy, systematically used after the crisis and even more in the pandemic, have distributional consequences and have contributed to the rise of private and public debts in recent years, hence probably to more risk-taking, by making the service of those debts easier. As such, an argument can be made that such operations require democratic representation rather than being delegated to a technical agency. However, this argument loses force when one considers that all monetary policy interventions have distributional consequences. All of them, regardless of whether they consist of interest rate changes or asset purchases, make debt raising easier or harder. This is, in fact, not a side consequence but the *very purpose* of monetary policy actions. We are dealing therefore more with a matter of degree than of kind, resolvable by clarity of mandate and proper accountability. As the intervention techniques become more forceful and new instruments are introduced, central banks need to explain their actions more thoroughly than otherwise and submit themselves to public scrutiny and debate. It must also be kept in mind that unconventional measures are undertaken in crisis conditions; that is, precisely when independent and swift action is necessary to preserve the resilience of the financial and economic system.

A related point is the relation between central bank independence and monetary-fiscal policy coordination. In its most extreme form, central bank independence may be interpreted as ruling out coordination, since the latter requires adapting one's behavior in accordance with other people's will or actions. In its 20-year history, the ECB has never embarked in policy coordination, at least explicitly. But here again, the contrast is more apparent than real. Coordination occurs when two policy actors, such as central banks and fiscal authorities, move together so that the combination of policies better attains some social optimum, rather than deciding in isolation taking the other's actions as given. The potential gains from such coordination increase in crisis conditions and when interest rates are close to their "effective" lower bound (zero or negative).[7] But such eventuality in no way implies a loss of independence by the central bank; what matters is that the latter decides independently, with the purpose of better attaining its institutional goal.[8]

3.   FINANCIAL STABILITY

"Resilience" is not a term often used by supervisors. A more frequent wording, typically to refer to the desirable condition of banks, is "safety and soundness." This expression features, for example, in the documents of the Basel Committee on Banking Supervision[9] and appears in a number of supervisory charters. Article 1 of the SSM regulation, the legal text establishing the tasks and purposes of ECB supervision, prescribes that the ECB exercises its supervisory function "(…) with a view to contributing to the safety and soundness of credit institutions (…)."

The problem with this formulation is that it is both slightly contradictory (a bank can never be fully safe if it conducts its business properly) and excessively vague (what does "sound" exactly mean?).[10] In its daily practice, ECB supervision has often mentioned sustainability as a desirable property of banking business models, a term which, as already discussed, embodies a time dimension (resilience which is sustained over time). Resilience and sustainability can apply both to individual institutions and to financial and economic systems as a whole, and the conditions to secure the two are not necessarily the same, as emphasized by the literature on systemic risks and macroprudential supervision.

For a financial institution, sustainability means ability to stay in business over a prolonged period of time even under adverse and unexpected conditions. The most important element to help guarantee that condition is often assumed to be the institution's capital. Capital measures the maximum unexpected loss which can be withstood by the institution without going bankrupt. Both quantity and quality of capital (ability to effectively cover losses) are important: it is the combination of the two that counts.

The experience of the great financial crisis shows, however, that capital alone is not sufficient; failures can occur even in well-capitalized banks if the composition of the rest of the balance sheet is excessively risky. It all depends on the nature of the shock. For maturity transformers like banks, liquidity – ability to cope with unexpected cash outflows or market liquidity dry-ups – and the stability and reliability of funding can be even more important than capital in certain situations, when financial markets malfunction and certain forms of loss of confidence occur.

Capital not only permits to cover losses, but also allows banks to promptly accommodate unforeseen increases of credit demand. The COVID-19 experience is important in this regard. Around mid-2020, non-financial firms and households in all major countries were hit by revenue shortfalls; banks helped them absorb the shock by extending more credit. Capital allows banks to perform a critical shock-absorbing function for the rest of the economy, at short notice, even in absence (or with lesser need of) supervisory forbearance. By doing so, banks contribute to the resilience of the economic system. By contrast, liquidity and funding issues were not important in the pandemic because the support of central banks and fiscal authorities resulted in a large increase of deposits balances held at banks. Banks became more liquid under the pandemic, not less, unlike in other crisis episodes.

These considerations suggest that in the face of high uncertainty, resilient bank balance sheets must include safety margins that offer protection along several dimensions. Banks which are well-capitalized, liquid and have reliable and stable funding sources are in a better position when adverse conditions materialize. This may sound like common sense, but its direct implication (that in good and normal times banks should make every effort to secure those conditions and supervisors should pressure them to do so) often proves more controversial than it should be.

Sustainability, securing resilience over time, is a difficult goal for banking supervisors. The reason is that the instruments available to supervisors cannot be used *directly* to ensure that banking business is conducted efficiently and prudently, which is a condition for resilience to persist over time. The business model is a decision pertaining to the shareholders and managers or the bank. The supervisor can only influence it *indirectly* by imposing a variety of prudential requirements, or, to some extent, by exercising moral suasion. Supervisors assess the business model of banks as an ongoing matter in regular examinations (in the ECB, the annual Supervisory Review and Examination Process, or SREP), contacts with bank managers and stress tests. Formal requirements and informal persuasion are both part of ongoing supervisory processes, giving rise to the so-called "Pillar II" component of banking supervision.

The key point which needs to be stressed here is that, in order for Pillar II to remain effective in promoting "sustainable" banks, its legal framework must grant sufficient leeway to the supervisor in order to exercise its function in a flexible and discretionary way. Frameworks which instead rely primarily on preset legal and regulatory requirements are unlikely to effectively ensure sustainability.

The COVID-19 experience in the euro area offers two examples that support this point.[11] The first regards the mechanism to govern the prudential provisions established against non-performing loans (NPLs). The SSM Regulation explicitly assigns the responsibility and power to set prudential provisions to the ECB in its supervisory function. In its early years, the ECB operationalized this task by issuing "expectations" to banks, regarding the timing and modality in which provisions should be set. Those expectations were not rigid requirements; they were adaptable to the specific conditions and risks faced by banks at each point in time.

This approach was challenged on legal grounds, based on the claim that the ECB was overstepping its powers and invading the field of the legislator. As a result, in 2019 the European legislators (Council, European Parliament, EU Commission) passed a legislative package prescribing minimum coverage levels ("prudential backstops") for NPLs, calibrated according to the type of loans and its seniority: the so-called "calendar provisioning." According to the law, the percentage of coverage increases with the time of non-performance, from one to ten years, and varies depending on the type of loan (with or without collateral). The timing of this legislative initiative proved particularly unfortunate: as soon as the new law was in force, the pandemic struck and provisioning calendars became unrealistic. Application of the law was de-facto suspended and replaced by public guarantees and moratoria which prevent NPLs from even materializing. As these words are written, it is unclear whether, when and in what form the law may be become operative.

Another example relates to the accounting treatment of NPLs. After the financial crisis, global financial reporting rules were changed to make them more responsive to ongoing and expected economic conditions, thus avoiding procyclicality. In the new rules, NPL recognition and provisioning by banks should be based no longer on past losses, but should rather match the time when the corresponding exposures and risks are undertaken. This de facto introduces a forward-looking element based on expected losses. The resulting mechanism, appropriate in case of demand-driven cyclical upswings, becomes inappropriate and in fact dangerous in circumstances such as those created by COVID-19, where a downswing (like the sharp recession which occurred in 2020) is accompanied by an increase in credit risks and massive future NPLs. The application of the new rule during the pandemic crisis would risk being seriously procyclical. For this reason, its application was postponed and it is unclear when and in what form will it be reinstated.

In truth, these two examples are different. NPL provisions are a prudential tool which can easily be handled in a flexible way depending on economic conditions and the state of the business cycle. Accounting rules, instead, are "structural," in the sense that they are linked to established and persistent business practices. As such, frequent changes of accounting rules are unadvisable. Yet, both cases contain a common lesson. Sustainable supervisory frameworks should avoid introducing elements which are not robust to different adverse contingencies. When the latter are particularly uncertain, overly rigid provisions, such as those enshrined in laws, should be avoided and preference should be given to granting discretion to supervisory authorities, with clearly defined goals set by elected representatives to which the supervisors are held accountable.

Before concluding this discussion on financial stability, a caveat is in order. Flexibility and discretion are powerful weapons in the hands of supervisors and can enhance the overall effectiveness of the banking framework, but, as all weapons, should be handled with care. This is especially the case if the regulatory framework is incomplete in other respects. Of particular concern is the fact that under current legislation the ECB is not formally entitled to use all the supervisory instruments listed in its charter, the Regulation establishing the Single Supervisory Mechanism,[12] unless there is a legal basis to it – other than the Regulation itself – either in European or in national law. National legislators are allowed to exercise significant prudential powers within their own jurisdictions, in force of the "national options and discretions" available in EU banking law.[13] Until these loopholes are removed, a change repeatedly advocated by the ECB, flexibility at national level may easily become an obstacle to banking integration, even if a single legal and supervisory framework applies.

4.   CONCLUSIONS

Is the world today increasingly uncertain and risky? Is it more fraught with existential threats than past times were?

Hearing economic policymakers often utter sentences like "… today we live in particularly uncertain times …," one is tempted to conclude, no: future life is as uncertain as it always was, and nothing is new in this respect. Yet, certain aspects of the world we live in – the globalization of political and economic phenomena, the increased reliance on information transmitted at light-speed, the growing role of capital markets which are by nature and irreversibly global – suggest that the answer is, yes: there is something out there which makes our future particularly fragile and vulnerable to systemic risks.

Policymakers need to build "systems," including economic and financial systems, which can survive and function in a variety of imponderable circumstances, and in a durable way. Recent contributions and debates have referred to these properties as "resilience" and "sustainability."

The preceding pages have offered some arguments along these lines regarding monetary policy and financial stability. A common thread is that in order to be resilient and sustainable, the policy architectures needs to rely significantly on discretionary decisions delegated to independent agencies – in the specific case, the ECB as monetary policymaker and banking supervisor. Rigid rules of legal and even constitutional nature constraining such discretion can become of hindrance, hampering or delaying crucial decisions when unexpected risks arise. Policy discretion can be, and should be, controlled by society by means of statutory provisions emphasizing the policy goals (rather than the means used to achieve those goals), and prescribing strict accountability processes on the ways those goals are pursued.

NOTES

1. See Ip (2015).
2. See the discussion in Peterson Institute for International Economics (2021).
3. SeeTett (2021).
4. Tett (2015) refers to these situations as "silo effects."
5. For example, at times in the 1970s and the 1980s administrative controls of credit flows or interest rates were used, in some countries, to complement and reinforce the more traditional open-market intervention techniques.
6. A forceful statement of this view was made years ago by Goodfriend (2012).
7. A point analyzed recently, with reference to the COVID-19 crisis, by Bartsch et al. (2020).
8. Angeloni (2020).
9. Basel Committee on Banking Supervision (2015).
10. Angeloni (2019).
11. More details are in Angeloni (2021).
12. Council Regulation (EU) No. 1024/2013 of October 15, 2013 conferring specific tasks on the European Central Bank concerning policies relating to the prudential supervision of credit institutions; available at: https://eur-lex.europa.eu/legal-content/EN/TXT/?uri=celex%3A32013R1024
13. Article 4.3 of the SSM Regulation is worth reading in full: "For the purpose of carrying out the tasks conferred on it by this Regulation, and with the objective of ensuring high standards of supervision, the ECB shall apply all relevant Union law, and where this Union law is composed of Directives, the national legislation transposing those Directives. Where the relevant Union law is composed of Regulations and where currently those Regulations explicitly grant options for Member States, the ECB shall apply also the national legislation exercising those options."

REFERENCES

Angeloni, I. (2019), Supervisory Independence. Speech at the ECB Conference on "Challenges for Supervisors and Central Bankers," March 22.
Angeloni, I. (2020), The ECB Strategy Review: Walking a Narrow Path, VoX EU Column, December 3.
Angeloni, I. (2021), *Non-Performing Loans: An Old Problem in a New Situation.* European Economy.
Bartsch, E., A. Bénassy-Quéré, G. Corsetti and X. Debrun (2020), It's All in the Mix: How Monetary and Fiscal Policies Can Work or Fail Together. *Geneva Report,* no. 23, December 15.
Basel Committee on Banking Supervision (2015), *Core Principles of Bank Governance.*
Brunnermeier, M. (2021), *The Resilient* Society. Endeavour Literary Press and PIIE.
Goodfriend, M. (2012), The Elusive Promise of Independent Central Banking. *Monetary and Economic Studies*, Bank of Japan.
Haldane, A. (2020), What Has Central Bank Independence Ever Done for Us? Speech at the UCL Economists' Society Economics Conference, November 28.
Ip, G. (2015), *Foolproof: Why Safety can be Dangerous and How Dangers Make us Safe*. Little, Brown and Company.

Peterson Institute for International Economics (2021), "The Resilient Society." Online seminar available at: https://www.piie.com/events/resilient-society-lessons-pandemic-recovering-next-major-shock

Tett, G. (2015), *The Silo Effect: The Peril of Expertise and the Promise of Breaking Down Barriers*. Simon & Schuster.

Tett, G. (2021), *Anthro-Vision: A New Way to See in Business and Life*. Simon & Schuster.

18. Central banks as emergency actors: implications for governance arrangements

David Archer

In 1920, the United Kingdom Parliament passed the Emergency Powers Act. In 1976, the United States Congress passed the National Emergencies Act, consolidating various presidential emergency powers granted by statute (filling a Constitutional gap). The 1958 French Constitution gives the President emergency powers. Frameworks for emergency powers are intended to balance the need for exceptional powers in exceptional circumstances with the democratic desire to constrain powers normally available. The main alternatives are not attractive. Without emergency powers legally provided, national leadership may hesitate undesirably, or break the law at the expense of the law's credibility when those actions are seen as appropriate. In contrast, without special checks and balances emergency powers may not be perceived as legitimate, given the reliance on the self-restraint of political leaders.

With respect to central banking, responses to the Great Financial Crisis of 2007–8 then the pandemic of 2020–1 may have revealed the absence of explicit emergency mandates as a gap in many central bank constitutions. Forceful and innovative action bore evidence of considerable flexibility in the way central bank mandates can be interpreted, and a far wider range of instruments available than previously understood. Latent emergency powers turned out to be more extensive than had been thought. This has raised questions about the legitimacy of them being in the hands of unelected officials whose self-restraint is also heavily relied on.[1]

This chapter considers whether explicit emergency mandates might be useful to have in central bank statutes. It points out that policy innovations in response to crises were extensive and largely unexpected. It argues that most policy innovations occurred within existing legal authorities, which contain significant and underappreciated latent powers. Even without mandates being breached, potential concerns about legitimacy of central bank independence arise. The proposition that explicit emergency mandates could better enable far-reaching departures from normal operations without bringing legitimacy into question is discussed. Examples are provided of (mostly partial) emergency mandates present in some central bank laws, and the desirable features of future emergency mandates are set out.

1. HOW MUCH DID CENTRAL BANKING POLICY CHANGE IN RECENT CRISES?

There is little doubt that the succession of crises since the Great Financial Crisis has prompted much innovation in central banks' monetary and financial stability policies. The Great Financial Crisis had 'a profound impact on the practice of monetary policy in a range of countries' (Blinder et al., 2017, p. 3) and greatly expanded central bank roles in financial stability space. Cantú et al. (2021) show that central bank policy responses to the COVID-19 pandemic typically further extended instruments developed in response to the Great Financial Crisis or were new. This is particularly true for lending operations. The extent of change can also be seen in the massive growth of central bank balance sheets, and the collapse in policy rates to the effective lower bound.

But perhaps more compelling are reflections of central bankers on the evolution of central banking during their professional lifetimes. Former Chair Bernanke recently remarked on 'the change in the set of tools and approaches that the Powell Fed uses that the Greenspan Fed would never have even thought about or would certainly not have even seriously considered'.[2] As Chair Powell himself noted, the Fed 'crossed a lot of red lines', adding 'this is that situation in which you do that, and you figure it out afterwards'.[3]

2. ACTION AND INACTION AND THEIR CONNECTION TO LEGAL MANDATES

The extent of change possible within existing mandates engendered surprise, which itself raises questions. What happened to the constraints part of the 'constrained discretion' granted central banks for independent action? Were they never there? Have they been dodged? Both possibilities would raise questions of legitimacy. Conversely, is there evidence that constraints caused mandate holders to hesitate to act even in circumstances where action would be consistent with objectives?

According to expert observers, the answers differ according to the jurisdiction. Although Chair Powell noted that some red lines were crossed, the two broad types of exceptional action undertaken by the Fed appear to have been within legal boundaries. The Fed's Act envisages its purchase of public obligations in open market operations. As for lending beyond banks, the Act provides the necessary emergency mandate (discussed further below). Where additional political cover was needed, there was close coordination with the

Treasury (Geithner and Metrick, 2018). In the context of the questions being considered here, concerns about political legitimacy centre on the extent to which Fed interventions could change within the existing mandate.

The Eurozone story is similar, but with a couple of twists. First, legal challenges to the expansion of instruments and facilities made legal boundaries practically relevant, while helping to identify their (evolving) location. Second, uncertainty about their location may have caused policymakers to hesitate at crucial points. Hesitation has been noted by several commentators (for example, Kang et al., 2016, Gros et al., 2012, Wyplosz, 2016). Relative slowness in acting has in turn been ascribed to various factors, including fear of breaching legal and legitimacy constraints (Honohan et al., 2019, Panico and Purificato, 2013, Schmidt, 2015), the separated consideration of financial stability and monetary policies (Honohan, 2018), differing perceptions of the scale of the threat (Kang et al., 2016), and policy mistakes (Hetzel, 2013).

Legal scholars suggest that the experience has made legal and political risk a bigger potential barrier to future action by the European System of Central Banks. The German constitutional court (Bundesverfassungsgericht, BverfG) and the European Court of Justice set out criteria that could stiffen future constraints even as they validated past emergency actions (Grund and Grle, 2016; Tober, 2015). Collectively these criteria act as restrictions that tighten the longer that unconventional policy stays in place (Mersch, 2016). The BverfG's criteria stress that actions easing government funding constraints need to be temporary in nature, with uncertainty about the central bank's future take up of new issuance (Viterbo, 2020). A published exit strategy is an important ingredient, from the BverfG's perspective (Viterbo, op cit.).

In short, in both these trans-Atlantic examples, significant innovations in instruments and operating procedures have raised questions, with the emphasis more on legitimacy in the United States and on legality in Europe.[4] The legality question appears to have been answered, for now. Future extensions might run into larger hurdles in both jurisdictions, hurdles that could be overcome by (respectively) the modification and creation of explicit emergency mandates.

3.   EMERGENCY POWERS FOR EXECUTIVE GOVERNMENT

Constitutional scholars have long debated how best to give emergency powers to governments within liberal constitutional regimes. Explicit allowance for crises was a feature of the Roman Constitution.[5] The checks and balances of that constitution could be sidestepped by a temporary dictator appointed by the senate for a maximum of six months. Handing back power and acting solely in the interests of the Roman state were expectations, but expectations that could not be enforced by another authority.

Knowledge of the Roman Constitution was available to the framers of the United States Constitution, yet, when it came to the development of United States version, notwithstanding extensive use of Romanesque checks and balances, specific emergency powers were limited (and given mostly to the legislature[6]). The limited reference to emergency powers in the United States Constitution has engendered much scholarly debate, as it did among the framers. For some the sparse provision of emergency powers was deliberate, intended to prevent their abuse. For others, it is because regular powers granted to the legislature and executive ought be considered expansively, as sufficient also to deal with emergencies. For yet others, the reconciliation lies in the potential for the legislature to act with sufficient speed to provide the needed extension of powers as and when required, for the time required. Extending powers by ordinary statute provides greater inherent legitimacy, allows a less expansive interpretation of normal powers, and allows the legislature to determine the exit when it 'thinks the emergency is finished or if the executive has proved untrustworthy' (Ferejohn and Pasquino, 2004, p. 218).

From these debates, a number of tradeoffs in the way emergencies are provided for can be identified. Making expansive powers suited to crises available, but not restricting their use to emergencies, invites overuse in normal times. Providing specific emergency powers invites the holder to 'kindle emergencies'. Not providing sufficient emergency powers invites discretionary overstepping of constitutional limitations, undermining their purpose and authority. Relying on the legislature to expand the boundaries of executive power as and when needed may limit that risk to cases where legislative delay and potential catastrophe coexist, but only if legislatures prove themselves able to act quickly most of the time (so the executive branch is willing to wait). Separating the authority to declare and undeclare a state of emergency from the person or group entitled to wield the emergency powers made available may reduce some of the risks, but with checks and balances come the risk of standoffs. When emergency powers are used, and especially when used properly and for the good, there is a risk that their use expands the envelope of normal powers – what requires a state of emergency to be reset to normal, and what defines the (new) normal? Finally, when it comes to accountability for the use of emergency powers, there is a risk of unreasonable hindsight being applied. Reviewers of emergency actions, having not ensured that suitable emergency powers were available, might not find themselves able to 'put themselves into [the rescuer's] situation'.[7]

4.   EMERGENCY POWERS FOR CENTRAL BANKS

Emergency power wielded by national leaders typically relate to threats of war, invasion and insurrection, but also natural disasters, pandemics and other threatened catastrophes. What about the more limited domain of central banking? Relevant laws also set out and constrain – with greater or lesser specificity – the scope of central bank powers, for the sake of political legitimacy. Yet emergencies also arise in this domain. As with national leaderships, central banks may have latent emergency powers already available within expansively written mandates, rely on parliament to grant additional powers when needed, have explicit emergency powers, or be expected to do whatever it takes notwithstanding legal prohibitions.

As already documented, the expansion in the range of central bank interventions since the Great Financial Crisis has been very substantial. Yet while there are examples of legislative initiatives enabling such an expansion, and examples of emergency mandates being deployed (both discussed later), these are comparatively rare. Emergency powers that were latent in central bank law even during the heyday of narrow central banking before the Great Financial Crisis is (by process of elimination) the main explanation.

4.1   Latent Emergency Powers: The Exceptional Use of Normal Powers

The use of latent emergency powers by central banks since the Great Financial Crisis is illustrated in this section by way of reference to the two biggest jurisdictions: the Eurozone and the United States.

The European Central Bank used quantitative easing to help maintain price stability, which its statutes permit it to do by trading in any 'claims and marketable instruments, whether in euro or other currencies', as it sees fit (van 't Klooster, 2018). Yet quantitative easing expanded the European Central Bank's activities in debt markets well beyond its previous range of practice. Commenting on the further expansion that came with responses to the COVID-19 pandemic, former Executive Board member Mersch said: 'We have disenfranchised ourselves from the previously self-imposed constraints so that these measures can address the uncertainty of the evolving crisis.'[8] The European Court of Justice ruled (in the Grauweiler and Weiss cases) that the application of statutory constraints depends on purpose and circumstances, with assessments of both being matters for the European Central Bank itself, so long as they meet certain criteria (necessary, proportionate, with safeguards, most effective available, non-distorting and in terms of impact on target markets consistent with the European Central Bank capital key).[9] In sum, as Mersch noted, European Central Bank statutes allow a wide range of tools but 'crisis measures must be temporary and targeted. They are justified only in the light of the exceptional circumstances seen during the pandemic.'[10]

On the other side of the Atlantic, the expansion in the range of instruments used in crisis fighting involved a mix of latent powers and emergency mandates. There, quantitative easing and unconventional monetary policy in general are mostly an extension of conventional monetary policy necessitated by the effective lower bound (Blinder, 2014). With respect to the use of its emergency mandate, Section 13(3) of the Federal Reserve Act allows Federal Reserve Banks in crises (unusual and exigent circumstances, as determined by a vote of five or more members of the Board of Governors) to make secured loans to parties other than those eligible for Fed facilities in normal times. Section 13(3) was used a number of times during the Great Financial Crisis to support individual entities in trouble (e.g. Bear Stearns, AIG) and critical markets (e.g. Money Market Mutual Funds, the commercial paper market) by way of asset purchase facilities structured as secured loans to Special Purpose Vehicles created for the purpose.[11] The reach of the powers available to the Fed under Section 13(3) alarmed enough members of Congress to result in additional restrictions being added in the Dodd-Frank Act. These included requirements that lending under Section 13(3) be through broad-based facilities (so not targeted on individuals or individual corporations), constructed with the approval of the Secretary to the Treasury, and with collateral sufficient to protect taxpayers against losses (rather than merely to the satisfaction of the lending Reserve Bank).

Though latent powers may exist within legal mandates, their existence might not generally be understood, and their use may come as a surprise, raising questions about the legitimacy of independent decision authorities granted to central banks. With respect to the European Central Bank's case, even former senior officials were surprised and concerned about legitimacy[12] and, as noted, the United States Congress moved to limit emergency authorities. These reactions illustrate the potential for surprise and subsequent attempts to restrict powers.

4.2   Dealing with the Legitimacy Problem

Tucker (2018), in his magisterial review of the role and place of central banking within the liberal democratic state, strongly argues for anticipating as much as possible the need to deal with emergencies. Emergency mandates might grant additional powers, but it should be clear whether they are to be wielded independently (in which case making the exceptional and temporary nature of the situation clear is vital) or whether the decision-making process has temporarily been adjusted to include the political authorities (as may well be the most appropriate course, given that such situations tend to encounter serious fiscal, debt management, distributional and regulatory questions). For Tucker, the least attractive option is to work without clear rules of the game, without which effectiveness and legitimacy cannot coexist.

Others have joined Tucker in calling for ex ante provisions that reconcile the need for constraints on independent unelected power in normal times with the inevitability that constraints may not leave enough room for emergencies. van 't Klooster (2018) and Viterbo (2020) argue that the revealed scale of the European Central Bank's latent powers calls for new emergency procedures in which the political authorities play a bigger role. Viterbo, for example, points out that the 1993 European Council Regulation defining what constitutes monetary financing and is thus prohibited by Article 123 of TFEU is amendable. The Commission can, after consulting the European Parliament, propose alternative definitions. Balls et al. (2018) also endorse involving politicians in crisis decision-making when distribution and fiscal risk issues arise – which is almost inevitable. Skinner (2021) suggests installing 'guardrails' to prevent legally inappropriate mission creep while legitimising the use of new tools to treat an economic emergency. Those guardrails might include greater involvement of the executive through an override (as in the United Kingdom). For all these authors, the extension of powers during crises should be governed by ex ante arrangements that allow the necessary powers while retaining checks and balances, thereby preserving legitimacy.[13]

4.3 Temporary Extensions of Authority Provided by Legislative Acts

While central banking folklore holds that legislatures are always and everywhere too slow to act, the COVID-19 pandemic in particular saw much speedy legislative action. The IMF's fiscal policy tracker is distinctly richer than any monetary policy one. Moreover, there are notable examples of legislatures acting to provide additional powers to central banks to allow them better to tackle crises. For instance, in Brazil and the Czech Republic legislatures acted to temporarily suspend certain legal constraints, and in the United States Congress passed the Coronavirus Aid, Relief and Economic Security (CARES) Act to fund the Federal Reserve's temporary provision of emergency facilities to smaller enterprises.

4.4 Explicit Emergency Mandates in Current Central Bank Law

A number of partial emergency mandates exist in current central bank law. Examples include:

4.4.1 Canada
In Canada, the law (S.18(b)(ii)) authorises the Governor to extend the universe of assets able to be bought or sold to include any financial instruments issued

by anyone, by declaring a situation of 'severe and unusual stress on the financial market or the financial system'.

4.4.2 Chile
In 2020 Congress passed a constitutional amendment to implement an emergency mandate:

- Allowing the central bank to buy and sell government securities in secondary market operations in 'transitory and exceptional' situations, though only if consistent with statutory objectives.
- The Bank must predefine the time period over which the emergency provision can be used.
- Decisions to declare exceptional conditions and set a timeline require a supermajority (four out of five) of the Bank's board. The Minister of Finance may suspend the decision for up to 15 days; the suspension can be overridden by a unanimous vote.
- Securities acquired in such an exceptional operation 'shall' be sold back to the open market, within a time frame determined by the board.
- The Bank cannot be directed to use these powers, or to cease using them.

4.4.3 Japan
In Japan, the law (Article 33: Regular Business) sets out the range of transactions permitted in order for the Bank of Japan to pursue statutory purposes, while Articles 34, 37, 38 and 39 provide for extensions in particular types of unusual circumstance, each involving some additional engagement with the political authorities. More generally, Article 43 allows for an extension of forms of business beyond those explicitly provided for in the 'regular business' provision, subject to prior authorisation by the political authorities, should that be 'necessary to achieve the Bank's purpose specified by this Act'.

4.4.4 United Kingdom
The Financial Services Act 2012 requires the Bank of England and the Treasury to maintain a memorandum of understanding (MOU) setting out respective responsibilities for financial crisis management. It also provides the Treasury with the authority to direct the Bank on the use of certain emergency and resolution powers.

The MOU assigns the prime crisis management role to the Bank. The Bank acts independently in crisis management within the bounds of its published rule book for liquidity management, including access to Bank liquidity facilities, so long as actions within those bounds do not involve fiscal risk. Should fiscal risk be anticipated, the Bank's Governor would notify the Chancellor, and decision responsibility would pass to the Chancellor.

4.4.5   United States

Section 13(3) of the Federal Reserve Act allows Federal Reserve Banks to provide liquidity directly to non-bank, commercial entities in times of crisis ('exigent and unusual circumstances') as determined by the Board of Governors.

The Dodd-Frank Act narrowed the scope of Section 13(3) by requiring that any discounting to non-banks be through facilities with broad-based eligibility; where facilities and terms are approved by the Secretary to the Treasury and ensure that the taxpayer is protected from loss. Such facilities must be terminated in a timely manner, requiring reauthorisation to extend beyond one year.[14]

5.   A WAY FORWARD: EXPLICIT FULL SERVICE EMERGENCY MANDATES[15]

Providing exceptional powers in advance has clear advantages over providing none. It reduces the need for the law to be broken in order to get the necessary done and – worse still – preventing the necessary being done, while giving legitimacy to those actions. Providing those powers by way of an emergency mandate that is distinct from the normal mandate in terms of its governance arrangements offers additional legitimacy, compared with relying on the self-restraint of unelected officials to prevent their inappropriate use. That approach also avoids the need to rely on increasingly polarised legislatures finding a way of coming together in the heat of the moment.

But what are the desirable features of such emergency mandates? Some seem obvious; others may require more imagination. Among the obvious ones are:

*   Require special procedures for unlocking exceptional powers. The declaration of an economic emergency by a qualified majority of appointed decision-makers is one illustration.
*   Involve the political authorities in the unlocking, if legitimacy so demands (for example, where fiscal risk exceeds some threshold; interventions would be significantly non-neutral; or involve a substantial increase in regulatory instruments). The state of emergency might need to be endorsed by the key economic minister(s); the political authorities or parliament might be empowered to negate the declaration within a certain number of days. Where fiscal risk is an issue, political endorsement might take the form of a financial indemnity for the central bank, or a public assurance of recapitalisation should that prove needed.
*   Extra requirements for transparency and for accounting for the use of exceptional powers.

- Facilitating timely exit from the state of emergency. Unpredictability means that hard time limits in law are unworkable, as are state-contingent resets based on thresholds for selected target variables. A workable alternative could be to require a sunset clause that could be deferred only with the express approval of parliament.

The question most obviously requiring imagination is a statement of which emergency powers would become available. The needed new instruments might not be foreseeable; much innovation occurred in response to the Great Financial Crisis and subsequently. Yet the broad character of instruments used was often already known. Balance-sheet policies, directed and subsidised lending, participation in markets, backstopping the financial system by underwriting some markets and assuming credit risk, regulation, directives, moral suasion, and so forth, have been deployed over the history of central banking; if not in each and every jurisdiction at least in some. Some of these instrument types are less objectionable on political or efficiency grounds than others, making them candidates for inclusion in an emergency mandate while other types remain excluded.

None of the existing emergency mandates satisfies all these features, though some go a long way, and all the desirable features listed above are present in at least one case, suggesting feasibility. The demonstrated ability of legislatures in Brazil, Chile and the Czech Republic to provide emergency powers – and in the form of a standing authority in the Chilean case – also suggests that the political process need not be an insurmountable hurdle to the creation of such mandates.

NOTES

1. Agustín Carstens, remarks delivered at the Bank for International Settlement's Annual General Meeting, June 2020 ('In the face of an unexpected adversary: the crucial role for central banks'), and results from a CFM-CEPR survey on 'The future of central bank independence' (den Haan et al., 2017).
2. CEBRA 2021, YouTube video available at https://www.youtube.com/watch?v=PmWB-dY7K28, especially 32:20 to 36:23.
3. Remarks made during a Princeton University webinar, 29 May 2020.
4. See Wallach (2015) for a discussion of the distinction, in the context of financial regulation and emergency actions in financial crisis.
5. Ferejohn and Pasquino (2004), on which this section draws heavily. See van 't Klooster (2018) for a discussion in the context of central banking.
6. The Roman constitution invested emergency powers in an individual, but one called into service from outside government. Modern constitutions tend to invest them in an elected president (Ferejohn and Pasquino, 2004).
7. From a letter from Thomas Jefferson to John B Colvin, September 1810.
8. Mersch (2020).
9. van 't Klooster (2018, pp. 278–9).

10.   Mersch (2020, op cit.).
11.   The use of SPVs to purchase paper that the Fed itself may not purchase itself raises legal questions (Mehra, 2011).
12.   'Ex-ECB chiefs criticise bond buying: The European Central Bank's two former chief economists have criticised the institution's announcement to buy unlimited amounts of government bonds'. www.express.co.uk/news/world/349354/Ex-ECB-chiefs-criticise-bond-buying, 03:43 (1 October 2012).
13.   Other authors also recommend procedural changes that expose central bank emergency actions to political and/or legal review, but without embedding these changes in an explicit emergency mandate (see, for example, Bateman, 2021, Egidy, 2021).
14.   Further restrictions have been written into the Consolidated Appropriations Act, 2021, but their actual impact remains uncertain (Landy, 2021).
15.   Emergency mandates are conceptually similar to proposals to create state-contingent macroeconomic policy regimes that in certain circumstances release peacetime constraints to better target abnormal situations (e.g. Wren-Lewis, 2020) and/or alter decision-making arrangements in ways that support the political legitimacy of resulting policies (e.g. Bolton et al., 2019).

REFERENCES

Balls, Ed, James Howatt, Anna Stansbury (2018), 'Central bank independence revisted: after the financial crisis, what should a model central bank look like?', Mossavar-Rahman Center for Business and Government Associate Working Paper No. 87.

Bateman, Will (2021), 'The law of monetary finance under unconventional monetary policy', *Oxford Journal of Legal Studies* 41(4).

Blinder, Alan (2014), 'Federal Reserve policy before, during and after the fall', in *Across the great divide: new perspectives on the financial crisis*, Martin Neil Baily and John B. Taylor (eds), Hoover Institution Press, chapter 5.

Blinder, Alan, Michael Ehrmann, Jakob de Haan, David-Jan Jansen (2017), 'Necessity as the mother of invention: monetary policy after the crisis', European Central Bank Working Paper No. 2047, April.

Bolton, Patrick, Stephen Cecchetti, Jean Pierre Danthine, Xavier Vives (2019), *Sound at last? Assessing a decade of financial regulation*, The Future of Banking 1, CEPR Press.

Cantú, Carlos, Paolo Cavallino, Fiorella De Fiore, James Yetman (2021), 'A global database on central banks' monetary responses to COVID-19', BIS Working Paper No. 934.

Carstens, Agustín (2020), 'In the face of an unexpected adversary: the crucial role for central banks'. Speech on the occasion of the Bank's Annual General Meeting, Basel, 30 June 2020.

den Haan, Wouter, Martin Ellison, Ethan Ilzetzki, Michael McMahon, Ricardo Reis (2017), 'The future of central bank independence: results of the CFM–CEPR Survey', VoxEU/CEPR.

Egidy, Stephanie (2021), 'Proportionality and procedure of monetary policy-making', I-CON 19(1), Oxford University Press.

Ferejohn, John and Pasquale Pasquino (2004), 'The law of the exception: a typology of emergency powers', I-CON 2(2), Oxford University Press and New York University School of Law.

Geithner, Timothy F. and Andrew Metrick (2018), 'Ten years after the financial crisis: a conversation with Timothy Geithner', YPFS Working Paper 2018/01, Yale University School of Management.

Gros, Daniel, Cinzia Alcidi, Alessandro Giovanni (2012), 'Central banks in times of crisis: the FED vs the European Central Bank', CEPS Policy Brief 276, July.

Grund, Sebastian and Filip Grle, The European Central Bank's Public Sector Purchase Programme (PSPP), the prohibition of monetary financing and sovereign debt restructuring scenarios (1 November 2016). *European Law Review* (2016), Available at SSRN: https://ssrn.com/abstract=2717105.

Hetzel, Robert L. (2013), 'European Central Bank monetary policy in the recession: a new Keynesian (old monetarist) critique', Federal Reserve of Richmond Working Paper No. 13-07.

Honohan, Patrick (2018), 'Real and imagined constraints on euro area monetary policy', PIIE Working Paper 18-8, August.

Honohan, Patrick, Domenico Lombardi, Samantha St Amand (2019), 'Managing macrofinancial crises: the role of the central bank', in *The Oxford handbook of the economics of central banking*, David G Mayes, Pierre L Siklos, Jan-Egbert Sturm (eds), Oxford University Press, pp. 619–52.

Kang, Dae Woong, Nick Lighart, Askoka Mody (2016), 'The European Central Bank and the Fed: a comparative narrative', VoxEU post, 19 January.

Landy, Douglas (2021), 'Unlucky: do the recent changes to the Federal Reserve's powers under Section 13(3) of the Federal Reserve Act inhibit future action?', White & Case Alert, 7 January.

Mehra, Alexander (2011), 'Legal authority in unusual and exigent circumstances: the Federal Reserve and the financial crisis', *University of Pennsylvania Journal of Business Law* 13(1).

Mersch, Yves (2016), 'Monetary policy in the euro area: scope, principles and limits'. Keynote speech at the Natixis meeting of chief economists, Paris, 23 June.

Mersch, Yves (2020), 'Legal aspects of the European Central Bank's response to the coronavirus (COVID-19) pandemic – an exclusive but narrow competence'. Speech to the ESCB Legal Conference, Frankfurt am Main, 2 November.

Panico, Carlo and Francesco Purificato (2013), 'The debt crisis and the European Central Bank's role of lender of last resort', Political Economy Research Institute (University of Massachusetts Amherst) Working Paper No. 306.

Schmidt, Vivien A. (2015), 'The Eurozone's crisis of democratic legitimacy: can the EU rebuild public trust and support for European economic integration?', European Commission Discussion Paper 015, September.

Skinner, Christina Parajon (2021), 'Central bank activism', *United Kingdom Law Journal* 71.

Tober, Silke (2015), 'Monetary financing in the euro area: a free lunch?', *Review of European Economic Policy* 50(4).

Tucker, Paul (2018), *Unelected power: the quest for legitimacy in central banking and the regulatory state*, Princeton University Press.

van 't Klooster, Jens (2018), 'Democracy and the European Central Bank's emergency powers', *Midwest Studies in Philosophy* XLII.

Viterbo, Annamaria (2020), 'The PSPP judgement of the German Federal Constitutional Court: throwing sand in the wheels of the European Central Bank', *European Papers*, June.

Wallach, Philip A. (2015), *To the edge: legality, legitimacy, and the responses to the 2008 financial crisis*, Brookings Institution Press.

Wren-Lewis, Simon (2020), 'Monetary and fiscal cooperation: the case for a state dependent assignment', Mainly Macro blog post, 14 January.

Wyplosz, Charles (2016), 'The six flaws of the eurozone', *Economic Policy* 31(87).

Index

ABLV Bank 17–18
Abrams, R. K. 127
accountability 3, 8, 10–11, 55, 91, 97,
    99, 103, 118, 124, 127, 129, 131,
    159–60, 165–6, 170, 173, 208–11,
    214–15, 221
activity-based rules 29–30, 185, 188–90
Adrian, T. 88–9, 98, 131
aggregate demand 91, 96, 101–3, 105
Ajello, A. 88–9
Altavilla, C. 148–9
Amazon 183, 187
Ampudia, M. 148
Andries, A. M. 130
Angeloni, I. 11
Apple 183
Araujo, J. 84
Archer, D. 11
artificial intelligence 181
Asriyan, V. 68
asset prices 7, 25
Asset Purchase Programme 210
Australia 1, 51
Austria 71, 73, 124
Azerbaijan 124, 126

backstops 5, 17, 20, 77, 135, 214, 227
Bafin 23, 53–4
bail-in 17–18
bail-out 5, 15–19, 162
Balls, E. 99, 224
Bank for International Settlements 104
Bank of England 8, 53, 103, 116, 124,
    126–7, 156, 160, 225
Bank Recovery and Resolution Directive
    15, 17, 72
banking union 4–5, 9, 12, 14–20, 27–8,
    37, 45, 56, 74, 137, 140, 147, 150
Baring, F. 158
Barth, J. R. 129
Bartholomew, L. 115

Basel Committee for Banking
    Supervision 72, 129, 131, 137,
    165, 212
Basel III 9, 150
Bean, Charles 8
Beck, T. 5
Belgium 23–4, 27, 72–3, 78, 124
Bernanke, B. S. 63, 219
BigTech 3, 10, 29–32, 181–91
Bitcoin 194, 200–201
Bitfinex 197–9
blockchain *see* distributed ledgers
Blunden, G. 165
Boissay, F. 88–9
Borio, C. 66, 68
Boyarchenko, N. 98
Brazil 227
Brunnermeier, M. 124, 207–8
Bulgaria 73
business models 4, 10, 52, 182–4, 186–7,
    189–91, 212

Cairo, I. 88–9
Calvo, D. 123, 129
Canada 84–5, 224–5
Cantú, C. 219
capital buffers 42–5, 62, 66, 76, 80, 99,
    138
Capital Conservation Buffer 43
Capital Markets Union 56–7
capital ratios 43, 101, 129
Carney, M. 182
Cecchetti, S. 68, 162
Central Bank Reform Act 124
central banks
    Bank of England 8, 53, 103, 116,
        124, 126–7, 156, 160, 225
    determinants of involvement 78–9
    Deutsche Bundesbank 53–4, 159
    ECB *see* European Central Bank
    as emergency actors 11, 218–27

Federal Reserve 8, 63, 90, 137, 156,
        165, 209, 219–20, 223–4, 226
    and financial crises 11, 135–51, 208,
        213, 218
    and financial stability 1–3, 24–6,
        35–6, 63, 66, 83, 122–31,
        156–67, 170–71
    independence of 1, 10, 108, 117,
        127–8, 171–3, 175–6, 211,
        218
    as lender of last resort 24, 35–6,
        53–4, 71, 75, 77, 96, 128,
        158–60, 208
    and monetary policy 35–7, 62–3, 71,
        74–7, 92
    policies in era of climate change
        108, 113, 115, 117
    and politicians 170–76
    pros and cons of involvement 7,
        71–81
    role in supervision 2, 9–10, 21,
        23–6, 34–7, 53, 99, 122–31,
        159–62, 170–76
    Sveriges Riskbank 65
    trust in 35, 91
centralization 4, 6, 17, 37–41, 56
Cerra, V. 64
Chile 225, 227
China 201
Christmas tree effect 52
CISS indicator 140–41
Claessens, S. 67
climate change 8, 12, 22, 31–2, 108–18,
    206
climate risks 3, 5, 8, 11–12, 22, 111–15
Colleges of Supervisors 14
Colombia 122
Committee of European Banking
        Supervisors 137
Competition and Markets Authority 189
conflicts of interest 7, 77, 80, 128, 138
Coronavirus Aid, Relief and Economic
        Security Act 224
corruption 36
Countercyclical Capital Buffer 42–4, 62,
    66, 138
COVID-19 pandemic
    challenges presented by 2–3, 5–6,
        8–9, 11–12, 19, 22
    consequences of 28–9, 32

ECB and 135–6, 138–42, 144, 146,
        151
    and emergency powers 218–19, 222,
        224, 228
    lessons from 44–5, 105–6, 206–15
    and macroprudential policy 96–7
    output slump during 7
    policy response 28–9, 34, 42–5, 62,
        71–2, 80
    role of new financial architecture in
        147–50
    and supervision design 49, 51, 53,
        55
credit booms 36, 64, 68, 85, 102, 161
credit crunch 29, 102, 147
credit cycles 4, 6, 62–6
credit ratings 23
crisis management 14, 18, 75, 126–7,
    135, 225
    see also financial crises
Croatia 73
cross-border banking 4, 14, 18, 45
Crypto Capital 199
cryptocurrencies 188, 194–201
currency peg 11, 195, 198–201
Cyprus 15, 73
Czech Republic 227

Darracq Pariès, M. 149–50
de Larosière Report 27
deadly embrace 5, 18–19
debt-service-to-income ratios 62, 66–8,
    84
debt-to-income ratios 23, 63, 66, 68
decentralization 2, 4, 6, 10, 28, 37–41,
    44, 56, 188, 194–6, 201
decision-making 11, 37, 44–5, 71, 76–7,
    97, 208, 223–4
deflation 91
delegation 8, 96–106
Dell'Ariccia, G. 63
Denmark 50, 73
deposit guarantee scheme 4, 72, 78
deposit insurance scheme 5, 9, 16, 20,
    39, 150
Deutsche Bundesbank 53–4, 159
Dewatripont, M. 18
Dexia 14
Diggle, P. 115
Digital Markets Act 30

Digital Operational Resilience Act 30, 189
Dikau, S. 108
Dincer, N. 129
distributed ledgers 194–6, 198–201
division of labour 4
doom loops 2, 4, 15, 56, 136, 147, 150
dot.com bubble 63, 86
Doumpos, M. 130
Drehmann, M. 68

Economic and Financial Committee 99
Economic and Monetary Union 137
economic growth 36, 74, 110, 115, 117, 135, 185
Edge, R. M. 105
Eichengreen, B. 129
Emergency Liquidity Assistance 77
emergency powers 11, 218–27
Emergency Powers Act 218
entity-based rules 29–31, 185, 188–90
Epaulard, A. 6
Estonia 16, 73, 78
Ethereum 200
euro debt crisis 2, 15, 19, 27, 49, 135, 139–40, 144
European Banking Authority 27, 56–7, 137, 188
European Banking Union 56
European Central Bank
 during COVID-19 pandemic 42–4, 207–15
 and emergency powers 222–4
 and financial crises 135–51
 institutional building within 58
 and macroprudential policy 4, 9, 23, 28–9, 31–2, 71, 79, 92, 99–100
 and microprudential policy 2, 28, 71, 74
 as observer in SRB 17
 policies in era of climate change 108, 110, 113, 115–16
 powers assigned to 4, 6, 71, 165
 strategy review of 7–8, 71
 Supervisory Review and Examination Process 213
 supervisory role of under SSM 16, 23, 37, 41, 100, 137–8, 213

see also Single Supervisory Mechanism
 tasks and responsibilities 9, 135–51
 top-up power of 41–2
European Commission 17, 30, 99, 137, 139, 190, 214
European Court of Justice 28, 220
European Economic and Monetary Union 22
European Financial Stabilisation Mechanism 139
European Financial Stability Facility 137, 139
European Insurance and Occupational Pensions Authority 27, 56–7, 137
European Parliament 214
European Securities and Markets Authority 23, 27–8, 56–8, 74, 137
European Single Market in Banking 15, 18–20, 137
European Stability Mechanism 139
European supervisory architecture 1–12, 21–2
 BigTech supervision 3, 10, 29–32, 181–91
 central banks *see* central banks
 current architecture 22–4
 deposit insurance scheme 5, 9, 16, 20, 39, 150
 financial stability *see* financial stability
 lessons from COVID-19 44–5, 105–6, 206–15
 of macroprudential policy 96–106
  see also macroprudential policy
 monetary and financial task interaction 71–81
 new elements 28–32
 policies in era of climate change 108–18
  see also climate change; climate risks
 and prudential policy 34–45
 puzzle of 14–20
 separation approach 7, 83–92
 and stablecoin 10–11, 194–201
 terms of debate 24–8
 trends in 6, 49–58
European System of Central Banks 110, 220

European System of Financial
     Supervision 9, 110, 137, 139, 150
European Systemic Risk Board 18, 62,
     72, 99–100, 137
European Union 1–2, 4–6, 21–2, 27–8,
     30, 41, 44–5, 51–2, 56–8, 72–3,
     99, 110, 116, 135–6, 139, 147,
     150, 186, 188–9, 208–9, 214

Facebook 183
failing banks 14–19, 26, 35
Federal and Trade Commission 189–90
Federal Reserve 8, 63, 90, 137, 156, 165,
     209, 219–20, 223–4, 226
fiat currency 11, 194–200
Filardo, F. 88–9
financial crises
     central banks and 11, 135–51, 208,
          212, 218
     consequences of GFC 2, 14–15, 17,
          25, 31, 37, 42–3, 51, 71–2,
          78, 80, 83–5, 96–7, 104–5,
          122–3, 129–30, 161, 170–71,
          174–5, 182, 212
     during COVID-19 pandemic *see*
          COVID-19 pandemic
     crisis management 14, 18, 75,
          126–7, 135, 225
     ECB and 135–51
     effect on policy 41–3
     elimination of 163
     and emergency powers 218–19,
          222–3, 225, 227
     euro debt crisis 2, 15, 19, 27, 49,
          135, 139–40, 144
     functional model in GFC 27
     lessons from GFC 63–4
     low frequency of 79
     mergers in run-up to GFC 19
     microprudential supervision after
          GFC 123–4, 126–30
     preventing 90, 92, 130
     probability of 140–42
     reducing probability of 76
     reforms following GFC 5, 14–15,
          17–19
     and supervision design 49–51, 53–6
     triggering of 36, 41, 64
Financial Policy Committee 103–4

financial regulation 9, 22, 43, 123–4,
     170, 184–7
Financial Services Authority 1, 50, 52–3,
     124, 126–9
financial stability 17, 29–30, 32, 35–7,
     49–50, 52–5, 58, 71–2, 108, 110,
     117, 135–6, 138–9, 148, 175,
     219–20
     and BigTech 182–90
     central banks and 1–3, 24–6, 35–6,
          63, 66, 83, 122–31, 156–67,
          170–71
     and the COVID-19 pandemic 206,
          208, 212–15
     and macroprudential policy 53,
          62–9, 83–8, 91–2, 96, 98–104
     and microprudential policy 4,
          122–31
     and monetary policy 24–5, 62–8,
          74–6, 122, 124, 127, 129, 131
     and price stability 3, 9, 24–5
     risks to 10
Financial Stability Board 72, 137–8
Financial Stability Oversight Council 99
Financial Stress Indicator 36
financial supervision *see* European
     supervisory architecture
Financial Supervisory Authority 124
Finland 72–3
FINTEC indicator 143–4
FinTech 10, 29, 181–7, 190
Fortis 14
France 19, 23–4, 218
full employment 110, 115, 117

G20 137
gatekeepers 184, 190
Gelain, P. 88–9
General Data Protection Regulation 186
Germany 19, 23–4, 53–4, 62, 73, 78,
     124, 220
Gertler, M. 63
Giannone, D. 98
Global Financial Crisis *see* financial
     crises
globalization 91
Goldman Sachs 128
González-Páramo, J. M. 10
Goodhart, C. 91, 124
Google 183, 187

Gourio, F. 88–9
governance 3, 5–9, 12, 16, 44–5, 56–7,
　　108–18, 129–31, 135–7, 150–51,
　　171–2, 176, 182, 186, 188, 226
Great Financial Crisis *see* financial crises
Greece 15–16, 73, 78
Greenspan, A. 63, 219
greenwashing 113

Hardy, D. 8
Hobelsberger, K. 9
Hong Kong 66–7
Houben, A. 7
household debt 64–5, 67–8, 85
Howat, J. 99
Hubbard, G. 106
Hungary 73, 78, 124

Iceland 124
inaction bias 4, 7, 23, 36, 79
independent agencies 8, 11, 21, 96–106,
　　215
inflation 36, 65, 74, 89–91, 98, 174,
　　210–11
insurance companies 1, 22–4, 31
interest groups 35, 68, 109
interest rates 3, 7, 25, 63, 65, 68, 71,
　　86–8, 90, 96
International Monetary Fund 98, 126
Ireland 73, 78, 124, 144
Italy 15, 19, 23–4, 73, 150

Japan 74, 122, 225
Jorda, O. 64
Juselius, M. 88–9

Kakes, J. 7
Kazakhstan 126
Khan, L. M. 190
Kohler, M. 68
Kok, C. 9
Korea 84–5
Kraken 197–8
Kuttner, K. N. 66–7

Lamfalussy approach 56
Larosière Report, 56
Latvia 17–18, 73, 78, 124
leaning against the wind 76, 86–92, 104

lender of last resort 24, 35–6, 53–4, 71,
　　75, 77, 96, 128, 158–60, 208
Liang, J. N. 105
Lim, C. H. 66
liquidity 15–16, 39, 41–2, 45, 53, 62, 71,
　　77, 84, 105, 115, 123, 126, 130,
　　137, 149–50, 157–9, 164, 166–7,
　　182, 186, 194, 212–13, 225–6
Lithuania 73
loan-to-income ratios 62, 66, 76, 99, 102
loan-to-value ratios 23, 36, 62, 66–8,
　　84, 99
Luxembourg 73

machine learning 181
macroprudential policy 3–8, 10, 12,
　　21–3, 25–6, 28–9, 32, 34, 44–5,
　　53–5, 62–8, 71–2, 74–80, 83–92,
　　112, 123, 126, 128, 137, 163–5,
　　186–7, 212
　　architecture of 96–106
　　and monetary policy 83–92, 96, 99,
　　　101–5, 170–76
　　and politicians 170–76
　　setting of 41–2
Maddaloni, A. 6
Malta 16, 73
Masciandaro, D. 10, 122, 130, 171, 174
Melecky, M. 123, 130
Memorandums of Understanding 14
microprudential policy 4–5, 22, 25–6,
　　28–9, 41, 71, 78, 80, 112, 122–31,
　　164–5
Microsoft 183
Millennium Bug 206
mission creep 8, 117, 224
monetary policy 1, 3–4, 6–9, 11–12, 19,
　　22, 50, 53–4, 96–104, 115, 126–7,
　　206
　　central banks and 35–7, 62–3, 71,
　　　74–7, 92
　　coordination with macroprudential
　　　policy 8, 28, 100–105
　　and the COVID-19 pandemic 28–9,
　　　34, 42–5, 62, 71–2, 80,
　　　208–11, 215
　　and emergency powers 219–20,
　　　223–4
　　and financial crises 135, 137–8, 144,
　　　147, 149–50

and financial stability 24–5, 62–8,
    74–5, 76, 122, 124, 127, 129,
    131, 156, 158–60, 162
and macroprudential policy 83–92,
    96, 99, 101–5, 170–76
policies in era of climate change 113
Monetary Policy Committee 103–4
money creation 157–8
money laundering 10, 30, 32, 185–6,
    188, 194
Mongelli, F. P. 9
Monte dei Paschi di Siena 19
Morais, L. S. 6
moral hazard 77, 128, 167, 207
Morgan Stanley 128
mortgages 62, 76
Müller, K. 68
multinational banks 39, 41
Mundell, R. A. 102

Narain, A. 131
National Emergencies Act 218
Netherlands 23–4, 27, 51, 71, 73, 78
Network of Central Banks and
    Supervisors for Greening the
    Financial System 113
New Zealand 85, 124, 126, 129
Next Generation EU 140
non-performing loans 16, 129, 138–9,
    213–14
Nord LB 19
Northern Rock crisis 127, 160
Norway 50, 84–5, 90

Pandemic Emergency Purchase
    Programme 46, 81, 210
payment system 11, 127, 195–201
Payments Services Directive 186
Peru 122, 126
Peterson, A. 7
Podpiera, A. M. 8–9, 123, 130
Poland 73
policy coordination 7, 37, 75, 80–81, 211
political economy 5, 8, 10, 12, 21, 91,
    108, 111, 114, 118, 171–3, 175–8
politicians 170–76
populism 10, 175
Portugal 73
Powell, J. 219

Pradhan, M. 91
price stability 1, 3, 6–7, 9, 24–5, 35,
    62–3, 65, 68, 74–6, 83, 87, 90–91,
    101–3, 110, 115, 138, 159, 165,
    171–3, 209–10, 222
Price-Based Indicator of Financial
    Integration 142, 144
prudential policy 8, 31, 34–45, 79, 126,
    131, 146
public interest 17, 109, 162

Rancoia, E. 150
regulatory arbitrage 7, 29, 164, 183
regulatory capital 3, 137
regulatory reform 5, 15, 18, 29–30, 85
Reinhart, C. M. 64
reputation 7, 35, 77, 160, 162, 181
Reserve Bank Act 129
resilience 6, 9–10, 16, 29–31, 45, 71, 74,
    76, 84, 99, 136, 138, 140, 144,
    150, 159, 162–6, 188–9, 191, 194,
    207–9, 211–13
resolution 4–5, 9, 14–28, 71–5, 77–8,
    126, 135–6, 140, 150, 162, 165–6,
    186, 188, 225
Restoy, F. 5
Richter, B. 67–8
Riksbank 122
ring-fencing 4, 15, 18, 45
risk management 9, 28, 39, 41, 96, 98,
    186–8
    see also climate risks
Rogoff, K. S. 64
Romania 73
Romelli, D. 122, 130, 174
Rungcharoenkitkul, P. 7, 88–9

Saxena, S. C. 64
Schlesinger, H. 159
Schularick, M. 63–4, 87
Scopelliti, A. 6
search-for-yield behaviour 7, 86
sectoral vs. functional supervision 26–7
Securities Market Programme 209
separation approach 7, 83–92, 138
shadow banking 68, 166–7, 187
Shim, I. 66–7
Sim, J. 88–9
Singapore 50, 123

Single Market *see* European Single
    Market in Banking
Single Passport Framework 55–6
Single Regulatory Framework 9, 150
Single Resolution Board 9, 17–18, 23,
    150
Single Resolution Fund 5, 17
Single Resolution Mechanism 4, 17–19,
    27
Single Supervisory Mechanism 9, 16–18,
    27, 34, 37, 39–41, 45, 56–7, 100,
    137–8, 147–8, 150, 212–13, 215
Skinner, C. P. 224
Slovakia 73
Slovenia 16, 73
Smets, F. 86
South Africa 126
sovereign debt crisis 2, 15, 19, 27, 49,
    135, 139–40, 144
Spain 15, 19, 23–4, 73, 144, 150
Stability and Growth Pact 139
stablecoin 10–11, 194–201
Stansbury, A. 99
State Aid Rule 139
Stein, J. C. 68
stress testing 16, 113, 137–8, 148, 163,
    165–6, 213
supervision design 5, 11, 49–58
supervisory architecture, European *see*
    European supervisory architecture
supervisory convergence 56–7
Svensson, L. 65, 87–9, 104
Sveriges Riskbank 65
Sweden 50, 62, 65, 74, 122
systemic risk 9, 18, 41–3, 62, 72, 78–9,
    98–100, 126, 129–31, 135, 137–8,
    142, 187, 212, 215
Systemic Risk Buffer 42–3

Taiwan 197
Taylor, A. M. 63–4
Taylor, M. 50–51, 54–5, 127

Taylor rule 36, 89–90
technological developments 29–31
    see also BigTech; FinTech
terrorism 10–11, 30, 32, 185–6, 188, 194
Tether 196–9
Thailand 85
Tinbergen rule 74, 102
too big to fail 10, 42
Total Loss Absorbing Capacity 18
transparency 37, 91, 112, 114, 131, 137,
    165–6, 181, 187–8, 194, 207, 226
Tucker, P. 9–10, 223–4
Turner Review 52
'twin peaks' model 1, 5, 21, 23–4, 26–7,
    50–51, 54–5, 58, 72, 124–6, 128

UN Environment Inquiry 108
unemployment 36, 63, 65
United Kingdom 1, 50, 52–4, 72, 74,
    78, 104, 116, 122–4, 126–9, 156,
    159–60, 165, 189, 218, 225
United States 36, 39, 63, 74, 85, 99,
    105–6, 122, 128–9, 137, 156,
    189–90, 209, 218, 220–21, 223–4,
    226

Van der Ghote, A. 88–9
van Oordt, M. 10–11
van 't Klooster, J. 224
veto powers 17
Viterbo, A. 224
Volcker, P. 9, 156, 158
Volpicella, A. 171
Volz, U. 108

Wallis Commission of Enquiry 51
Wells Fargo 197
White, W. R. 104
World Bank 123, 127

zombie banks 15